# TRAVELER

# THE JOURNEYING BOY

# THE JOURNEYING BOY

## Scenes from a Welsh Childhood

## JON MANCHIP WHITE

THE ATLANTIC MONTHLY PRESS
NEW YORK

*Published simultaneously in Canada*
*Printed in the United States of America*
FIRST EDITION

Library of Congress Cataloging-in-Publication Data
White, Jon Ewbank Manchip, 1924–
    The journeying boy: scenes from a Welsh childhood / Jon Manchip White.—
1st ed.
    ISBN 0-87113-460-8
    1. White, Jon Ewbank Manchip, 1924–    —Biography—Youth.
2. Authors, Welsh—20th century—Biography—Youth. 3. Wales—
Description and travel—1981–ㅤ4. Wales—Social life and customs.
I. Title. II. Series: Traveler (New York, N.Y.)
PR6073.H499Z465   1991      828'.91403—dc20      91-7751

THE ATLANTIC MONTHLY PRESS
19 UNION SQUARE WEST
NEW YORK, NY 10003

FIRST PRINTING

FOR VALERIE

*Bare ruined choirs,*
*where late the sweet birds sang*

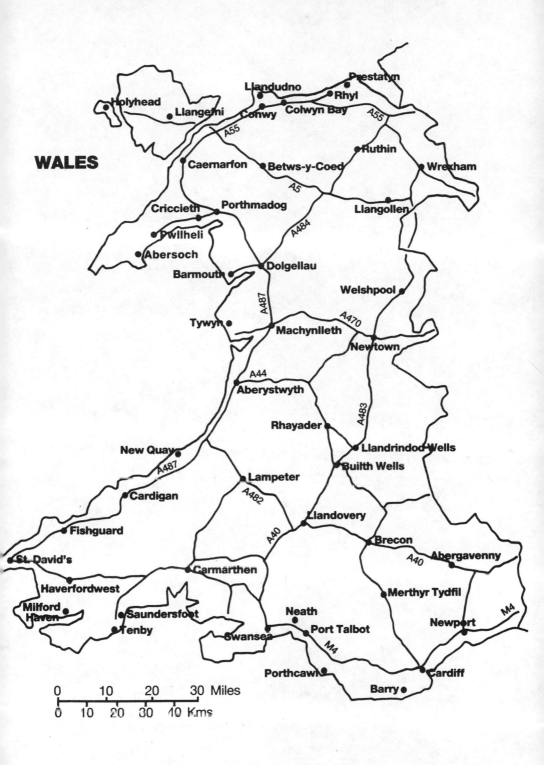

# THE JOURNEYING BOY

Humping my single bag, I make my way across the concourse of Paddington Station to the platform where the train to South Wales stands waiting.

Already, a full twenty minutes before the train is due to leave, I feel a surge of that anxiety, almost a sense of panic, that I felt on the plane two nights ago, coming over from America. Flying the 4,000 miles across the Atlantic from Atlanta to Gatwick, I had already found myself questioning the wisdom of setting out across "the bitter, salt, estranging sea" from my place of exile in Tennessee.

Wasn't this visit to Britain, and especially to my native Wales, bound to be painful? Why stir up old memories? Why pick at ancient scabs? What was the point of it? Though I was still a British citizen, this would only be my fourth trip to Britain since I had left it twenty years ago, to spend ten years in Texas and another ten years in Tennessee. How long was it since I was last in Wales? Twelve years, was it? Thirteen? Wouldn't it have been more sensible to leave the thing alone? Why risk resurrecting old griefs, or expose myself to the even greater sadness of revisiting places where I once was happy? Perhaps it was such fears that in the last twenty years had led me to visit Mexico, Canada, Egypt, Italy, France, Spain—anywhere but Britain, and especially Wales.

I remember that when I last returned to Britain I made a special point of avoiding Wales. I was born and grew up in Wales. I spent my adolescence in Wales. I called Wales my home until my twenty-first year. Since then my inclination has been to roam.

If there are two grand divisions of the human race, the nomads and the stay-at-homes, then I am emphatically a nomad. "Why should we be of the tribe of Manasseh when we can wander with Esau?" I have always been incurably restless, chronically curious about odd corners of the world. Yet obviously I dreaded going back to Wales because I was afraid of what the impact of those early recollections might be. I knew they might hit me with the force of those waves that would rear suddenly out of the Bristol Channel when I was playing as a child on the beach at Cold Knap or Lavernock and knock me down.

It is therefore a relief, as I am crossing the concourse with my bag, to observe that the basic features of Paddington Station have remained the same. I am still on familiar ground. The great overarching glass canopy still lets in the watery English sunlight the way it did when Frith painted it in the 1860s, or when I used to travel back and forth to Wales as a small boy in the 1930s. The same smoky, liquorish smell still lingers on the grimy panes. The same big clock still shovels along the hours with its fat, black fingers. True, there are many minor changes, and these, as I have already discovered since landing at Gatwick yesterday evening, can be more disconcerting than the major ones. It is the little things that have altered or vanished that can cause you a more immediate pang. For instance, why should I have been so oddly dismayed when the man behind the ticket counter handed me this flimsy paper printout instead of the stout oblong of thick, green cardboard that I had been expecting? And I am also dumbfounded by the price that I had to pay for it: four to five times the price that it was when I last stood at that ticket window only a dozen years ago. Nor have I got used to the chunky little pound pieces that have replaced the old pound note. Where are the farthings and three-penny bits, the elegant florins and half crowns of days gone by?

Weaving my way between the carts and trolleys piled high with mailbags, I realize that there is one feature of England, though, that hasn't changed. The bags are crammed with the undelivered mail that has been lying around in this and every other British station for several weeks. The Post Office is on strike. Am I, I wonder, a sort of Jonah? Whenever I come back to Britain I seem to arrive in the middle of a strike: an airline strike, a rail strike, a bus strike, a newspaper strike, an electricians' strike, a dockers' strike, a steel strike, a coal strike. This time it is a mail strike. All over the country the blue or red letter boxes stand with their poor little mouths sealed over with sticky tape, like visitors from another planet who have been seized and bound and gagged by the Trades Union Congress. Even today, ten years after the country was hit by the wave of strikes that culminated in the Winter of Discontent in 1979, when the garbage was uncollected and the dead went unburied, the atmosphere of Britain is still tainted by the threat of strikes. Is this why this morning I find Paddington so eerily empty of passengers? I always remember it thronged with masses of Welshmen, coming up to London on the spree or returning raucously to their hills and valleys. Has the fare become too expensive? Has the glamour of London worn off? Or do people still flock to London, but use the new motorways instead of the railway, because of resentment of the continuous dislocations of the sixties and seventies, or from fear of being caught out by a sudden strike and decanted from the train at some wayside station?

Certainly Paddington has a subdued air about it. Heaving my bag aboard, I realize what it is that I chiefly miss. The shining silver train I am now boarding, headed by a locomotive whose electric motors are already busily ticking over, will get me down to Wales more than an hour faster than the old steam-powered engine of the 1930s was able to do, yet there was something much more noble and uplifting about those old steam trains of the long-defunct Great Western Railway. Those old trains were war-horses, tricked out in a shining livery of green and gold, their big-bellied bodies shod with massive wheels and bogies and connecting rods. The driver and his fireman sat high up, like gods, while below them scurried a whole army of workers and acolytes, tapping and polishing, greasing and oiling. The trains hissed and they growled. Vast plumes of smoke shot out of their nostrils and went twisting away toward the girders overhead. They quivered with power, they strained to be off, they bore proud names on their glittering flanks: *Cardiff Castle, Harlech Castle, Pembroke Castle, Caernarvon Castle.* The station stank with their hot and sulfurous breath, and on the platforms around them stalked the stationmasters, the timekeepers, and the porters, decked out in uniforms that gleamed with gilt buttons and were spangled with gold braid. Those were the last of the heroic days of travel. The fact that the journey was longer, more clamorous, more redolent of soot and dirt and ashes only gave it, especially to a small boy, an added spice of adventure.

It was also a great deal more comfortable. The seats were plumper and softer. The windows could be raised and lowered by means of thick, soft leather straps. There were pictures of cathedral towns and seaside resorts. The luggage racks were capacious, made of good-quality string mesh instead of a cheap metal. During the war, traveling between my home port at Portsmouth and my corvette or destroyer at Plymouth or Glasgow, on trains teeming with other servicemen, I could hoist myself aloft into one of those string racks and enjoy a good sleep. And glancing around the carriage, as I wedge myself into a seat behind a plastic table, I remark how bleak and sterile it is compared with the carriages of the old GWR. Like so much else, modern travel is efficient, but not much fun.

But now we are beginning to move. We start to glide away, very softly, very silently. There are no preliminary roars and jerks and grindings, as if the engine is pawing at the rails and lowering its head and preparing to charge out of the gate. There are no earsplitting blasts on the whistle as the stationmaster consults his watch and brandishes his flag. Nor is there an answering snort of steam from the footplate, where the driver leans far out like an old-time racing driver and the stoker is wreathed with scarlet flame as he tops up his firebox with good Welsh coal. Today we sneak out upon the road to the west almost apologetically. I realize that I am not to be transported to my native place with the old triumphal slam and bang. I am not to be deposited on Welsh soil breathless and dizzy, with a sense of achievement at having survived a prolonged and perilous ordeal.

We gather speed. We begin to slide past the suburban stations whose names are a roll call that I once knew by heart: Royal Oak, Westbourne Park, Ealing Broadway, Southall, West Drayton. These were joyful landmarks on my journeys home from school. Now as then, they appear curiously secret and mysterious. No train ever seems to want to stop at any of them. Their platforms are permanently empty and deserted. However, I am glad to see that most of the ancient slums with which they used to be surrounded, the rows of rotting back-to-back houses that once disfigured this part of the trip, have disappeared. What the Blitz began, the bulldozer finished. True, what has taken their place is only one degree more appealing—car lots, factories, gasworks, acres and acres of scrubby, weedy waste ground—yet even these are an improvement on the squalid spectacle that once greeted the traveler.

London, in many noticeable ways, has spent its last few years, as they say in America, literally cleaning up its act. The Thames runs more sweetly. Whole unsanitary areas have been torn down and rebuilt. Then why, in what I have seen of it before catching the train to Wales, have I felt so disappointed with it? I am fond of London. I lived in London for eight years. Like many young Britons, it was for London I headed when I left the university. My younger daughter was born a Londoner. So why, as I stare from the carriage window as the suburbs wheel by, haven't I really enjoyed my brief stay there? Of course, the city has changed drastically since my last visit. We usually resent changes in places we were once familiar with and where we were happy. Still, cities exist to change. They are changing even while we are living in them. And certainly London was changing rapidly throughout the 1950s, when we were living in Hamilton Terrace in St. John's Wood. But it is only when there has been a long break in continuity, when we come back after a prolonged absence, that the changes become obvious, and painful. I have to be careful not to judge the London from which the train is taking me too subjectively and unfairly.

Even so, I can see that the changes of the 1980s have been far more extensive than the changes of the 1950s to the 1970s. Mrs. Thatcher has prevented Britain from sliding down the European league table to the level occupied by Greece, Portugal, and Ireland, but at the same time she has given unbridled rein to that unlovely crew, the speculators and developers. London and southern England have grown bloated, while the North has shriveled. Still, I suppose that represents a definite improvement. When I was last home, the entire country was miserable; now only half of it is. I imagine that must be some sort of progress.

Half a century ago, when I made this same journey from London, its population was 3 or 4 million. Now it is nearly 7 million. As in modern Tokyo, New York, São Paulo, Mexico City, you can read in the faces of its citizens that its amenities are stretched too thin, that its services are growing fragile, that there is the specter of breakdown. I thought the people I passed in the streets of London lacked their old perkiness and good cheer. They struck me as overburdened and glum. But once more I have to be on my guard: I have reached that stage in life when I would find it difficult to live in any capital city, indeed in any sizable city, even one I have known and liked.

Then, of course, there are the cars. Who was it who said that all power corrupts, but that horsepower corrupts absolutely? Certainly London, like most of the world's once comely capital cities, has been corrupted by the monstrous growth of its traffic.

My impression is that buses and taxis in London have become proportionately fewer and harder to come by, while private cars have multiplied at least twentyfold. There are traffic jams everywhere, even on the new motorways and ring roads. Like everyone else, Londoners have taken in a major way to the car, and, indeed, people who work in London now appear to think nothing of commuting from distances that would have been unthinkable thirty years ago, when the hardiest commuters were those who traveled up and down on the *Brighton Belle.*

I suppose it is just conceivable that London's traffic jams may ease a little in the years ahead, though it will probably take another gasoline shortage to do it. A much more serious problem, I think, and one which seems even more critical, is London's latest architecture. This is where the speculators and developers, abetted by the bureaucrats, have excelled themselves. Not only is London cluttered horizontally but it is constricted vertically. The city has contracted a severe case of architectural pollution.

After the war, when the Blitz had laid waste entire regions of London, there was a unique opportunity to rebuild the city in a fashion worthy of a great capital. Professor Richardson, for one, dusted off Christopher Wren's original plan to surround St. Paul's with splendid piazzas and boulevards which would embrace the whole area of the City and extend far beyond it. Instead, London chose to regress to the city of Defoe and Dickens, to the London of crooked corners, fetid alleyways, and bad air. There seems to be something in the English soul, stemming from the dank and huddled villages of the Anglo-Saxons, that prefers its dwelling places to be cramped, teeming, and higgledy-piggledy rather than airy and radiant. The English climate, admittedly, has a great deal to do with it: it is difficult to envisage an Urbino or a Salamanca in England. However, after World War II, London muffed its finest architectural chance since Wren and the Great Fire.

Of course, I wouldn't be trying to define my impressions of

England in this way if I weren't making this autumn journey to Wales. What am I going to find when I reach Wales? Will Cardiff, its capital, my birthplace, have come to resemble London? More speedily than I could have expected, we are darting clear of the suburbs and shooting into the countryside. My mood begins to lighten as we run between the broad, brown fields of Berkshire, their soil already cleared and combed by the harrow, and between the high banks of the cuttings, still strewn with burdock, loosestrife, cow parsley, convolvulus.

> *If England was what England seems,*
> *An' not the England of our dreams,*
> *But only putty, brass an' paint,*
> *'Ow quick we'd drop 'er! But she ain't!*

No—there is a lot more to England than the blank, bland modern buildings that confronted me in London, and that confront me now as we pass through Reading and Swindon, moving swiftly toward the midpart of the journey. The smooth motion is beginning to induce a dreamlike state. The wheels hiss suavely over the rails, their seamless welding no longer giving out the old, familiar galloping rhythm. The wheels whisper over the points instead of thundering, while the trains on the up line no longer slam past with the breath-stopping roar and bang that once made me cringe back with delighted terror.

And something else, too, some other ingredient of my boyhood journeys, is lacking. But what? It is only now, after nearly an hour on the train, that I am able to identify it. It is the telegraph poles. There are no telegraph poles. The cables have been taken down and buried. There are no more tall, black poles to watch, each of them bringing me 30 or 40 yards closer to the land of my heart's desire. There are no more strands of wire strung between the poles like great undulating tresses of hair, caught up and held in place by gleaming white porcelain insulators. I realize how much I miss my tarry old telegraph poles.

Still, as I gaze at the view, my chin cupped in my hand, it seems to me that I can recognize many of the same landmarks, the streams, the rivers, the country pubs, the Georgian farmhouses, the Saxon and Norman churches. They strike a buried chord. In spite of the clutter of housing estates that now imprison or encroach on them, they remain the fixed points that used to enliven my journeys when I was a small boy. They are long-lost images, swimming up to the surface. They are the notes of a forgotten piece that a pianist or a violinist instinctively recalls by means of what is known as neural memory. The churches, the farmhouses, the streams, and the hamlets are deeply overlaid impressions, brushed from the bottom of the mind, detached from the depths of some dark core so that they can struggle up once more into the daylight.

They are releasing other memories, also. Superimposed on the glass of the window I can glimpse the small ghost of the boy who once used to make this journey. Three times every year, between the ages of eight and sixteen, I was set free from England and my boarding school to return to Wales and my family. The glass reveals a small boy with smooth forehead and clear eyes, wearing an ugly and ill-fitting school uniform. The uniform consists of a coarse gray shirt with an unruly collar, rumpled gray shorts, thick gray socks, black boots with badly tied laces, and a cap and a blazer bearing the school colors of dark blue and light blue. Attached to his buttonhole is a large luggage label, on which is inscribed his name and address in big block letters, and in his damp little hand he clutches a crumpled ticket. Altogether he bears a startling resemblance to the boy in Thomas Hardy's poem, *Midnight on the Great Western*:

> *In the third-class seat sat the journeying boy,*
> *And the roof-lamp's oily flame*
> *Played down on his listless form and face,*
> *Bewrapt past knowing to what he was going,*
> *Or whence he came.*

> *In the band of his hat the journeying boy*
> *Had a ticket stuck; and a string*
> *Around his neck bore the key of his box,*
> *That twinkled gleams of the lamp's sad beams*
> *Like a living thing. . . .*

The forlorn little figure on the window pane, with the fields and villages swimming along behind it, seems to be growing gradually sharper. But what I can't hope to recapture is the sense of joy, the primal intensity of emotion with which the child made that journey. Just as there has never been any misery in my life that has matched the despair and the homesickness that I felt as a small boy banished to an institution in distant England, so there has never been anything to compare with the savage elation that accompanied my return to my native Wales.

How can I describe the feverish eagerness with which, at school, I used to tick off on an elaborate chart the final lessons, meals, chapel services, games of cricket and rugby, and cadet corps parades of the term? How can I convey the delirium of the last night in the dormitory, when I lay awake all night, giggling and whispering, wriggling into my clothes under the blankets long before dawn, bounding out of bed the instant the bell went off? Or the way we were marched by our masters in unruly groups, singing and shouting, to the local station, where we were shepherded to the terminals of central London, to be carried to our final destinations by the Great Western, the Midland, the Southern, or the London and North Eastern Railway? Often I was so overwrought I couldn't bear to sit in the compartment, but spent the whole of the three-hour journey patrolling the corridor like a small, unkempt animal, with frequent visits to the lavatory ("Do not operate the lever while the train is standing at the station").

Not that I was totally unhappy at my English school, or even unhappy most of the time. Small boys are infinitely adaptable. I made some lifelong friends there. I found masters who taught me how to temper my Celtic impulsiveness with Anglo-Saxon patience, how to balance a hot Welsh heart with a cool English head. Over the years I have come to believe that the combination of Celtic nature and Anglo-Saxon nurture may be a useful one. All the same, I had to learn to be tough and resourceful, to survive as a lone Welsh boy among several hundred English boys. To English boys of the late imperial era, the 1930s and early 1940s, the Welsh, Scots, and Irish were still numbered among the lesser breeds.

What made being at an English boarding school especially irksome to me was that I knew it was only sheer bad luck that had landed me there in the first place. My parents had only agreed to send me away because my father had come home from a sanatorium to die of tuberculosis, and the doctors had advised him that his condition was far too contagious to risk keeping a child in contact with him. Accordingly, I was dispatched to the land of the Saxons to water the bread of exile with my infant tears.

I am beginning to feel a little oppressed by the emptiness of the train. These big, open carriages are cold and cavernous in comparison with the intimacy of the old compartments. There, you were squeezed in knee to knee and thigh to thigh with cheerful and curious Welsh folk who, an hour out of Paddington, would have pried out of each other the most intimate details of their lives: how many times they had been married, how many children they had, what religion they practiced, what operations they had undergone and whether they had left any spectacular scars (if so, these may have been shown), their shoe size and their hat size, and whether their teeth were original or whether they were not (false teeth might have been taken out at this point and passed around for inspection). The Welsh appetite for personal information is unconcealed, unashamed, and bottomless.

Today there are only a handful of listless passengers, seated widely apart. I get up, deciding to have a cup of coffee, and walk through the train to the dining car, or rather the café space, since dining cars appear to be a thing of the past. The selection of buns and biscuits on the counter looks uninviting, and the coffee is lukewarm, muddy, and served in a Styrofoam cup. As a boy, of course, when my family had lost its money and was in deep financial trouble, I could not afford to eat in the dining car; the school provided us with a cardboard box containing a meat pie, a sausage roll, an apple or an orange, and a carton of milk—and, really, deciding at what point in the journey to open the box, fingering its contents, biting into the pie, were magical moments, more enchanting to a small boy than eating in the dining car would have been. Later, however, as a man, traveling between London and Cardiff, or Gloucester and London, I would love to eat breakfast or dinner in the dining car, with its red velvet curtains, its crisp napkins and tablecloths, its silver cutlery and crested china, its fresh flower in a silver vase, its handwritten menu, and its white-jacketed waiters performing miracles with their serving spoons as the train rocked and pock-pocketed about. Toast and marmalade, tea and coffee, poached haddock and kippers, bacon and eggs never tasted so good, and *The Times* and *The Telegraph* never contained such titillating news.

Sipping without enthusiasm at the gritty, brownish fluid in my Styrofoam cup, I happen to glance sideways through the glass in the doorway that leads to the next carriage. It takes me a moment to recognize what I am seeing. At first sight it appears very strange. A group of men, perhaps a dozen in all, are gathered in a tight knot on one side of the carriage, some standing, some crouched sideways on the seats. They wear suits of sober black, with white shirts and dark ties, some of them with ties loosened and their jackets laid across their knees. They strain forward, with their eyes fixed on the figure of a man standing facing them a few feet away, on the other side of the carriage, swaying, gesticulating, sculpting the air with his hands.

Now that I can see the mouths of the men opening and closing, I realize that I am watching not a group of demented accountants, but members of a Welsh choir returning from some contest or engagement in London, or a London Welsh choir going down to sing in Wales. This is only a practice, an impromptu session, but they are singing their hearts out, totally absorbed, their faces shining. One of them stands up, edges forward a little, starts to sing a solo. He is younger, taller, more slender, fairer haired than the others, who are thickset and black haired in the typical Welsh way.

I wish I could hear what they are singing. The sound of the train and the thick glass in the intervening door drowns out their voices. The Welsh are singing in there, and it makes me sad to be deaf to it, to be shut out. I watch them, wistful. The soloist throws his head back, his eyes half closed, the cords standing out in his neck. I try to guess from the movements of his lips what Welsh song he is singing . . . for somehow I know that he is singing a Welsh song, and in Welsh. Most Welshmen now cannot speak the Welsh language—but they still know the old Welsh songs, and how to sing them in their ancient tongue. Is he singing "Bugeilio'r Gwenith Gwyn"? "Aderyn Pur"? "Hwylio yr Heli"? . . .

Surely they wouldn't mind if I opened the door, slipped through, took a seat unobtrusively at the rear of the carriage? It would ease me to listen to the Welsh singing again—a promising start to the trip.

I move toward the door. But at that moment the song, whatever it was, comes to an end. The conductor drops his hands, smiles, relaxes. The group, smiling too, stirs about, stretches, putting on jackets, straightening ties, patting backs. As always, a session of song has put them in a good humor, set the world to rights, restored its harmony.

I sigh, my shoulders sagging a little. I put my half-empty cup of unconvincing liquid on the counter and make my way back to my own seat, reflecting that it is much easier to walk along the aisles of these trains than it was to walk the aisles of the old Great Western, where you got tossed about like a sailor in a storm. But I miss the old rackety jerk and jolt that made the journey home so thrilling as a boy.

Glancing at my watch as I resume my seat, I realize that the train has already carried me past the halfway mark. I feel a strange impression that with every mile I am becoming increasingly Welsh. I am shedding the English Dr. Jekyll; the elemental Welsh Mr. Hyde is beginning to emerge. Only an hour to Cardiff. I sense that my rising excitement is tinged with a prickle of panic. What on earth am I doing, allowing the train to suck me back so slickly into the past? What am I going to find there? Is it too late to gather my gear and make a dive out of the train? Why am I exposing myself to so much soul-searching and distress? At my age and in my present personal situation, these things are not easy to cope with. Haven't I had enough personal trauma in these past three years? Why am I permitting myself to be whirled back into the turmoil of an existence I thought I had long ago sloughed off and come to terms with?

I must try to clear my thoughts. First and foremost, I tell myself, I am going home because of a simple love of country, the desire to see the land of my birth once more before I die. At sixty-four, I cannot expect to make too many trips back to Wales. This may be my last. I have reached that time of life which, as Dante puts it in a nautical metaphor that would please my seafaring ancestors, "cautions every man to lower his sail and gather in his lines." The moment has come to take stock. Kierkegaard says somewhere that the irony of life is that we have to live it forward but can only understand it backward. If I am to make any sense of my own life, to tease some sort of a pattern from it, then I have to make this reverse journey to my Welsh starting point. When you are young, or even middle-aged, you are far too busy and impatient to bother about glancing back over your shoulder. Sixty-four is a suitable age to start. Yet the prospect causes me to shudder. In spite of the Delphic prescription to Know Yourself, how much of ourselves can we really ever hope to know? So much of ourselves is permanently hidden from us. And how much of ourselves, if it comes to that, *ought* we to know? The springs of action and imagination may be strongest and most effective when least understood. In any case, how much of ourselves do we actually *want* to know? What if we look into ourselves and don't like what we see? Stare down into that precipice and who knows what monsters we might glimpse paddling around in the murky waters? And surely I've left it a bit late, haven't I, seeking to understand more of myself, at over sixty?

But, of course, there is also the plain matter of family piety. Not that I intend to visit the actual graves of my parents and my forebears, where they lie in their wet Welsh churchyards. Even though, like most Welshmen, I am prone to thoughts of death and dissolution, I abhor churchyards. I turn my head away whenever I drive past one. In all likelihood I shall be buried in Texas, though I tend to change my mind about it. For a long time I had a hankering to be buried in Salamanca. But who can foresee such things? Someone has said that life is what happens to you while you are making other plans. Those who live a vagabond life must expect a vagabond death.

> *O little did my mother think*
> *The day she cradled me*
> *The lands I was to travel through*
> *The death I was to die.*

But what of the living? What of my Welsh friends? In spite of time and distance, I have always tried to observe Dr. Johnson's advice to "keep one's friendships in good repair." I shall visit my old friends and haunt my old haunts. I shall prowl around the docks and parks, the pubs and museums, the cricket pitches and football fields. I shall see if my villages and towns and cities have changed, and how, and why. I shall revisit the elements that won't have changed: the hills, the valleys, the rivers, the Bristol Channel. Perhaps I shall repeat a portion of the wild Welsh rambles of my youth. Twice as a young man I walked the length and breadth of Wales, first from north to south, then from south to north. Each time I followed the route taken by one of my early heroes. With a friend from Cambridge, I walked around Wales in the footsteps of George Borrow, who toured the country in the 1850s and published in *Wild Wales* one of the most enchanting of all travel books. We went in the third summer of the war. The weather was wretched, most of the hotels and boardinghouses were closed, and there were virtually no cars or buses on the road because of petrol rationing. So, except for the very occasional lift, we walked every mile of it. But we were two high-spirited young men whose morale remained unaffected by the rain or the Blitz or the disasters abroad. Ten years went by before I went again. This time it was a solo effort, again mainly on foot, but now with more assistance from lorry drivers and buses. I seem to remember that I had some important decision to make and needed some breathing space. So I set off, this time in the other direction, tracing the itinerary of another and much earlier hero, Giraldus Cambrensis. Gerald the Welshman had made his famous journey, which he turned into a book as lively and quirky as Borrow's, in 1188, but the personality that emerges from its pages is as vivid and racy as if he had been writing in our own time. Gerald the Welshman and George Borrow: men who were fearless, opinionated, credulous, tireless, dogmatic, and eaten up with an unappeasable curiosity about everything and everybody under the sun. As with Borrow, I wanted to see my native country through Gerald's eyes, to compare what he had witnessed with what I was witnessing.

I can claim to have known the face of Wales pretty thoroughly in my youth and early manhood. Will I still recognize it, or at least the smaller South Wales portion of it on which I intend to concentrate in the days ahead, now I have reached latish middle age? What if I am destined to find myself a stranger in what was once a dear and familiar place? Maybe I should have left it all well alone?

Too late now to change my mind. I am being hurled back, willy-nilly, a prisoner in a speeding silver capsule, into the past. And all at once, with a heart-stopping violence, I feel the capsule bolt into a deep cutting, diving into a long, dark tunnel.

I time it. Three minutes at 70 miles an hour. Again neural memory enables me to identify the tunnel. It is the tunnel built beneath the Duke of Beaufort's land, when the railway line was first driven through. His Grace refused to allow the view from his windows to be ruined by the uncouth spectacle of a sooty and rowdy locomotive.

Then, as we thrust back into the daylight, a mile away on the right I see a splendid sight: the pylons and girders of the new Severn Bridge, carrying the motorway across the broad reach of the river and into the heart of Wales. New to me, that is. When I drove down to Wales in the 1950s and 1960s, I had to make the wide circuit via Cirencester and Gloucester and along the left bank of the Severn. The bridge has cut two hours and a very sweet slice of country from the journey.

I sit up straight behind my plastic table. I am on my home ground now. For ten years I lived only a few miles upstream from the bridge, at The Court in Minsterworth. The thought of it brings on a dizzying surge of emotion.

And then the vista of the bridge and the river is whisked away as we shoot into a second tunnel. No difficulty in remembering what this one is. The Severn Tunnel. The longest tunnel in the British Isles. Isambard Kingdom Brunel's masterpiece of burrowing and earth shifting. With unnerving abruptness, I am once again bustled back fifty years. The Severn Tunnel was the peak and climax of my childhood journey. The whistle would give a howl, and the train would bucket into the bowels of the earth. Smoke would fill the carriage, and everyone would cough and splutter. We would lunge for the windows and tug on the leather straps. The dim lights of the carriage would skim the cyclopean blocks of the tunnel walls, streaming with damp, and we had a thrilling feeling of the deadly weight of water pressing down above our heads.

Today I scarcely have time to register that the train no longer whistles, that the lights are brighter, the motion steadier. We swoop up from underground, the daylight suddenly banging into the carriage like a slap in the face, with none of the old fume and fuss, and find ourselves not only in the upper world but in the county of Gwent: in Wales.

We have arrived. In obedience to an obscure impulse from long ago, I perform the ancient ritual of collecting my luggage and carrying it down to the end of the carriage, opposite the door. I always used to complete the last twenty minutes of my journey standing up, craning out the window, watching for the long curve of Cardiff platform. I do that now.

The Welsh air stings my face. Mixed with my exhilaration is a sense of sadness. No one today will be standing on the platform waiting to run and wrap her arms around the small, grubby schoolboy in his rumpled uniform, clutching his damp and dog-eared ticket, his cap over one eye, the knot of his tie under his ear. No house with the bright fire and the familiar furniture. *Tempus edax rerum.* All those rooms in our lives which were once central to us and which we took for granted, which seemed so solid and so permanent—nothing more than flimsy stage sets, broken up and flung into some cosmic limbo. And as I lean out, eyes smarting, it is only now that I admit to myself that I am nursing another, secret reason for returning to Wales, and as soon as it wells up in my mind I try to dismiss it. Time enough to wrestle with it in the days ahead.

The platform is coming up. No time to struggle with personal problems. Long before the train has come to a halt, I have got the carriage door open.

Cardiff General. Signs in the Welsh language. CROESAW Y CYMRU. WELCOME TO WALES. I jump down onto the platform with my bag. I walk toward the well-remembered stairs, the subterranean passage with the white tiling.

My heart flutters. My legs tremble. I walk fast. Then faster.

I hadn't anticipated that the return of the native was going to be so terribly hard on the feet. I must have walked 20 miles on the pavements of Cardiff today. I promised myself before I left Tennessee that most of my present pilgrimage around southwest Wales and Glamorganshire would be performed on foot. Pilgrimages shouldn't be undertaken in cars or on public transport. Can you imagine Tannhäuser arriving in Rome in a Porsche, with his pilgrim's staff in the trunk?

At any rate, here I am in my bedroom on the second floor of my hotel, seated in the big bay window with the lace curtains looped back. My feet are soaking in a basin that I have borrowed from the management. The water is as hot as I can stand it, and as I was limping home I stopped at a chemist's shop to buy a packet of Epsom salts. I wonder if medieval pilgrims knew about Epsom salts? Gerald the Welshman, during the course of his circuit of Wales, could have done with some when he pulled off his sandals and dangled his feet in the waters of one of the many streams he forded. So could George Borrow, when he pulled off his big, black boots and thrust his aching feet into the mountain pools.

It is a relief to settle back in an easy chair, while the dusk begins to settle over the Cathedral Road. A soothing warmth is beginning to creep up from my toes, and I am nursing a glass of Swn y Môr that I have brought up from the hotel bar. Swn y Môr: Sun and Sea. Welsh whiskey. Made in Brecon, not many miles away, and very potable too. How could I have imagined, in the bluenosed and puritanical Wales of my youth, that the day would dawn when not only could people openly enjoy a glass of whiskey, but the stuff would actually be distilled in Wales itself? Every swallow gains an added savor from the thought of all those Baptist and Methodist and Calvinist elders turning in their graves. *Iach y da!* (Mud in your eye!)

It seems oddly appropriate, in view of the fact that I have just come from America, that I should find myself staying at an establishment called the Lincoln Hotel. The owner, whoever he is, apparently possesses a singular devotion to the sixteenth president. Lincoln's knobby features adorn the hall, the staircases, the rooms, the hotel notepaper. A curious preoccupation for a Welsh hotel keeper. Of course, it may merely be bait for American tourists, but I don't think so. I think it springs from one of those warm and unpredictable enthusiasms to which the Welsh are prone. The Welsh have a predilection for men like Lincoln, who are capable of making the larger gesture.

In fact, it is by pure chance that I have hit upon this small but extremely comfortable hotel. I had had the fixed idea, before leaving, that I would stay at the Angel, in the center of town. In my youth the Angel was the grandest and most prestigious of the city's hotels. I had been looking forward to taking up my quarters there and playing at being Local Boy Makes Good. Then I got to chatting with my taxi driver, as we were driving away from Cardiff General, as to whether the Angel was likely to be full. (You talk immediately to everyone in Wales—usually in sheer self-defense, since everyone is immediately going to start talking to you. If talking were an event in the Olympics, the Welsh would win most of the medals hands down.) At any rate, the taxi driver gave it as his opinion that I would find the big downtown hotels much too chilly and impersonal. Silence and standoffishness were all right for an Englishman, but for a Welshman like me (he had established my Welshness before I had slammed the door) somewhere chummier was called for. The Welsh, in addition to being loquacious, are incurably gregarious. So he suggested that I try one of the smaller hotels that had sprouted up in recent years in many of the former private mansions along the length of the Cathedral Road. Naturally, I jump at this: the Cathedral Road, after all, was where I had lived as a boy and where I had done most of my growing up.

But chance—or something more than chance—hadn't just landed me at the Lincoln Hotel; it had landed me, I soon realized, in the house that stood exactly and precisely opposite my old home. Can you blame a superstitious Celt for feeling that there was something rather uncanny about such a coincidence? What were the chances of flying 4,000 miles and ending up outside what used to be my own front door?

In any event, here I am, nursing my sore feet and sipping my Swn y Môr, in one of the front rooms of the Lincoln Hotel. The size of these houses, built in the 1870s and 1880s, when Cardiff was approaching its heyday and shipowners like my father were beginning to flourish, can be gauged by the fact that the two houses occupied by the Lincoln Hotel have been converted into thirty good-sized bed–sitting rooms, each with its private bathroom. The room I am now occupying, with its wide bow window, its lofty ceiling, its ornate plasterwork, corresponds in every way to its counterpart in the house across the street, just visible behind the row of majestic chestnut trees.

I feel a strange little shiver as I gaze out through my lace curtains at the lace curtains of the other drawing room across the way. It is as if I were still behind those other curtains—me, myself—playing around on the carpet at my parents' feet with my toy soldiers and model ships. Time is performing one of its conjuring tricks: it has turned my world deftly around by a hundred and eighty degrees. At the beginning of our lives we look forward; at the end of them we look back. The youth I once was and the aging man I am now are staring out and confronting each other across the years. Creepy. I feel as if I have fallen under a sorcerer's spell, or as if I am a voyeur, peeping through the lace curtains to spy on myself.

I take a long pull at my whiskey and flex my toes in the warm water. All told I must have been strolling around the city for nine or ten hours. When we recall our youth, it always seems to have been sunny weather, though for most of the time it must really have been like the weather today, gray and overcast, with a biting wind. Still, at least it didn't rain on this first day of my homecoming. South Wales has the highest rainfall in Great Britain, not itself renowned for mellow weather. In the atlas, South Wales is mantled by a solid black pall. Could the vile weather of Great Britain have been one of the reasons I eventually decided to leave, removing myself to the American Southwest, where the sun shines for three hundred and sixty days in the year? I have always hated rain and been made miserable by it. I used to laugh when people in the Southwest asked me if I didn't miss it. And so, since Cardiff didn't punish me today with its worst weather, I was able to have a good prowl around and see how the old place is looking and faring.

I must say I am astonished to find how much it has been transformed since my last visit. Not that the central area and its surroundings have changed so much that I cannot recognize them; the main landmarks are more or less fixed and immutable. But the entire city has been smartened up and rendered more trim and tidy. In Great Britain as a whole one would have done very well, during the 1980s, to have invested in the paint and varnish business. And Cardiff seems to have been more lavish with the paintbrush than most cities—a sign not just of prosperity but of a positive lifting of the spirits. It signals a growth, since the dismal days of Harold Wilson, of confidence and self-respect.

Cardiff has always been a fascinating city, right from its ancient beginnings. From the mid-1800s until as recently as the 1950s, it had served as one of Britain's major ports and one of the principal ports of the world. Like all ports, it had a flair and character of its own. Ports are brash, energetic, cosmopolitan, individual; their gaze is directed outward, toward the oceans and the continents. Ports are exciting. Cardiff, in its port days, was an exhilarating place to live.

Its history as a port actually extends back for at least two thousand years. Almost immediately after the Emperor Claudius's conquest of Britain in A.D. 43, the Romans built one of their so-called Forts of the Saxon Shore here, in an effort to protect the people of South Wales from the depredations of Irish and Scandinavian pirates. It also served as a way station on the highroad that led into South Wales from the great legionary fortress of Caerleon. As was their habit, the Romans built thoroughly. By the midpoint of their four-hundred-year occupation of Britain, they had replaced the earth-and-timber defenses of their earlier fort with massive stone walls, 20 feet high and 10 feet thick. The square fortress, covering 9 acres and equipped with bastions and two towering gateways, still constitutes the magnificent central focus of the city. When the castle was restored by the Bute family in the nineteenth century, the remaining courses of Roman masonry, marked off by bands of darker stone, were cleverly incorporated into the walls that were raised above them and are clearly visible to passersby today. When I was a boy, the sight of that Roman masonry excited and moved me. It is something, after all, to have been born in a city founded by Imperial Rome and occupied by a Roman garrison for four centuries. I have always felt privileged to be able to make the double boast: *Civis Romanus sum et civis Britannicus sum.*

When the Romans withdrew in the middle of the fifth century, the castle, like life in Britain in general, fell upon evil times. However, the Dark Ages that followed provided my youthful imagination with an equally powerful stimulus. How, for example, could I fail to feel personally involved when I learned, from the copy of Geoffrey of Monmouth's *History* in my father's library, that King Arthur, who had defended Britain against the Saxon hordes who surged in to fill the vacuum left by the departure of the Romans, had personal associations with Cardiff? The name *Caertyf*, the "Fortress on the River Taff," rang through Geoffrey's pages. It was from the port of Caertyf, said Geoffrey, that Lancelot had hastily embarked, with King Arthur hot on his heels, when he had fled to France after the discovery of his fatal passion for Queen Guinevere. Mustn't the ships of Lancelot and Arthur have pushed off from the very quay, looking out on the Bristol Channel, where my father had been born fourteen hundred years later? Think of that. And what did it matter that my particular hero, Gerald the Welshman, writing later than Geoffrey (and scarcely more reliable as a historical authority), would pour bitter scorn upon the poor monk of Monmouth and his *History*? Gerald liked to tell the story of a magician called Meilyr, who lived near the ruins of the Roman fort of Caerleon and was tormented by demons: "And when," says Gerald, "St. John's Gospel was placed on his lap, the demons vanished immediately. But if Geoffrey's *History of the Kings of Britain* was placed there instead, then the demons alighted all over his body and became even more troublesome."

The Dark Ages brought two important developments to the city and its neighborhood. First, the Celtic tribes of Wales and the West Country, who had fiercely resisted the Romans and the Saxon interlopers who succeeded them, gradually emerged as well-defined and well-regulated princedoms. The Celts had begun as bands of warriors, related by blood, who during the Iron Age, about 500 B.C., had left their homes in western and central Europe and quickly infiltrated the whole of Britain. They had rapidly absorbed the original and never very numerous inhabitants and become the warrior overlords of Briton. It was these Celtic tribesmen whom the Romans had conquered and who, when the Romans had retired, had been steadily pushed back by the invaders from Scandinavia into the north and west of the British Isles. Ultimately, as the Anglo-Saxons took over the area which was to become known as "Angle-Land," or England, the Celts were penned back into present-day Wales and Scotland. For a thousand years the Celts had held sway in Britain; now, despite the best efforts of folk heroes like Arthur, half their realm had been shorn away.

The Dark Ages, of course, were by no means as dark as historians once made them out to be. On the contrary, the courts of the newly emerging princes, both in the Celtic West and in the Saxon East, were often places of notable splendor and culture. In South Wales, the Celtic kingdom became known as Morgannwg or Gwlad Morgan, the Land of Morgan, giving its name to the present tripartite counties of West Glamorgan, Mid-Glamorgan, and South Glamorgan, in the last of which the capital city of Cardiff is situated. The Morgan in question was Morgan Mwynfawr, a shadowy figure thought to have died about 970. His family claimed descent from no less a person than Maximus Magnus, a Roman general who had served as commander in chief in North Wales before leading the British legions across the Channel in a successful attack on Rome in 387, only to die in battle at Milan in the following year. As Macsen Wledig, he is commemorated by a story in the *Mabinogion*, the medieval epic that is to Wales what the *Iliad* is to the Greeks.

The closing years of the Dark Ages, between 800 and 1000, were marked in South Wales by incessant raids by the Vikings and other freebooters, operating from bases in Ireland (where Dublin began as a Viking settlement) and western Scotland. The Vikings set up a string of bases or trading posts along the whole length of the South Wales coast: the name of Swansea, for example, derives from the Viking *Sweynsey*, the Island of Sweyn. The word *Holm*, in Flat Holm and Steep Holm, the two islands opposite the entrance of Cardiff harbor, is also Scandinavian. The Vikings entrenched themselves on the islands, and there are also lingering traces of Viking occupation in several names of Cardiff streets.

However, even in the turmoil of the Dark Ages, softening influences had begun to make themselves felt with the arrival of Christianity. Christianity first took root in the Celtic kingdoms—in Brittany, Ireland, Wales, and Scotland—and was carried by priestly missionaries, many of whom were martyred, into pagan England. Wales itself, succumbing to another of its many outbursts of religious fanaticism, became positively infested by battalions of holy men and hairy hermits. Saints were two a penny. In many parts of Wales whole families, from grandfather to grandson, consisted of saints. Place names such as Llanpumpsaint, the Town of the Five Saints, suggest that there were entire villages where it was impossible to walk down the main street without tripping over one. The Celtic saints made an indelible impression on the country, even though in recent years the Catholic church has been busily demoting and desainting them by the cartload. (Llanpumpsaint, in the county of Dyfed, is the site, incidentally, of a Roman gold mine that continued in sporadic production into modern times. Gold, pearls, furs, greyhounds, and slaves were the staple Roman exports from Wales. My father, always a romantic, was co-owner of the mine when it was in very fitful production in the 1920s. He had to shift whole mountains to obtain sufficient nuggets to furnish a royal wedding ring. Like many of his enthusiastic bylines, it went bust and was closed down. However, it wasn't my father's fault that there has never been any Welsh gold rush.)

It was during the heady epoch of the saints that imposing monasteries and churches were founded, particularly in the lush lowlands of South Wales. The monasteries of Llantwit Major and Llandough, and later Llandaff, grew into celebrated religious and cultural centers. Llandaff (the *Llan* or parish on the river Taff) was rather given in later days to making exaggerated claims to antiquity. Although it claimed as patrons a remote King Lucius and an equally remote St. Dyfrig—one of that swarm of saints just referred to—it was probably the creation of a St. Teilo in the sixth century. In course of time it would become the largest of Wales's four cathedrals (Llandaff, St. David's, Bangor, St. Asaph), though it would always be tiny St. David's in West Wales whose bishop would exercise religious primacy. Llandaff is the cathedral approached by the Cathedral Road, where I now sit soaking my feet as the night comes down. Set in its rolling parklands, it is only a mile or two away. Sipping at my Swn y Môr, I am as conscious of its presence and proximity as I was when I was a boy in the house across the way.

The task of transforming the modest church of Llandaff into a cathedral was taken in hand by that great race of cathedral builders, the Normans. It had taken the Normans a quarter of a century after landing in Britain to turn their attention to South Wales. First they had to complete the crushing of Saxon England that they had begun at the Battle of Hastings, where, as a schoolboy once wrote, "Duke William told his archers to shoot their arrows at the thickest part of the English, so they aimed them at their heads." The Normans were not only great cathedral builders but great castle builders, and the first thing the Norman baron Robert FitzHamon did when he reached Cardiff was to take over what remained of the old Roman fortress and use it as his center of operations. FitzHamon, who styled himself the Prince of Glamorgan, was one of the flood of military opportunists that the Conqueror loosed on Britain with permission to grab whatever they could. Inside the tumbledown Roman walls he threw up a huge earthen mound, or *motte,* 40 feet high, on which he perched a solid stone keep, or *bailey,* from which he had a clear view of the surrounding countryside. His motte and bailey still stand and dominate the interior court of the castle, and during the course of my stay I mean to climb it, for old times' sake. In course of time FitzHamon was created Earl of Gloucester, as his fellow toughs on the Welsh frontier were created Earls of Chester, Shrewsbury, and Hereford. He was an able and formidable man, and eventually died leading the armies of Henry

I in Normandy at the Battle of Falaise—a town whose name is only too familiar to soldiers of my own generation. His body was brought back to England and interred at Tewkesbury Abbey, which he had founded.

FitzHamon's heir and successor was his son-in-law, Robert Beauclerc. Beauclerc was Henry I's illegitimate son by Nest, a beautiful and provocative Welsh princess who was the daughter of the Welsh ruler Tudor ap Rhys (and the grandmother of Gerald the Welshman). He added extensively to Cardiff Castle and, as the possessor of both Welsh and Norman blood, acted with such success as a go-between among the boisterous Welsh princelings in South Wales that he became known as Robert the Consul. In the stone keep of his rebuilt castle, he incarcerated his uncle, the Duke of Normandy, the Conqueror's eldest son, whose army had been defeated by Henry I at the Battle of Tinchebray. The Duke remained a prisoner there for the last eight years of his life, when his body was taken for burial from Cardiff Castle to Gloucester Cathedral. He was said to have been a man of intelligence and culture, who spent his captivity writing poetry in both English and Welsh.

There is a tradition in my family that the name *Manchip* is derived from the Norman-French word *manciple* (as in Chaucer's "Manciple's Tale") and that an early Manchip had been the manciple or steward to this Robert of Normandy. He was reputed to have helped the Duke, one rainy Welsh winter day, to escape from the castle, though they only managed to get a few yards from the walls before becoming ignominiously stuck in the mud in what is now Duke Street. Granted that my family has ancient associations with Cardiff, I doubt if the tradition has any real basis. Probably it stems from that genealogical mania which is a specialty of the Welsh, resembling one of those legendary descents that the Tudors, a Welsh dynasty, employed their Welsh heralds to "erect" for them, as the technical term puts it. Thus Henry VIII and his daughter Elizabeth I liked to claim descent from Noah, Solomon, Achilles, Hector, King Arthur, Charlemagne, the Seven Worthies, and anyone else whom they fancied might shed luster on their line. So why shouldn't I be allowed to claim descent, in the Welsh way, from the humble steward of Duke Robert? Certainly Norman influence and Norman-Welsh intermingling have played a potent part in the history of Cardiff and Glamorgan. My father's first name, *Gwilym*, for example, clearly derives from the French *Guillaume* rather than from the English *William*. As it happens, I possess another and rather piquant connection with a Gwilym, in that Minsterworth Court, near Gloucester, which was my home for ten years, and which was originally part of the Duchy of Lancaster, had passed into the possession of Elizabeth I and was given by her to the court herald who had "erected" an impressive if almost wholly imaginary genealogical tree for her. She also appointed him to be the first Rouge Dragon Pursuivant, one of the four official royal heralds, one each for England, Wales, Scotland, and Ireland, whose business is still to attend to all matters pertaining to rank, title, pedigree, and the like. At Minsterworth, I devoted a corner of what had once been his library to Gwilym the Herald, as he was called, and furnished it with a nice copy of the third edition of *Gwillim's Display of Heraldrie*, "For the Use and Delight of Gentlemen," printed in 1638 and with hundreds of illustrations of coats of arms exquisitely hand painted.

By the time the FitzHamon family passed out of history, in the thirteenth century, the Norman hold on Cardiff and its environs had been firmly consolidated. Indeed, it would endure for another three hundred years, until the waning of the Tudors. The Clares, the Monthermers, the Despensers, the Nevilles, the Beauchamps, the Plantagenets, all boasted Norman descent and assumed in turn the style of Earls of Gloucester and Lords of Glamorgan.

The city of Cardiff has always been conscious of the Norman contribution to its history. Many of its streets, parks, and public buildings are graced with Norman names. These names my father, a close student of history, would explain to me. Indeed, Cardiff owes much to the stability which its Norman overlords were able to exert at a time when the rest of Wales was experiencing the death throes of the independent Welsh princedoms, at the hands of the Welsh themselves as much as at those of their Norman and English enemies. The sense of apartness from, even superiority to, the rest of Wales which Cardiffians have always been accused of, stems not only from the city's size and its cosmopolitan character as a port, but also from the distinct caste imparted to it by the years of Norman settlement.

The Tudor era, beginning with the accession of Henry VII or Henry Tudor (*Tudor* is the Anglicized version of the Welsh *Twdr*), would be one of general pacification and organization. This would be particularly so in Wales, since the Tudors, being of Welsh origin themselves, knew far too much about the combative and quarrelsome proclivities of the Welsh to ride them on too easy a rein. Cardiff Castle was seized by the Crown at the end of the Wars of the Roses, and in 1551 was bestowed on one of the outstanding statesmen and soldiers of the age, William Herbert, who was simultaneously created first Earl of Pembroke. Herbert's principal residence was not at Cardiff but at Wilton in Sussex, the magnificent manor house which he built on land given to him at the dissolution of the monasteries by his patron, Henry VIII. As the Lords of Glamorgan and Earls of Pembroke, the Herberts would dominate South Wales for the next century and a half, dividing their time between Cardiff and Wilton. William Herbert's son Henry was deeply interested in the arts, and it was to Henry's sons William and Philip that the First Folio of Shakespeare's plays was dedicated in warm terms in 1623.

With the exception of the violent but relatively brief upheaval caused by the Great Civil War in the 1640s, the history of Cardiff over the next three hundred years was quiet and uneventful. The town settled down as one of the Bristol Channel's fishing and trading ports, one of those sleepy little market towns you see in the watercolors of Rowlandson and Paul Sandby. Its castle, greatly expanded during the Middle Ages and the Tudor era, still overshadowed it, and its inhabitants carried on their activities beneath its walls and within the enclosure of the town wall, with its five gates, two of them sea gates that opened onto the wharves beside the river Taff. A shire hall and a guildhall were built, and two parishes were established, centered on the churches of St. John and St. Mary. Two friaries, one Dominican and one Franciscan, alternately flourished and foundered as religious fashions changed, and always there was the reassuring presence of the cathedral at Llandaff, a short distance from the West Gate and the bridge across the Taff. The Herberts merged peaceably with the Windsors, and between 1550 and 1850 the town prospered in its own unique Anglo-Welsh way, its population of between four and five thousand making it by far the largest town in Wales.

Around 1850, however, a truly astonishing change was destined to take place. The aggressive Scottish dynasty of the Butes, which had recently allied itself with the diffident Windsors, quickly seized the initiative in the development of the area's rich iron and coal resources. In almost no time at all Cardiff metastasized into one of the most phenomenal boomtowns of the Industrial Revolution. Within a mere half century its population swelled by a staggering thirtyfold, and the nature and appearance of the town were forever altered. Yet it is to that older Cardiff, the Cardiff of the FitzHamons and the Herberts and the Windsors, that the foundation of my own family's relationship to the city essentially belongs.

My ancestors the Manchips were something of a fugitive breed. The name is very rarely encountered, though it crops up occasionally all around the Bristol Channel and in the basin of the river Severn. The shores of the Bristol Channel, like those of the Mediterranean, have always constituted a cohesive cultural area. There were Manchips in Bristol, in Weston-super-Mare, in

Clovelly on the north coast of Devon. The Whites, on the other hand, were firmly anchored in Cardiff itself, though they too had relatives who were scattered throughout South and West Wales and around the Bristol Channel littoral.

As a family, the Whites demonstrated that fissiparous tendency which has been a marked feature of Welsh society. Living within the same small town, half the Whites were landlubbers and stay-at-homes, while the other half were a wandering and restless lot who followed the tides. Of the stay-at-homes, Edmund and John White were burgesses, another John White became the Bailiff, and in the eighteenth century an Emmanuel White served as Sergeant of the Mace. In Victorian times, a Henry White was a member of the city council and a Justice of the Peace, but alas, many other members of the tribe would appear to have been rank bad hats. In 1577, for instance, we achieved a rare double: two members of the family, Florence White and Thomas White, were hanged together for murder, the nature of which I would love to know but which has unfortunately not been recorded.

The year 1577 was altogether poorish for the Whites. In that year a member of the seafaring branch of the family, Matthew White, was arraigned on a charge of piracy and seems to have been lucky to have dodged the death penalty. In this he was more fortunate than Maurice White, a couple of centuries later, who was hanged for piracy at Bristol. Probably the piracy in question was fairly small beer, more akin to smuggling and similar skulduggery than stirring stuff with cannon and cutlass. I am, though, able to claim, by marriage, a connection with a far grander pirate than either Matthew or Maurice. My wife's mother was a Morgan, one of those Cardiff Morgans among whom was numbered the famous Henry Morgan of Cefn Mably. As a boy, I would often take a Sunday-morning stroll from my home across the fields to the rambling old mansion at Cefn Mably, which by that time had become an inn celebrated for its generous platters of ham and eggs. Now, I believe, it has been turned into an old people's home and is engulfed by the wastes of one of the new housing estates.

Henry Morgan was one of the greatest buccaneers and seamen who ever lived. He served, while still in his twenties, as chief lieutenant to the notorious Edward Mansfield, who flayed the coasts of the Caribbean with a fleet of no fewer than fifteen ships. On Mansfield's death in 1667, Morgan succeeded to his command, and as a privateer commissioned by the British government went on a four-year rampage that began with the capture of Camagüey in Cuba, continued with the destruction of Maracaibo in Venezuela, and ended with an extraordinary march across the isthmus of Panama to put the city of Panama to the fire and sword. "His operations," one of his biographers tells us, "were always marked with indescribable brutality and debauchery, but they were executed with skill and bravery, often against great odds." The British authorities in the Caribbean, alarmed by his success, managed to take him into custody and send him as a prisoner to England, where they confidently expected him to be put on trial and executed. But the citizens of London accorded him such a hero's welcome that Charles II, ever sensitive to the popular will, knighted him instead and sent him back to the Caribbean as Lieutenant Governor of Jamaica, of which he eventually became Governor. Not bad for a country boy from Cefn Mably.

These seafaring Whites, while not aspiring to the heights and depths of a Henry Morgan, nevertheless possessed something of his gamy character. They were a contentious bunch. A William White, in the eighteenth century, had numerous complaints for violent behavior sworn out against him, and another William White, my own great-grandfather, a sea captain and Bristol Channel pilot, was summoned for inflicting damage on the property of his neighbors. The most prominent of the Whites, Rawlins White, owner of a Cardiff fishing fleet, whose story I shall be touching on later, suffered a hideous death which, though glorious, was largely brought about by the bloody-mindedness which is entirely typical of the Whites. My own personal favorite among this dubious crew is Captain Joshua White, who sailed the seas in the 1750s in his ship the *Tryton*— though on second thought it might be better to draw a veil over his entertaining but shady activities.

"Why," I had asked myself on the way down from Paddington, "should I be of the tribe of Manasseh when I can wander with Esau?" Taking my feet out of the basin, padding across to the phone to call down for another Swn y Môr, I reflect that there isn't much doubt as to which portion of the tribe I belong to.

Wales is my country, my *patria grande,* as the Spanish would say, but it is Cardiff and the county of Glamorgan that I really consider to be "my" Wales, my *patria chica,* my country within a country.

At noon today I gave myself a short respite from my wanderings to visit the Reference Room at the Central Library. It struck me that it might be interesting to look up the copy of the *Western Mail* for June 22, 1924, to see how the world was wagging on the day I came into it. I thought it would also be amusing to sit once more in the handsome Reading Room where I had spent so many hours during my school holidays, working myself into a cold sweat to prepare for my university entrance exam.

In those days, because of the Luftwaffe's nightly hammering of the South Wales ports, I was never sure from one day to the other whether I would find the Library in a shambles or even in existence. At noon today I have something of the same sensation: the Reference Room looks as if a bomb has dropped on it. The paint is faded, the windows dirty, the plaster peeling off the lofty ceiling. The books are piled in heaps, waiting to be carted off to a new facility nearby. I knew I would have to say good-bye to many things on this trip to Wales; this is the first of those good-byes. It confirms my queasy feelings about the random and shifting nature of things, as if we were all involved in some kind of a game in which everything is aimless and jumbled and eventually thrown carelessly into the discard. Nor am I reassured when, after a good deal of difficulty, the file for the *Western Mail* for 1924 is eventually located and I turn up the relevant copy. All that busy cast of characters: vanished. All the scenery of the play: dismantled, hauled away, disposed of God knows where.

> *Dead, we become the lumber of the World,*
> *And to that mass of Matter shall be swept*
> *Where Things destroy'd, with Things unborn are kept.*

Leafing through the tindery pages, I discover that I was inserted into British society at a peculiarly grim period. The June of 1924 was less than six years away from the end of World War I, in which the great states of Europe virtually committed suicide, and only fifteen years away from World War II. In 1924 the country, after a brief boomlet, was about to enter what the British call the Slump, and the Americans the Depression.

On this high summer day in 1924, increasing numbers of miners are being laid off in the South Wales coalfields. There are renewed strikes over wages in the collieries of the Afan Valley. The rise of dictatorships and the onset of World War II are foreshadowed by the protests that are taking place on the Continent over the murder of the Socialist deputy Matteotti by Mussolini's Blackshirts. Few people can have been reassured by the declaration of the British Prime Minister, the ineffable Ramsay MacDonald, that "the Entente is safe with Monsieur Herriot in command in France." The tidings that Mallory and Irvine have been lost on Mt. Everest have been conveyed to their parents.

The steamship *Clan Macmillan* has disappeared off Rangoon with the loss of more than seventy hands. The Irish Mail has been held up and robbed at Dublin by armed bandits.

The items of Welsh news particularly intrigue me: the bits of the mosaic that form the immediate background of my own existence. In North Wales, the Welsh Wizard, Lloyd George, is once again teasing the man who is now his nominal leader, the egregious Asquith, in a typically mischievous speech, though the Liberal Party is already foundering, thanks largely to Lloyd George's own shenanigans. The financier Sir Alfred Mond (with whom T. S. Eliot hoped to lie in heaven "wrapped in a five percent Exchequer Bond") has been speaking at the South Wales seaside town of Barry in favor of "Empire co-operation." A quick man with a cliché, Sir Alfred does not realize that the Empire has little more than forty years to run. The paper's leading article attacks "the rising star of Labour" (the *Western Mail*, like Cardiff, is strongly Conservative) and speaks darkly of the "Red Money from Moscow that is pouring into the country."

The members of the Carmarthen Archaeological Society have made a pilgrimage to the shrine of St. David. Mr. A. J. B. Wace and Mr. Mortimer Wheeler have been short-listed for the post of Director of the recently opened National Museum of Wales. Dr. Adrian Boult has conducted the Welsh Symphony Orchestra at the Aberystwyth Festival. There has been a spectacular fire at the Porthcawl Casino. Lady Rhondda is threatening to create a schism in the Welsh Rotary Club. Next year's Eisteddfod, or National Festival, will be held at Pwllheli. Nature lovers should watch for the wild asparagus on Worm's Head. The column devoted to literature contains a correct but dull poem in Welsh by "Brynfor" and a routine denunciation of Caradoc Evans, whose stories of rural Wales have made him the target of the same kind of spiteful attacks that are being leveled at James Joyce and D. H. Lawrence.

❋     ❋     ❋

What kind of people are these Welsh? How can I set about describing the character of such an idiosyncratic nation?

It is often difficult to convince my American friends, and even some of my more obtuse English friends, that Wales is indeed a separate nation and not simply a province or region of England. Americans tend to look skeptical when I tell them that the Welsh are as different from the English as the Greeks from the Swedes, or the Poles from the Portuguese, and that it is one of nature's little jokes to have confined two such utterly contrasted peoples side by side upon the same small island. Nor do they quite believe me when I point out that only a couple of hours and a hundred miles west of London (a fleabite in terms of time and distance in America) they could find themselves in a place where they could not understand a word of the language, or be able to read the newspapers or the street signs, or make any sense of the radio and television programs: where in fact they might feel that they had landed on another planet.

The English know the Welsh as well as anyone, but even the English don't really know the Welsh very well, as they will often be the first to admit. The word *Welsh* is derived from the Anglo-Saxon word *waelisch,* meaning "foreign," and to most of the English, Wales is still foreign territory, almost as foreign as France or Belgium. Relatively few English people travel to Wales, cheek by jowl though it runs with their own country, and the Englishman venturing into Wales for a vacation regards himself as almost as much of a tourist as an American would. It is possible that the average Englishman feels rather less comfortable with the prospect of going to Wales than he does with the prospect of going to Scotland or Ireland, despite the antipathy of the Scots to the English and the sempiternal troubles in Ireland.

These old racial antagonisms die hard. And antagonism there still is—more so on the Welsh side than on the English, because the Welsh have more to forgive. For me this is something, inevitable though it is, to deplore and regret. I always want to knock the heads of the Welsh and English together and ask how many more generations it will take for them to realize how much they need each other, complement each other, balance each other, constitute two halves of what could be a fruitful and productive whole. The English are predominantly head, the Welsh predominantly heart. Head and heart should go together.

Speaking for myself, I have always been grateful that I was to a large degree the product of a Welsh nature and an English nurture. It was Wales that gave me the sense of romance, England that gave me the sense of reality. I am always amused by the fact that, when I am in Wales, and eventually grow irritated with all that Welsh extravagance and melodrama, I turn my back and look longingly east toward England. Similarly, when I am in England, and grow sick of all that thick-skinned and thick-souled Englishness, I turn toward the west and yearn for Wales. The more extreme of my nationalistic friends in Wales would regard my Anglo-Welsh bipolarity as a sort of mongrelization, even a kind of treason, but to me it has always represented a source of strength.

The Welsh word for themselves is the very opposite of "foreigner." They call themselves *Y Cymry*, or "the comrades," living in a land called *Cymru*, which can be translated as "The People." There are profound differences between the inhabitants of the various regions of Wales, yet the Welsh as a whole feel a strong sense of nationhood, a clear idea of their individuality and separateness. Their feeling of comradeship is very definite: every Welshman considers himself connected in a deep and immediate way with every other Welshman. Indeed, the country is so small that most people in Wales can quickly establish some sort of family kinship with everybody else. There is a sense of a common blood tie. Perhaps I am exaggerating a little, since there are now, after all, getting on to nearly 3 million Welsh people, up by almost a million from when I was born; but family feeling, a passionate and almost mystical regard for one's immediate personal relationships, is a highly marked feature of Welsh existence, and this personal and private feeling is readily extended to one's fellow countrymen as a whole. Wales is one of those small countries where you can easily picture the citizens turning out to form a human chain. No doubt the fact of having a common enemy, of continual friction and confrontation with the English, has been a powerful factor in implanting in the Welsh a sense of togetherness. The Welsh have never quite lost the feeling of what they were, fifteen hundred years ago, in Arthurian times: refugees. They still have something of the refugee mentality: a whole people displaced by barbarian invaders and sent huddling back into a tiny corner of its ancestral domains. Whenever I used to cross the border into England as a boy, I had a dim sense of issuing forth into some lost and larger homeland, a country that in ancient times had belonged to us and that, after bitter battles, had been taken from us.

I have to acknowledge that this view of the comradely character and essential unity and homogeneity of the Welsh might be strenuously contested by many of both my Welsh and my English friends. I must admit that there hasn't been much appearance and evidence, to the objective eye, of sweetness and comradeship in Welsh domestic history. Even in the heady days of Welsh independence, the princes of Wales and their subjects were prone to set about one another with a lethal relish; their preoccupations were a good deal more sanguinary than sanguineous. All the same, I would assert that these conflicts were basically familial, dissensions within the same family rather than quarrels with outsiders, even though quarrels between brothers are notoriously more lethal than quarrels with strangers. I certainly cannot bring myself to agree with the current fashion among Welsh historians of representing the Welsh nation as perpetually divided against itself: north against south, east against west, Welsh speaker against non–Welsh speaker, agricultural worker against industrial worker, religious believer against non-believer. Contemporary Welsh scholars strike me as being rather too fond of inventing crises for the Welsh nation, even though Welshmen, with their excitable tendency, certainly possess a decided appetite for crises and insist on detecting them in the most unlikely places. One can scarcely open a recent commentary on Wales without encountering a crisis on every other page. The "crisis of identity" seems to be particularly in vogue. Some writers would have us believe that the Welsh people have done little since the Iron Age except indulge in one long crisis of identity, or at least lurch from one minicrisis of identity to the next.

The fact is, however, that you cannot talk to a Welshman for three minutes without receiving the impression of a very firm and positive self-image. Whether he is a North Welshman or a South Welshman, Welsh speaking or non–Welsh speaking, a Christian or an atheist, a soccer fan or a rugby fanatic, your Welshman is first and foremost a Welshman, and proud of it. It does no good to pronounce, with the Welsh Nationalists, that one Welshman is a "good" Welshman and another a "bad" Welshman, one a genuine Welshman and another a suspect Welshman. This can only create mischief. Ultimately the difference between one Welshman and his neighbor is no greater than the difference between a Yorkshireman and a Lancastrian, or a Devonian and a Cornishman. No one can deny that the Englishman has been having a great deal of trouble in the latter half of the twentieth century in adjusting to his altered political and economic status in the world, but it would be silly to claim that he is having difficulty with his actual identity. Indeed the complaint made against him by his colleagues in the Common Market is that, as Gilbert and Sullivan put it, "in spite of all temptations to belong to other nations, he remains an Englishman." What is history, in any event, but one colossal, continuing crisis? The Welsh can't lay claim to any monopoly on crisis.

Nevertheless, we Welsh have certainly had our due share of

it. It has been said of our Celtic cousins the Irish that they manufacture a lot more history than they can consume locally. The Welsh are more inward looking and hermetic than the Irish, and have not chosen to impose their miseries on the consciousness of the world to anything like the same extent, but Welsh history is every bit as highly colored and inflamed as the history of Ireland. Moreover, Wales is only a third the size of Ireland, and is physically a very small country indeed. It is not much more than 40 miles across and 130 miles deep: a little larger than Connecticut, but not quite as large as Maryland, New Hampshire, or Vermont. So it is astounding, really, what an immense freight of triumph and tragedy such a tiny corner of the earth has given rise to, and has managed to support.

The history of Wales is the hectic product of the restive nature of its people. From the outset, the narrow territories of Wales were disputed by successive waves of turbulent adventurers. Some centuries before 1000 B.C., the so-called Beaker Folk entered this westernmost portion of the British mainland. They were seamen, traders, skilled makers of pottery and bronze tools, conversant with the practices of herding and agriculture which their forebears had adopted, seven or eight centuries earlier, in the eastern Mediterranean. They buried the more distinguished of their dead in elaborate stone passage graves, often massive and spectacular, which exist in much the same form in Malta, Sicily, Corsica, the Portuguese Algarve, Brittany, Cornwall, Wales, Ireland, Scotland, and as far north as the Orkney Islands. As the Bronze Age progressed, in addition to passage graves they raised many smaller and circular graves, and also imposing circles in stone and wood which were known as henges—Stonehenge, Woodhenge, et cetera. They also erected a large proportion of those standing stones or monoliths that are such a familiar and mysterious feature of the Welsh landscape. Altogether the Bronze

Age culture of Europe and Britain appears to have been well organized and generally pacific, its widely spaced communities headed by a shrewd and sophisticated merchant class.

Around 500 B.C., however, these peoples began to be displaced, or dominated and absorbed, by a much more combative and militaristic breed. These were the Celts, who, pushing out in their war bands from their original heartlands among the lakes and highlands of central Europe, quickly took control of the rest of the Continent. They were smelters of iron, and their iron swords and spears were as far superior to the bronze weapons of their predecessors as bronze weapons had been to the flint and fire-hardened wood of the Stone Age and Neolithic peoples. Indeed, the story of Arthur drawing the sword from the stone is probably a parable of the shift from the Bronze Age to the Iron Age, and of how some superior individual demonstrated to his people the method of smelting the new material and manufacturing the iron sword which would replace the old-fashioned bronze weapon. The incoming Celts were also able to cultivate the land in a more systematic fashion than their forerunners; whereas the bronze ax head was only good for felling trees, the iron plowshare of the Celts was able to tackle the clayey soils of northern Europe. These warrior-farmers not only settled down to plow the soil with their oxen but ranged far and wide in their war chariots, to the wheels of which they attached fearsome knives. In battle they fought naked, their bodies painted with frightening designs. Their shrill war cry petrified even the disciplined ranks of the Roman infantry. Confident of their superiority, acquisitive and land hungry, they eventually reached the shores of northern France and the Low Countries. Then, when they had taught themselves to become expert seagoers like the Beaker Folk, they contrived to transport themselves across the Channel into Britain.

The first wave (between 500 and 100 B.C. there would be three waves of them altogether) had landed in southeastern Britain. It was the second and largest wave, sailing two centuries later and heading for the westerly shores of Britain, that colonized the western portion of the island. They first ruled then mingled with the indigenous population of Wales, losing no time in carving out distinct tribal areas. In these areas they constructed hill forts, the precursors of the later castles of Wales, some of them, like the famous Maiden Castle in Wessex, so beloved of Thomas Hardy, boasting multiple lines of ramparts and ditches and intricate entranceways guarded by high wooden towers. Probably they did not live permanently in these hill forts but retired into them with their families, their possessions, and their livestock in times of peril, as Spanish communities did into the local Alcázar and Greek communities into their Acropolis.

What was the legacy that these horsemen and charioteers, this martial elite, added to the life-style of the more temperate folk who had gone before? For one thing, they brought to Wales its language, the individual voice that has endured from that day to this—endured in spite of the fact that from time to time the English made determined efforts to suppress the tongue of their diminutive neighbor. Geography, and increasingly lopsided de-motics, would allow the English to subjugate the Welsh, despite their ferocious resistance, more thoroughly than they would ever manage to conquer and subjugate the Scots or the Irish; yet somehow it was the Welsh who clung to their language more obstinately and successfully than either the Scots or the Irish were able to do. During many of the troughs in their national history, it must have seemed to the Welsh that their language was the only thing they had, the only thing the English had grudg-ingly left them.

Scots Gaelic, Irish Gaelic, and Welsh may originally have had a similar origin, in what philologists call Common Celtic. In course of time, circumstances brought about modification and specialization, and Common Celtic split into two branches: Goidelic or *q*-Celtic (so called because of its characteristic hard *q*-sound) and Brittonic or *p*-Celtic (because of its softer *p*-sound).

Goidelic was spoken on the northerly and westerly fringes of the Celtic world, in northern Scotland, Ireland, and on the Isle of Man, while Brittonic (or Brythonic) became the language of the heartland of British Celtdom, in England, southern Scotland, Wales, Cornwall, and (after Cornish settlers had carried it there) Brittany. In time, all these regions developed compartmentalized versions of Celtic that became mutually incomprehensible. (It might be interesting to note that the name *Great Britain* was not originally coined, as most people assume, to glorify the over-weening Britain of the British Empire; it was merely meant to signify the British Isles as Great or Greater Britain, in contrast to Brittany, otherwise known as Little or Lesser Britain.)

Whether one is minding, as it were, one's p's or one's q's, the languages of Celtdom, like Celtic art, all share a striking particularity: they are exceedingly complex, able to absorb a great weight of dense and subtle meaning. Such languages lend themselves readily to poetry, which, with its sister art of music, has always supplied a vital spark of Welsh existence. The Welsh poets of the seventh to the ninth centuries A.D., whose work was written down some centuries later in such collections as the Red Book of Hergest and the Black Book of Carmarthen, would provide northern Europe with its earliest recorded specimens of literature. It is intriguing to note, incidentally, that the earlier of these poets—Aneirin, Taliesin, Llywarch Hên, and the woman poet Heledd—lived and wrote not in Wales but in Calydon or Caledonia, that is, in northern Britain or southern Scotland, which, before Britain was broken up by the Anglo-Saxon inter-lopers, was an integral part of a unified Celtic realm. I always enjoy the shocked look on the faces of my Scottish friends when I tell them that Edinburgh was once a Welsh town.

The best way for a non–Welsh speaker to appreciate some-thing of the intricacy of the Welsh formal meters, and of the chiming rhyme scheme springing from the earliest days, which is called *cynghanedd,* is to read the poetry of Gerard Manley

Hopkins and Dylan Thomas. Thomas did not speak Welsh, but in some instinctive fashion, genetically or by osmosis, he inherited the Welsh poet's obsession with consonance and assonance, with alliteration, with internal rhyming, with half rhymes and slant rhymes and all manner of stanzaic devices. Hopkins, who had a modicum of Welsh blood, actually taught himself to write very passable poetry in Welsh, and the most artistically fruitful years of his life were spent in Wales, at the seminary in Flintshire named after the Welsh saint St. Beuno. Hopkins's "inscape" and "instress," his "sprung rhythm," can readily be recognized as a close approximation of *cynghanedd*. It should also be noted that many of the English poets who belonged to the most linguistically labyrinthine school of English poetry, the Metaphysical, were partly Welsh by blood or possessed direct links with Wales. John Donne, George Herbert, and Thomas Traherne had such connections, while the poet who once spoke most intimately to me, Henry Vaughan, spent all his life and was buried in the Breconshire valley that I intend to visit as part of my present journey to Wales.

The same tendency toward complexity that characterizes Celtic poetry is typical of Celtic art. The gold, silver, and bronze horse trappings, weapons, bowls, drinking vessels, neck rings, bracelets, and armlets that have been discovered in Europe and in Britain demonstrate that the Celts were absolute masters of design and decoration. If it were not for a fine sense of overall control, and a certain geometrical rigor, the decoration of these artifacts would degenerate into a mere riot of aimless and extravagant forms. As it is, one is overwhelmed by the impression that these objects convey of vehemence and urgency; the artists who wrought these vivid pieces did not possess a cool view of the world, though clearly they felt the necessity, as the Celtic poets did, of anchoring their propensity toward abstraction and over-exuberance in a firm aesthetic armature. Once again, the fundamental motifs and stylistic manner of ancient Celtdom have persisted in Wales throughout the centuries and are discernible in our own century, for example, in the spirited paintings of Ceri Richards and in David Jones's close-meshed and calligraphic watercolors depicting the Arthurian legend.

Celtic art, and what historical data we possess from early sources, testifies to the fact that the Celts were mystics, nature worshipers, shape shifters, passionate dreamers. These characteristics are embodied in the earliest recorded utterances of the Welsh. Taliesin, an exemplary figure whose persistent image gave Emyr Humphreys the title for his cardinal study of the Welsh character, *The Taliesin Tradition,* wrote an extraordinary poem in which he declares: "I have been a blue salmon. I have been a dog. I have been a stag and a buck in the hills. I have been a spade and a hoe and a tool in the smithy. Neither father nor mother gave me birth. I sprang from God's root, from the primrose and the mountain blossom, from the bloom of bush and tree, from the earth and from the flower of the nettle, from the foam of the ninth wave."

I think the response of most Welshmen, on hearing these strange words, would be a queer little shudder of recognition. They touch obscure but never far from the surface emotions that must surely stem from the pantheistic worldview of the original Celts, and of the Bronze Age folk who went before them. The remote and impenetrable terrain of Wales, the last bastion of Celtdom, has lent it a historical continuity from Neolithic days to our own. When you walk the Welsh landscape, you are permeated with the atmosphere of antiquity that suffuses it. It is King Lear country. In addition to its huge inventory of castles, dating from every epoch, the countryside is thickly strewn with cromlechs, cairns, quoits, dolmens, barrows, tumps, circles, henges, hill forts, wayside crosses, holy wells, haunted caves, sunken cities, and subterranean passages. Above all it is sprinkled with standing or recumbent stones of every kind: stones with carved inscriptions in Celtic, Latin, and Ogham; stones crowning the peaks of mountains, ridges, escarpments, or standing in mysterious isolation by the sides of streams or in the middle of the woods; stones on which fires were lighted and sacrifices were made; stones that rock, fly, walk, and talk, and that on May Day or Midsummer's Eve go down to take a bath in the river. Wales is a small but richly stored repository of physical remains and folk customs that stretch back beyond the Iron and Bronze Ages to the ages of Copper and Stone.

The very stones of Wales are immeasurably ancient, since the rocks of rocky little Wales are among the most venerable in the world. Most of the country consists of rocks that are at least 200 million years old, while three of the earliest periods known to geology—the Cambrian, the Ordovician, and the Silurian— actually take their names from the Welsh formations where they were first identified. The Welsh inhabit the world's bedrock. And in the waters of Wales exist organisms that are even older than the rocks. One of them, the weirdly named *Kakabekia barghoon- iana,* discovered off Harlech in 1964, is said to be the earth's oldest surviving life-form.

Cambrian is the anglicized version of the word *Cymro*, while the Ordovician and the Silurian are named after the Ordovices and the Silures, two of the four Celtic tribes that had consolidated their individual regions in Wales before the onset of the Romans. The Ordovices and the Deceangli held sway in North Wales, the Silures and the Demetae in South Wales. These four, like the other Celtic tribes in Britain and southern Scotland, fought incessantly among themselves. There was also constant civil war between the two grand divisions into which the British tribes were divided, the western Celts and the easternmost Celts, the latter still flooding into southeastern England from the Low Countries, at the expense of their older, established rivals in the midlands, the north, and the west. When Julius Caesar made his reconnaissance in strength, in 55 B.C., the whole situation was highly fluid, and it was equally volatile a century later, when in

A.D. 43 the Emperor Claudius judged the British islands, with their reputed mineral and agricultural riches, ripe for plucking. His expeditionary force of no less than five legions encountered fierce preliminary resistance, but under the command of the tough future emperor Vespasian soon made headway, and within a short time the majority of the Celtic tribes had been subdued and had made their peace with Rome.

Not so in Wales. The legions managed to push their way along the southern and northern coastlines, and Tacitus has left us a vivid description of the Druids of Anglesey, in their flowing white robes, leaping or being hurled by the legionaries off the cliffs onto the rock beneath. Nevertheless, the central portion of Wales held out, and it was ten full years before the Romans could make any progress there. The Ordovices and the Silures came together under the leadership of the gifted and determined Caratacus, or Caractacus, one of the two sons of Cunobelinus (Shakespeare's Cymbeline), the king of the powerful Catuvellauni of the eastern Midlands. Caratacus and his equally famous brother Togodumnus had vehemently resisted the Romans when the latter made their original landing, and now Caratacus had fled to the west to continue a guerrilla campaign in the mountains of Wales. He kept the west aflame and conducted a successful rear-guard action until A.D. 51, when his forces were eventually run to earth and crushed in the Malvern Hills, which King Arthur was to make the center of his own operations five centuries later.

Caratacus managed to fight his way free and evade capture when his men were trapped, and he sought refuge with the Brigantes, the Celtic tribe that straddled the whole of northernmost Britain. Unfortunately Cartimandua, the queen of the Brigantes, who had concluded an alliance with Rome, handed him over to Claudius, who had him led captive, chained, through the streets of Rome. Claudius, not otherwise famous for generosity, then pardoned Caratacus and restored him to the wife and family who had been captured along with him. However, even after the downfall of Caratacus, the embers of revolt still glowed in Wales, and it would be more than another generation before the Romans would be able to exploit the country's deposits of lead, copper, iron, and coal, and to dredge its rivers for gold and pearls. Indeed, although they were finally able to enmesh Wales with their usual systematic network of roads and trackways, interspersed with forts and marching camps, the only part of it that they (like the Norman invaders after them) were truly able to subdue was the lush and easily accessible coastal area of South Wales, in particular the Vale of Glamorgan.

We have seen how the Romans built a substantial fortress at Cardiff, and how in the course of time prosperous Roman villas and farmsteads began to sprout in the rich farmland surrounding it. For the most part, however, the Romans sealed off the bulk of Wales from their eastern dominions in Britain in much the way that they sealed off the remote and savage Picts in the north of Scotland. To contain the Picts, the Romans first built the massive stone defensive line of Hadrian's Wall, then created a neutral zone by building the earthen Antonine Wall a hundred miles to the north of it, depopulating the territory in between. In Wales, nature did not provide the Romans with a handy narrow point stretching from sea to sea, so to bottle up the Welsh they devised a military frontier that was anchored in the north, in the country of the Ordovices, by the great fortress of Deva (Chester), and in the south by the equally imposing fortress of Isca (Caerleon). Between these two major strong points they placed a line of secondary forts, of which the most substantial were Viroconium (Wroxeter—A. E. Housman's Uricon) and Magna (Kenchester).

In accordance with their habit, the Romans planned clearly and executed carefully. In fact, the frontier that Rome established for Wales, from Deeside in the north to Severnside in the south, has remained the frontier demarcating Wales from England for the past two thousand years. The respect in which the Romans held these early Welsh fighting men can be judged by the fact that, once Roman rule had taken firm root throughout the whole of Britain, only three cities were designated as permanent legionary headquarters. Two of these were Deva and Isca, guarding the borders of Wales. Deva became home to the Sixth Legion, and Isca the Second Legion, while the third city, Eburacum (York), served as the main supply depot for the northern frontier.

Not only did Queen Cartimandua of the Brigantes bring odium on herself for so slavishly collaborating with the Romans and for her betrayal of Caratacus but, also in A.D. 51, she committed an even more shameful act by refusing to come to the aid of her fellow queen Boudicca or Boadicea of the Iceni. Boudicca, provoked beyond endurance by the rapacity and callousness of the imperial tax gatherers, had raised her people in revolt and marched on London. On the way she utterly shattered and routed a Roman legion before she was finally cornered and killed. The borders of the Iceni, in East Anglia, marched with those of the Brigantes: but Cartimandua chose to sit tight and watch her Celtic neighbors go down to defeat. For this she would later lose her throne and be driven into exile among her Roman patrons.

It is interesting to mark the existence of women at the head of sundry Celtic tribes. Nor were they titular leaders, but forceful figures in their own right. Women have always played a consequential role in Celtic life, and conspicuously so in Wales—much more so, I think, than in England. It seems a fair guess that the Celts were in fact matrilineal, while the Anglo-Saxons were patrilineal. Although the Saxon kings possessed their share of formidable and assertive consorts, we do not find among the Saxons independent queens like Boudicca or Cartimandua, or like the great Queen Maeve in Connaught. Welsh women have never been loathe to thrust themselves forward, and in the circle of the family the ascendancy of the woman can be absolute. Indeed, Welsh men rather seem to enjoy being bullied, and in their later years often tend to become lazy and complacent and to let their wives do the work and make most of the decisions. When the young Welsh man decides that the time has come to cut the umbilical cord and fight free from maternal influence, the act is frequently accompanied by prolonged and impassioned battles. Nor are Welsh mothers noted for approving of their sons' girlfriends. Often the mother's belligerence will prevail, with the result that, both before and after marriage, the son can remain a somewhat passive mother's boy. The same mettlesome quality can be shown by a sister toward her brother, or by one sister toward another. Nevertheless, the Welsh woman's tendency to domineer and be overprotective is only the expression of her fierce and all-consuming love for her family. I speak of this with some feeling, since my mother was one of eight sisters, and I was largely raised by females. There was no lack of Boudiccas in my household. However, I have always been grateful for this early experience, stifling though it was at times, since I think that it gave me not only an insight into women's artfulness and guile but also an appreciation which many of my English friends might have lacked of their courage and resourcefulness, together with a deep respect and tenderness for them and a sense of ease in dealing with them. One of the pleasant things about the Welsh, in comparison with the English, is their genuinely egalitarian instinct, and nowhere is this more apparent than in the relations between Welsh men and Welsh women.

The role of women in Celtic religion was as significant as their role in everyday affairs. Side by side in the Celtic pantheon with the sun god Lugh, and with the horned god Cernunnos, King of the Stags, presided the female deity known as the Great Goddess. The Great Goddess was the spirit who ruled over nature, a creator, although she could also assume a Kali-like aspect and wreak destruction. Sometimes she manifested herself in the guise of the Divine Mothers, three goddesses portrayed as seated or standing side by side, bearing baskets of fruit and sheaves of corn. The Divine Goddesses possessed a particular appeal for the Romans, who called them the Matronae and raised shrines and votive tablets to them throughout Britain and Gaul. At other times the Matronae might appear as the Genii Cucullati, the Hooded Ones, three somber figures swathed from top to toe in cloaks. It was the Great Mother who, under different names, was the protectress of rivers, waterfalls, lakes, and wells, for the Celts recognized water as the mysterious source and sustenance of all life. The lakes and streams of Britain and Europe have yielded up a glittering trove of Celtic artifacts, deposited there as ritualistic offerings. The Rhine and its tributaries all have names with Celtic derivations, while the river Marne is named in honor of the Matronae, the Seine in honor of the goddess Sequana, the Clyde in honor of the goddess Clota, and the Severn in honor of Sabrina.

It must have been the tug of some Celtic instinct that prompted me, when I lived at Minsterworth Court, where my lawns ran down to a broad reach of the river Severn, to enact a curious little ceremony with each returning spring. With my wife and my two small daughters, I would go down to the riverbank to strew the surface of the river with armfuls of the earliest daffodils. And as they were borne by the current down into the heart of the waters, we would recite the lines from *Comus*:

> *Sabrina fair,*
> *Listen where thou art sitting*
> *Under the glassy, cool, translucent wave,*
> *In twisted braids of lilies knitting*
> *The loose train of thy amber-dropping hair:*
> *Listen for dear honour's sake,*
> *Goddess of the silver lake,*
> *Listen and save!*

I might mention that the names of our daughters, Bronwen and Rhiannon, can be traced back to Celtic antiquity. Bronwen and Rhiannon figure prominently in the stories of the *Mabino-gion,* the collection of tales rooted in Celtic lore. *Bronwen* is an earlier form of *Branwen,* "one of the three great Queens of the Island of the Mighty," who has one of the eleven stories in the book entirely to herself. Rhiannon too is an important character in the *Mabinogion,* a princess half human and half divine, incomparably beautiful, and destined to become the mother of the hero Pryderi. She possesses magic birds which, if you were beguiled into listening to them, would hold you captive for seven years, even though it would seem that only as many minutes had passed. Her name is probably linked with that of Rigantona, a Celtic goddess who presided over the welfare of horses, those creatures to whom the Celts were so passionately attached.

The collapse of Roman rule in Wales must have been as painful as it proved throughout the rest of the Empire. As it happened, it was a figure I have already mentioned briefly, a soldier whom the Welsh came to regard as their first great national hero, who was largely responsible for the debacle. Maximus Magnus, a capable and ambitious general of Spanish origin, had served with distinction in Wales and Scotland. We have seen how, in A.D. 383, he took Britain's best army, containing a sizable Welsh contingent, to the Continent in pursuit of the imperial crown, only to be defeated and killed near Milan, at the Battle of Aquileia. Thus, at this critical time, Britain was left bereft and defenseless in the face of increasing piracy and lawlessness, although no blame was attached to Maximus, or Macsen Wledig, as the Welsh called him, by the Welsh themselves. In the *Mabinogion* he is honored with a short but glorious tale, largely devoted to his infatuation, which the Welsh as a romantic people thoroughly approved, with a girl he had glimpsed in a dream. "I have had a dream, and in that dream I have seen a girl, and because of her there is neither life nor being nor existence for me." The tale describes how the lovesick general sallies forth from Britain, conquers France and Burgundy, and with the aid of his Welsh battalions takes Rome and becomes Emperor. He then rewards his Welshmen by making over the rest of his army to them, whereupon they have a fine time "going out and conquering lands and castles and cities, killing all the men but sparing all the women."

Macsen Wledig was, of course, the direct forerunner of King Arthur; in fact, they lived only a century apart. The ruins of an imperial polity survived for a generation or so on the fringes of the Empire after the Goths had sacked Rome in A.D. 410, but by A.D. 450 the Saxons had begun their systematic incursions into Britain, and Arthur would appear to have been one of the native Britons who became leaders of an organized resistance. He may not have been an actual king but, like Caratacus before him, the gifted leader of a war band, a kind of Robin Hood or perhaps the general and right-hand man to some legitimate ruler. Possibly he was a *dux bellorum*, a professional soldier trained as a cavalryman in the methods of the Roman army. Possibly also he was a legendary figure compounded and amalgamated from several of those gallant captains who strove to stem the tide of the Saxon advance. He has been tentatively identified with a man of Roman descent called Ambrosius Aurelianus, but that he may not have been a real and identifiable person is suggested by the fact that the historian Gildas, a West Country monk who wrote only a short time after Arthur would have been active, nowhere mentions Arthur in his copious pages. Indeed, hints and references to Arthur and his Round Table and his twelve battles against the Saxons, culminating in the great victory of Mt. Badon, only begin to appear three hundred years after his putative death, while the grand flowering of the Arthurian story into an epic that would spread into every corner of Europe did not take place until Geoffrey of Monmouth, a British monk living in Wales, wrote his *History of the Kings of Briton* in 1136, seventy years after the

Norman Conquest. Geoffrey's *History,* combined with other Franco-Norman materials, took Europe by storm and very quickly alerted the Welsh themselves to the existence of a potentially valuable national property. Arthur was swiftly elevated to the dignity of Wales's secular guardian, her Once and Future King, the guarantor of her survival and the pledge of her eventual freedom and independence.

The Arthurian legend, of course, would eventually assume proportions that would dwarf its Welsh origins and its appearance in the pages of Geoffrey of Monmouth and the *Mabinogion.* But it was there, in Welsh legend and literature, that the names and exploits of the lords and ladies of King Arthur's court would be forever fixed in their original form. There we encounter, before they would become transfigured by Sir Thomas Malory and Chrétien de Troyes, the names of Queen Gwenhwyvar (Guinevere), Peredur (Percival), Gwalchmei (Gauvain), Kei (Kay), Bedwr (Bedivere), Lawnslot (Lancelot), Myrddin (Merlin), and the rest. Where Camelot may actually have been situated has been for over a thousand years the subject of earnest debate, but it has always been situated in the Celtic West or its immediate environs. Tintagel in Cornwall has asserted a tenuous claim, based on its picturesque atmosphere and situation, and so has Caerleon in Gwent, the former headquarters of the Second Legion, while Glastonbury in Somerset will forever be associated with Arthur's death and his final voyage to the Islands of the Blessed. In 1278, Edward I of England disinterred what he had persuaded himself were the bones of Arthur and Guinevere from a grave in the grounds of Glastonbury Abbey, and he and Queen Eleanor solemnly carried them in procession for reburial within the walls of the abbey. Modern archaeologists have likewise speculated that Somerset might have been home to Camelot, at the substantial hill fort of Cadbury Rings, with its impressive Great Hall raised on wooden pillars. As for the site of the Battle of Mt. Badon, which may have been fought somewhere around the year 500, most authorities place it somewhere to the east of the Celtic heartland that Arthur was defending. The village of Baydon in Wiltshire has been suggested as a likely candidate.

The troubled era that followed the collapse of Roman rule was by no means distinguished, however, solely by chaos and destruction. The Christianity that had begun to flourish in the Roman Empire during its later stages took firm root in Wales, and it was Welsh missionaries who in the sixth century prompted a surge of Christian enthusiasm in Ireland and Brittany that in turn flowed back to nourish the church in Wales. This was the time during which a network of religious houses sprang into existence all over Wales, giving shelter to such prominent men of God as St. Beuno, St. Illtyd, St. Padarn (St. Patrick, a Welsh boy supposedly kidnapped by Irish pirates from the famous West Welsh seminary at Lampeter and transported to Ireland), and above all Wales's patron saint, St. David. The names of these holy men are repeated again and again in the names of Welsh towns and villages. The tradition and the rites of the Celtic church remained quite distinct from those of Rome, and indeed its leaders were so confident, and so resolute in their opposition to Rome, that according to the Venerable Bede they rebuffed St. Augustine, who for five years had been working to convert the Saxons and wished to bring the Celtic bishops under Roman rule, at two separate conferences on the Welsh border in 602 and 603. The body of the Welsh church was not persuaded to accept Roman usage until over a century later, and even then there remained pockets of ecclesiastical resistance that held out until the Norman Conquest.

It was during these obscure and ill-recorded centuries, between 500 and 800, which Welshmen like to call their Heroic Age, that both Wales and England began to emerge as well-defined ethnic and geographic entities. In both regions clear-cut dynastic houses began to emerge. At first it was the Welsh, if anything, who were the most important. In the sixth century Maelgwyn, of the nascent North Welsh royal house of Gwynedd, appears to have exercised broad rule not only over Wales but over Scotland, Cornwall, and a substantial swathe of southwest Britain. Then, within the space of a half century, two shattering defeats lost Wales the predominance it was never destined to regain. The southwest was shorn away at the Battle of Dyrham in 577, and North Britain at the Battle of Chester in 615. Until the end of the seventh century, Gwynedd continued to produce powerful kings, in the persons of Cadfan, Cadwallon, and Cadwaladr, the last taking his place in Welsh memory and esteem beside the figure of King Arthur himself. Nevertheless, Wales was now coming under heavy pressure from the Saxon kingdoms of Northumbria and Mercia, and later Wessex, which themselves were struggling to resist pressure from the east in the shape of the incoming Scandinavians.

In the same way that the English were beginning to adopt such firm groupings, the Welsh were simultaneously starting to arrange themselves into distinct and recognizable kingdoms, each with its own dynasty. Indeed, the kingdoms of Wales would long outlast those of Saxon England, remaining in existence for virtually seven hundred years. Nor have they vanished yet. When the new county system was introduced throughout Great Britain in 1974, the names of the ancient kingdoms were revived, and once again the map of Wales is embellished with the proud names of Gwynedd, Powys, Dyfed, and Gwent, while the names of Meirionydd, Ceredigion, and Glamorgan had never vanished from it. Whenever I write *Gwynedd* or *Powys* on the address of a letter to Wales, I cannot repress a strange little shiver.

Of these late Dark Ages and early medieval kingdoms, four were predominant: Gwynedd and Powys in the north, Deheubarth and Morgannwg in the south, and various minor dependencies of all four kingdoms usually existed. During the entire span of their lengthy existence, these Welsh realms would be locked in rivalry among themselves, just as an England supposedly united by the Norman Conquest would be constantly engaged in combat in England and Ireland, in the Hundred Years' War and the Wars of the Roses. At any given moment, one Welsh prince would be in league with or at odds with another, or in league with or at odds with some king of England. Too seldom would they unite to repel one of the frequent English attempts to subdue them, to pen them into their own corner of the islands, to put an end to their endless razzias and encroachments. Nonetheless, secure in their mountain bastion, the Welsh would become conscious of their own identity, and would exert themselves strenuously to protect it.

The construction of Offa's Dyke by King Offa of Mercia, around 780, signalized the hardening of Wales and England into separate nations and the establishment of a boundary between them. Significantly, the dike traversed the present Welsh border from north to south along more or less the same line that had been drawn by the Romans between their legionary fortresses at Chester and Caerleon. However, if the Romans and the Saxons, and the English after them, were in the process of defining their frontier, so were the Welsh. What remained of Western Celtdom was saying, "Thus far and no farther"—and this is the boundary that they have maintained ever since. Even in decay, Offa's Dyke is in places an impressive sight, and long stretches of it can still be easily traced. When you drive from England along one of the roads that cut it, you have the definite feeling that you are entering a different country. You know you are now in Wales.

With the construction of the dike, Wales may be said to have embarked on the first phase of its imperial period, which historians designate the Rule of the High Kings. During the earlier, three-hundred-year part of this phase it was Gwynedd and the north which came to the fore, thanks to the efforts of such monarchs as Rhodri Mawr, or Rhodri the Great (847–878). It then became the turn of Deheubarth and the south, under the leadership of Hywel Dda or Howell the Good (c. 920–950) and Gruffydd ap Llewellyn (1039–1063). One of Wales's most illustrious modern historians, Gwyn A. Williams, observes rather tartly that Rhodri was the only Welsh king called *Great*, and Hywel the only Welsh king called *Good*. However, Hywel was truly a remarkable man. He was responsible for promulgating a code of laws that figures in the legal textbooks alongside such pioneer codifications as that of Hammurabi. That his code was widely approved and applied is indicated by the fact that it has come down to us in over thirty medieval manuscripts. It testifies to the civilized level of life in Wales at this time, in contrast to the authoritarian and coercive atmosphere of England.

Indeed, it is worth repeating that Welsh life appears always to have been more comradely and easygoing than life in England, perhaps because of the fact that Welsh life has been based on the Celtic idea of the extended family rather than, as in England, on a legacy of serfdom and feudalism. The feudal spirit is entirely absent in Wales—as can be sensed, I think, in the different attitudes of the Welsh and the English toward monarchy. In Wales, the monarch is traditionally regarded in a somewhat formal and irreverent light, as the head of a large, noisy, and sprawling family, whereas in England the monarch is still perched in chilly isolation at the top of a seemingly indestructible class system. The English are always apprehensive that the sacred person of the monarch may be subjected, during a tour of Wales, to casual and undignified encounters accompanied by slaps on the back. The Welsh are altogether a more egalitarian people— which may help to explain, among other things, why they seem to feel more at home in countries like America, in marked contrast to the English, with their strong feeling for caste and hierarchy.

It is clear from the nature of his system of laws that Hywel Dda was no authoritarian, discharging his office by force and terror. Women, for example, were treated in the customarily respectful Welsh way, in a manner that must strike the reader as surprisingly modern. Marriage was a civil rather than a religious arrangement, divorce was by consent, and in the case of divorce the joint possessions were divided equitably and by mutual agreement. Illegitimate children were treated on exactly the same footing as legitimate ones. The code even anticipated a national health service, in that all doctors were required to treat most ailments gratis and could charge only for complicated ones. Fair and sensible guidelines were laid down for the buying and selling of property, livestock, horses, and even dogs and cats. In the case of crime—again a modern touch—the emphasis was on restitution and compensation rather than on punishment. As Jan Morris observes, in her splendid *The Matter of Wales*, "The intention was to re-establish social harmony, and the more terrible penalties of English law, the torturings, the gibbetings, the disembowelments, were unknown in independent Wales—even public whippings entered the country only with the Tudors." When the English finally, after a thousand years, succeeded in crushing the Welsh, they quickly sought to expunge every trace of Welsh custom and jurisprudence in order to substitute their own iron system. But old habits die hard (if indeed they die at all), and a modern visitor to Wales will not need to stay there very long before he hears, in the home or the public house, in the workplace or the football stand, the words which are among the most commonplace of Welsh expressions, words that reach back to Hywel Dda: *"Chwarae teg! Chwarae teg!"* "Fair play! Fair play!" The notion of fair play, of a simple, natural justice and forbearance, is deeply ingrained in the Welsh character.

After nearly three centuries, the epoch of the High Kings terminated in the penetration of Wales by the Normans. In 1063, outside the walls of Brecon Castle, the Normans killed the last of the High Kings, Rhys ap Tewdwr of Deheubarth, who had vanquished Gwynedd and ruled all Wales for nearly thirty years.

But although the Normans seized most of the choice and fertile portions of the country, and drastically reduced the area of the traditional kingdoms, during the remaining two centuries of the royal era in Wales, the so-called Period of the Princes, the Welsh monarchies managed not only to survive but to flourish. This they did in what had now become their time-honored fashion: fighting the English and fighting each other—though perhaps *skirmishing* would be a more accurate word than *fighting*, since the Welsh had learned to avoid pitched battles whenever possible. They also became adept at contracting alliances, often by means of intermarriage, between their own royal houses and those of the Norman and English barons and kings. They performed this diplomatic dance with great adroitness, and their deftness enabled them to hold the Normans and Plantagenets at arm's length in the same fashion that they had previously dealt with the successive waves of Angles, Saxons, Jutes, Franks, and Friesians. If eventually they found it expedient to acknowledge the kings of England as their overlords, they did it in such a way that they were able to preserve their native rights and privileges virtually intact and were left undisturbed within their own sphere of influence.

The Normans, nonetheless, did contrive to make grievous inroads into the country. The took over its entire southernmost sector and nibbled away determinedly at its eastern borders. The Welsh lords of Deheubarth and Morgannwg were pushed back into the mountains and became virtual vassals of the great Marcher families, who bestrode the most productive parts of Wales. In Glamorgan, the Welsh language began to die out. The barons of the Welsh Marches, practiced land grabbers by training and inclination and by royal encouragement, emulated the Romans by protecting their new territories with a system of *bastides*, a military network of major fortresses interspersed with minor ones. Powys and Dyfed were reduced to a condition of impotence, and it fell to Gwynedd, in the remote and hilly northwest, to serve as the main bulwark of Welsh freedom.

In essence the Marcher barons were regarded by the English monarchs in much the same way they regarded the Welsh kings: as quasi-independent but subject rulers. The courts of both the barons and the Welsh kings became, in the two centuries after the Conquest, centers of notable culture, the barons patronizing poets and scholars who wrote mainly in French, their Welsh counterparts in their own tongue. Every aristocratic Welsh household, major or minor, had its officially appointed chief bard, the *pencerdd,* devoting his talents to elevated themes, and its secondary bard, the *bardd teulu,* celebrating more vulgar and racy ones. In fact, the last Welsh poet in full private employment, Siôn Dafydd Las, died in 1694, while well into the nineteenth century the Welsh country gentleman felt an obligation to keep the local poet remunerated.

The *pencerdd* in particular was a person of great consequence. From Celtic times onward he had served the dual, Homeric function of historian as well as poet, preserving and transmitting to posterity the triumphs and disasters of his people. He was a member of a nationwide guild or trades union, which protected him whether he served a single master or roved about in the guise of a wandering minstrel. He guarded his professional practices jealously and was required to serve a long and rigorous apprenticeship before he was deemed to have mastered all the intricacies of Welsh prosody. He may even have had to submit to formal examinations before he could advance from one grade to the next, and it has been suggested that the tales of the *Mabinogion,* for example, were the set pieces which he was expected to master during his apprenticeship. Some idea of his exalted status can be gathered from the fact that to strike him was a very serious offense, punishable by a stiff fine. Welsh poets were prized and privileged people, as indeed they have ever afterward continued to be. Perhaps the greatest honor the Welsh nation can bestow on a man (apart, of course, from selecting him for inclusion in the nation's rugby football team) is to crown him as the Bard in the poetry contest at the yearly national Eisteddfod or festival, which itself originated in the centuries-old gatherings when the poets and musicians of the country would congregate to recite, to sing, and to play.

The princes, then, managed to maintain a workable if precarious accommodation with their Anglo-Norman neighbors to the east. From time to time the fragile truce would break down, and the English Crown would decide on a major effort to invade Wales. Several such attempts, mounted by the first three Henrys, were beaten back, usually with the assistance of that vile weather for which Wales was notorious, General Rain being as useful to Wales as General Snow was to Russia. Much of the reputation of the Welsh as wizards, able to command the elements, stems from these providential interventions by storm and tempest. Forty years after the Norman invasion, however, Henry I achieved a major stroke by contriving to insert a colony of Flemings into Pembrokeshire, at the westerly tip of South Wales, thereby ensuring that the Welsh would always be conscious of a hostile foreign enclave seated on their back doorstep. This was the same technique, of course, which the English were to employ elsewhere, notably in Northern Ireland. Even today Pembrokeshire bears the nickname "Little England Beyond Wales," and its inhabitants possess a noticeably different ethnic composition and different social habits.

In addition to the Norman and Flemish presence, the Welsh princes were also plagued by the never-ceasing raids of pirates and freebooters from overseas. Sovereign Wales nevertheless persisted, each Welsh ruler energetically transforming his own earthen stronghold into a robust stone castle in imitation of the Normans. By no means all of Wales's six hundred castles are testimony to the presence of an alien occupier; a good proportion of them are of native construction. The economy, of course, was wholly rural, based primarily on those activities with which the Welsh nation is primarily associated: sheep and cattle raising, and dairying. Whenever in my journeys through Texas, Tennessee, and other American states I encounter a dairy, I very often find it is owned by someone of Welsh descent: a Jones, a Jenkins, an Edwards, a Prosser. I daresay it is the same in the rest of the English-speaking world. The princes of Gwynedd nevertheless managed to keep hold of the island of Anglesey, the fecund "granary of Wales" that had provided wheat for the Romans and for the Bronze and Iron Age folk before them. The grain of Anglesey eked out the more exiguous crops of grain elsewhere, in whatever fertile strips of land the Normans had failed to seize, and provided the princes of Gwynedd with a good part of the economic resources that they needed to survive.

It was Gwynedd that brought the princely period to a splendid and honorable climax, ensuring that Welsh independence should not be snuffed out with a whimper but should conclude with a glorious bang.

For the last seventy-six years of its existence, Gwynedd was ruled by two outstanding princes: Llewellyn ap Iorwerth, called Llewellyn Mawr or Llewellyn the Great (1196–1240), and Llewellyn ap Gruffydd (1246–1282), known to history as Llewellyn Olaf or The Last Prince. The former, taking advantage of Richard the Lion-Hearted's troubles abroad and in the Holy Land, and of King John's struggles with his barons, succeeded in making himself the overlord of two-thirds of Wales. He set up Powys as a buffer state to protect Gwynedd and extended his conquests in an eastward direction virtually to the English border, even acquiring land from the Normans by treaty. Only the far south of Wales still held out against him.

Worn out by his exertions, Llewellyn the Great retired to a monastery to die, and it was only after six years of dispute and civil war that Llewellyn ap Gruffydd was able to accede to his grandfather's throne. By now the Welsh princes had become realists, and Llewellyn ap Gruffydd's ambition was not to rule over a Wales that was totally and unequivocally independent but to realize Llewellyn the Great's dream of ruling over a Wales which, though nominally acknowledging the suzerainty of England, would nevertheless be united, prosperous, peaceful, and free to govern itself in its own way.

For the first twenty years of his thirty-six-year reign, all went deceptively well. In his tenth year he successfully fought off a challenge from Prince Edward, the son of Henry III, who although he was only sixteen at the time was already proving to be the royal terror he was later to become as Edward I. His father had created him Earl of Chester, and he immediately seized and sought to exercise permanent control over four adjacent counties or *cantrefs* that had become detached from Gwynedd and that were being clumsily administered by the English Crown. When war broke out, and Henry sent his armies into Wales, the English were soundly defeated. At Chester in 1257, after a meeting with Henry, Llewellyn had the *cantrefs* reunited with Gwynedd and made Henry expel the troublesome Prince Edward from Chester.

For a further fifteen years Welsh fortunes soared high. Henry and his son, embroiled in civil war, were captured by Simon de Montfort at the Battle of Lewes and, although they liberated themselves at the subsequent Battle of Evesham, were in such a weakened state that they had to compound everywhere with their enemies. By the Treaty of Montgomery in 1267, Henry recognized Llewellyn as the undisputed Prince of Wales, a titular vassal of the English Crown but in actual fact an authentic power in his own right.

Such was the high-water mark of the Welsh monarchy. It was a euphoric interval that would last a scant five years. Prince Edward, who succeeded to the English throne in 1272, possessed a long memory and a killer instinct. He had a score to settle with

Llewellyn. Llewellyn wisely ignored repeated summonses to London to do homage to his new suzerain and put himself confidently on his guard. But the new Edward I was resolved to settle, once and for all, the Welsh problem that the last eight kings of England had failed to solve. No sooner had he mounted the throne than he assembled and sent into Wales—not just into Gwynedd in the north but into the whole of Wales—a well-organized and well-equipped army of four divisions under his most efficient and energetic commanders. The isle of Anglesey he devastated by means of a powerful fleet. Obviously he had only been awaiting his father's death to unleash this onslaught on the Welsh prince who had humiliated him when he was Earl of Chester.

Clearly he intended that the English should put up with no more nonsense from the Welsh. Within a year he had seized all the castles in the country that were in Welsh hands and had bestowed them on his own officers. In 1273 a humbled Llewellyn had to sue for peace and sign the Treaty of Rhuddlan, whereby he was reduced to the status of an English servitor and compelled to pay a crippling indemnity. Needless to say, Gwynedd was stripped of the four *cantrefs* that had been the cause of the original quarrel sixteen years before.

It was not quite the end of Welsh opposition. The Welsh quisling whom Edward had set up as a rival to Llewellyn, Llewellyn's own brother Dafydd, developed notions of grandeur, defied the English, and had to be hunted down and dragged at a horse's tail through the streets of Shrewsbury to be hanged, drawn, and quartered. Llewellyn himself then essayed a last campaign, with pitiful forces, and in the dead of winter in 1282, after losing a one-sided skirmish in the mountains of mid-Wales, he was ambushed and killed at Cilmeri near Builth. The circumstances of his death are obscure. It seems that he was either riding away from the battlefield or was engaged on a reconnaissance when he accidentally encountered an English man-at-arms called

Adam de Frankton. Frankton does not appear to have known who the lone horseman was, and probably Llewellyn died as the result of a one-sided tussle between a young and eager man and a wearied and much older one. When Frankton's victim was identified, the head of the Last Prince was cut off, washed in the well of a nearby farmhouse, and sent to Edward I, who had it derisively crowned with a wreath of ivy and stuck on a spear outside the Tower of London.

The slaying of the Welsh king by the English foot soldier was an awesome and tragic event. Recent years have witnessed a resurgence of Wales's interest in its early history, and in 1966 a large boulder was placed beside the road to mark the approximate site of the spot where Llewellyn ap Gruffydd fell.

When Edward I extinguished the Welsh monarchy, he was extinguishing a line that had existed longer than his own. From Edward's day to our own is seven hundred years, the same span of time that the institution of Welsh kingship had existed. And if one reflects that these kings of Wales were the descendants of the kings who had ruled the Celtic tribes, then the span is longer still, stretching back beyond the birth of Christ. Nor was Edward expunging the leadership of some savage hill tribe; he was expunging a royal strain whose courts had known glory. No doubt there was a great deal of squalor mixed in with all that splendor: cruelty, betrayal, cowardice, all manner of foul deeds. No doubt some of the more romantic Welsh Nationalists of our own day, including the most illustrious of them all, my old acquaintance Saunders Lewis, have exaggerated the splendor at the expense of the squalor. Yet an undeniable splendor there was, a grace and elevation not unworthy of the radiance of Arthur's Camelot. That is what passed away, what perished at Cilmeri.

For the Welsh, it was a body blow. They were fully alive to its implications, long term as well as short term, psychological as well as physical. Here are some lines from a lament for Llewellyn ap Gruffydd written by the bard Gruffydd ab yr Ynad Coch:

*A hand has killed the head of our court.*
*  I have lost my lord. I feel a long fear.*
*Lord Christ! how grieved I am for him.*
*  Oh God! kill me with him.*
*This is the deathsong of Britain, the deathsong for our*
*    leader.*
*  Many a tear runs down the cheek,*
*Many a flank is red and torn,*
*  Much blood is soaking into the ground,*
*Many a widow cries for him,*
*  Many a mind breaks down in sadness,*
*Many a son is left fatherless,*
*  Many a house goes up in flames,*
*Many a ruin is left by the pillager,*
*  Many a piteous moan, as once at Camlan.*
*Don't you see the lashing of the wind and rain?*
*  Don't you see the oak trees crashing together?*
*  Don't you see the waves scourging the shore?*
*The handsome head of resolute Llewellyn:*
*It shocks the world an iron stake should pierce it:*
*  The head of the king who wielded the iron spear,*
*The head of the king as proud as the soaring hawk,*
*  The head of the king as fierce as the prowling wolf.*
*A splendid king, lost with the flower of his army,*
*  May he find rest in the white kingdom of heaven.*

The young Edward I now embarked on a policy of refurbishing the key castles in the areas that had been occupied by his armies in the year before the hunting down of Llewellyn. Builth, Caerphilly, Aberystwyth, Denbigh, Dinas Bran, Chirk, Rhuddlan, and others were all enlarged and strengthened. It was from within the sinister and sprawling walls of Rhuddlan that, in 1284, he issued a Statute that tersely stated: "The land of Wales has been annexed and is united to the crown of England as a member of the same body." And with the overrunning of the kingdom of Gwynedd he immediately put in hand a master plan that he must already have drawn up. Gwynedd, as the ringleader in the Welsh fight for independence, was now to be literally sat upon by the heaviest single chain of castles that would ever be constructed in Europe. At enormous, almost crippling cost to the English treasury, workmen were recruited from all over Europe and dispatched to North Wales to build the huge, terrifying new castles at Conway, Caernarvon, Harlech, and Beaumaris. Christendom's leading military architect, Master James of Saint-Georges-d'Esperanche, was brought across from Savoy to superintend the program.

Britain had never seen anything like it. It took three thousand men to build Beaumaris alone, and the cost and bulk of the raw materials, not to mention the expense of transporting them, stagger the imagination. Whole Welsh communities were uprooted and English settlers brought in to take their place. The enterprise had the lunatic air about it of an attempt at a Final Solution. The Welsh were to be permanently suppressed, and the symbolic instrument of their suppression was to be made pitilessly manifest. Today the great castles of Gwynedd are Wales's main tourist attractions, but the Welsh could have seen little that was attractive about them when they were built. They were the flinty badge of bondage. Caernarvon Castle in particular was intended to impress upon the Welsh that their time was gone. Caernarvon had been a sacred site to the Welsh, with its fabled associations with Maximus Magnus and the Emperor Constantine; now those hallowed associations were buried beneath an immense weight of stone. To rub the lesson in, it was Caernarvon that Edward chose as the place to present his son publicly to the Welsh people as their first English master and governor-general. Customarily Edward is depicted in sentimental fashion as offering to the Welsh people their infant Prince of Wales upon his shield; though since the future Edward II was seventeen years old at this time, this would have been a considerable feat, even for someone as athletic as his father. Any conciliatory considerations Edward may have felt were secondary to his principal purpose of displaying their new overlord to the "meri Wallaci," the "mere Welsh" as he had termed them in Statute of Rhuddlan. At seventeen he himself had been a seasoned soldier, fully capable of serving as a regional Gauleiter. He intended his own son, and his son's sons after him, to do the same.

It was, I think, a remarkable tribute to the spirit and fighting qualities of a very small nation that it was considered necessary to apply this enormous apparatus of restraint in order to hold it in check. Edward and the English were acting, of course, out of a sense of historical imperative. Unlike the Welsh, who as the heirs of the Celtic British had a strong perception of their own nationhood, the English were still struggling to create a national identity from the melting pot of Anglo-Saxons, Scandinavians, and Normans. One of the ways to forge and define a national identity is in opposition to other and dissimilar national groups, and the English at this epoch were engaged in defining themselves in relation to the Welsh, Irish, Scots, and, across the Channel, the French. Exceptionally vigorous, and with an instinct for hierarchy and discipline that served them well in war, they felt themselves capable not merely of defeating their Celtic enemies to the west and north, and their Latin enemy over the water, but of subjugating and even absorbing them. Except for brief periods, like the half century since the end of World War II, the English have never lacked nerve and confidence.

It was the unfortunate lot of the Welsh, as the smallest, closest, least populated, and most accessible of their four enemies, to be quashed first. Even so, the English had to exert every ounce of their strength to bring it about. The task would have taken much longer if in fact the terms of the contest had not already gone against the Welsh. Though we must remember that we are talking of tiny numbers, and that the population of

England during the reign of Edward I was probably not much more than a million and a half, the population of Wales would have been only a third or even a quarter of that. Within the next hundred years, however, the population of England was destined to quadruple, while the population of neighboring Wales would remain stagnant. Even when the Black Death would cut back the population of England from 5.0 to 2.5 million, the sheer numbers of the English would still tell hopelessly against the Welsh, and the disparity would keep widening. It was therefore not lack of courage but cold mathematics that overwhelmed the Welsh. From the time of Edward I onward, with one or two sporadic interruptions, the Welsh have never been in a position to pose a major threat to English interests. And today the gap yawns even wider: there are over 47 million Englishmen to under 3 million Welshmen. Indeed, even when you add the Scots and the Northern Irish to the Welsh, the sum total of the Celtic population rises to only somewhat more than 9 million: a ratio in favor of the English of over five to one. The Welsh represent under 5 percent of the present population of the United Kingdom.

Military, dynastic, and nationalistic factors aside, it has to be admitted that there has always been a strident racial element in the relationship between the English and the Welsh. Given their radically different origins, temperaments, and habits of thought, this was to a great degree inevitable, and if the English have indulged in racism, the Welsh have enthusiastically reciprocated. On the other hand, the English do seem to possess a more pronounced gift for this sort of thing than the Welsh. It was already discernible in the Saxons and was greatly augmented by the arrival of the Normans, who regarded themselves as innately superior to everyone else, with a God-given right to grab and bully. And, of course, the tendency was immeasurably intensified by the creation of the British Empire, in which Wales, Scotland, and Ireland were relegated to serve in the ranks alongside the other colonial dependencies. Yet there has been something that goes deeper than that—something in the attitude of the English to the Welsh that resembles the attitude of the Americans to the American Indians. Of course, in these recent years of imperial decline, the English have found it tactful to treat the Welsh with somewhat more politeness than they were previously accustomed to do, but the Welsh remember that it was not too long ago that the crop of jokes about the Irish which have come into vogue since the troubles in Ulster were precisely the jokes that the English used to tell about the Welsh.

All the same, if the English inclination to chauvinism can sometimes appear ugly, often it can seem comic, even endearing. The English themselves play it for laughs. One thinks of the bogus headline attributed to *The Times:* "Fog in Channel, Continent Isolated." If the chauvinism of the English is deeply ingrained (and there are good reasons, after all, for the English antipathy toward certain other European nations), it is commonly expressed in a more or less amiable fashion. Also, if we Welsh grouse about the English, and the injuries they have inflicted on us, we have to admit that we ourselves can be a pretty irritating lot. On the whole, we ought to recognize that we have been exceedingly fortunate that it is the English with whom, down the centuries, we have been condemned by fate to live cheek by jowl. We might, for instance, have been sentenced, like one of the smaller Baltic nations, to be a next-door neighbor of the Russians—or of the Germans. We Welsh have been lucky, really, to have on our front doorstep a nation which, for all its fault, pompous and thick-skinned though it can be, is also decent and magnanimous, and not one of those nations with whom it would have been truly terrifying to have had to associate.

Whether the Welshmen of the time liked it or not, and whether the Welshmen of today like it or not, the presentation of the Prince of Wales at Caernarvon in 1301 marks the moment of the indissoluble association of Wales with England. The presentation was in fact a stroke of genius. The lofty-sounding title Prince of Wales had been bestowed on no mere earl or baron but on the heir to the throne, the second highest person in the land. It gave the Welsh a sense of having a permanent friend at court and a permanent entrée into the royal family. In due time the Welsh would transfer their passionate, Celtic sense of loyalty to their own royal leaders to the throne of England, a process facilitated by the fact that the kings and queens of England have often possessed Welsh blood.

For the first Prince of Wales, however, the ceremony at Caernarvon did not prove auspicious. His father had put in train, by his intemperate actions in Wales, Scotland, France, and in England itself, a cycle of violence that would persist for the next two centuries. The violence would proliferate into further wars against the Welsh, Scots, and Irish, into the Hundred Years' War, and into the almost perpetual civil struggle that would culminate in the Wars of the Roses. Prince Edward, coming to the throne as a young man of twenty-two, ruled only until his early forties, when he became the first English king since the end of the Saxon era to be deposed; he was subsequently done to death in Berkeley Castle. If the final act of Marlowe's *Edward II* is to be believed, his murder was particularly hideous. When I lived in Gloucester, across the Severn from Berkeley, I was several times told of the local legend that the king's dying screams could be heard in Gloucester, 10 miles away:

> *The shrieks of death, thro' Berkley's roof that ring,*
> *Shrieks of an agonizing king!*

Edward II had been popular in Wales, since he had attempted to soften the rigorous policies of his father. At the end of his reign, when he was flying for his life, it was among the Welsh, always sympathetic to defeat and disaster, that he found a temporary refuge. On his unlucky Scottish campaign of 1314 he had taken a contingent of five hundred Welsh bowmen with him, and at the catastrophic Battle of Bannockburn it was his Welshmen who had almost saved the day. For the next hundred years, indeed, the archers of Wales, whose skill had been largely responsible for prolonging the existence of the native Welsh monarchies, were to be the backbone of the English armies and perhaps the most feared single body of soldiery in the whole of Europe.

The Welsh had been addicted to the bow and had been practicing with it for several centuries. Writing over a century earlier, Gerald the Welshman had described the bowmen of South Wales, who hailed principally from the wooded region of Gwent, at some length. "The bows they use," he wrote, "are not made of horn, not of sapwood, nor of yew. The Welsh carve their bows out of the dwarf elm-trees in the forest. They are nothing much to look at, not even rubbed smooth, but are left in a rough and unpolished state." He records that a Welsh arrow was capable of penetrating an oaken door, and that Norman knights fighting the Welsh were frequently pinned to their saddles with an arrow through their armored thigh—sometimes through both thighs. In the Middle Ages a Welshman was seldom seen walking about without his bow slung over one shoulder, and often his harp over the other. He would no more forget to take his bow when he went out in the morning than a Mousquetaire would forget to take his sword or a Texas Ranger his pistol.

Gerald says, "You can't shoot far with them, but they are powerful enough to inflict very serious wounds at close quarters." That was soon to change. The knotty little bows grew in size until they were a full six-foot-four long, much taller than their stocky Welsh owners. The string was now drawn back to the ear, instead of to the chest, which made for accurate aiming, and the range increased to no less than 400 yards and was unerring at 250 yards. The arrows too, flighted with goose feathers and tipped with iron, became specialized, and the Welsh bowman on active service carried seven different types. It must have been an impressive and amusing spectacle, watching the diminutive South Walians wield these gigantic weapons. (The continuing shortness of stature of the Welsh is indicated by the fact that, whereas the height requirement for the other four regiments of the Brigade of Guards is six feet—or was in my time—the height requirement for the Welsh Guards was five foot ten. Since I was six feet, I was immediately nominated for the King's Company.) But if the South Walians were short, they were wizards with the bow. They were trained to it from boyhood. It took a strong left arm to pull that mighty bowstring, and the Welsh continually strengthened their arms by means of incessant tourneys and competitions. Archery was, by royal decree, the only sport that could be indulged on a Sunday. All kinds of fancy shooting were in vogue: standing, kneeling, firing over the shoulder, aiming at targets held above the head or even between the legs. The Welsh have always been show-offs.

Edward III, coming to the throne at the age of fifteen in 1327 (he was to reign for fifty years), resembled his grandfather Edward I. He immediately launched a series of *chevauchées*, or raids by armed columns (the word gave us the word *cavalcade*), deep into France. He took his Welsh longbowmen with him, and at the Battle of Crécy in 1346, when he smashed the French army and took the King of France prisoner, he had five thousand of them. When the mounted French knights and the Genoese crossbowmen began their advance, the Welshmen put a preliminary shower of sixty thousand arrows into the air. The cloud of aerial death obscured the sun. The sound of it was indescribable. Each archer could get off sixteen arrows a minute. The enemy were sitting ducks, since in the battles of the period the cavalry did not come on at a thunderous charge but at a trot, in order not to outdistance the crossbowmen, who were walking beside the horses, firing as they came. But even had the horsemen charged at a dead run, the Welshmen, with that ferocious firepower, would still have knocked them out of their saddles long before they could have reached the English line. As for the Genoese and their metal arrows, though they had dominated most of the battlefields of the Continent, and though their crossbows had equal penetrating power with the longbow, they suffered from fatal disabilities. With their cumbersome cranking machinery, crossbows could only fire two bolts or quarrels a minute, and wet or foggy conditions played havoc with the mechanism. In bad weather, on the other hand, the Welsh archer simply unstrung his bowstring and coiled it up snug and dry under his cap.

Edward III was a capable general, and his dispositions at Crécy were highly effective. The predominance of archers in his ranks called for defensive tactics, with his bowmen massed together to form a thick, bristling hedge. Ahead of them he dug protective pits and garnished his front with *chevaux-de-frises,* sharpened stakes thrust point-forward into the ground. The Welsh bowman, in fact, had enrolled in the army of his former English enemy at the moment when the old, haphazard feudal levy, given to milling around ignorantly on the battlefield, was being displaced by the small, disciplined, tightly knit regular army. Instead of requiring his nobles to do service by bringing their peasants into the field, Edward exacted scutage or shield tax from them, monies that he could use to raise and train a professional force. Such a force did not come cheap; by the end of his reign a Welsh bowman had to be paid as much as sixpence a day, an enormous wage at that time.

The Welshman gave value. His weapon was the reigning queen of the battlefield, and he himself was incredibly tough and hardy, as compact and sinewy as the Welsh hill ponies that had been much sought after by the Romans, the Saxons, and the Normans, and that can still be seen wandering the fells of mid-Wales today. The Welsh foot soldier was wonderfully well adapted to the grim slog of the *chevauchée.* If you have only recently abandoned the business of dodging, tracking, and ambushing the English among the mountains of Wales, you are not likely to be dismayed by the mud and rain of France, or to be unable to keep up the pace set by your mounted English officers. That Crécy had been no fluke the Welshmen proved ten years later, under the command of Edward's son, the Black Prince, at Poitiers. It was at the victorious conclusion of that battle that the Black Prince adopted as his emblem the device that the Prince of Wales has borne ever since: three feathers enclosed within a diadem. It would be pleasant to think that it was suggested by the goose quills on his Welshmen's arrows.

The longbow was not destined to enjoy its undisputed primacy much longer. In 1260 Friar Bacon had written down his formula for gunpowder. Artillery was on its way (a few primitive bombards had been employed even as early as Crécy) and would change the face of the battlefield as drastically as it would render useless all those arrogant castles, Caernarvon and Conway, Harlech and Beaumaris, that Edward I had so recently and so laboriously erected in Wales and elsewhere. They were more or less superannuated even while he was building them. But the Welsh archer would still achieve one grand and culminating triumph: at Agincourt, in late October of 1415.

Henry V's army at Agincourt numbered a mere 5,320, of whom only 730 were knights and men-at-arms and the 4,590 who constituted the remainder were bowmen. His men were in a bad way, weary, cold, famished, soaked through, seemingly at their last gasp. He drew them up in the same defensive posture his forebears had adopted at Crécy and Poitiers, with his wings anchored on the woods to the left and right of them. To shore up his meager ranks he dismounted his handful of knights and dispersed them among his archers.

His chances of survival seemed nonexistent. The French numbered 25,000: 15,000 dismounted knights, 3,000 crossbowmen, 7,000 cavalry. Every soldier in France had been thirsting for sixty years for this day. The odds were five to one. The

French could not wait to come on. And—as they advanced—in the first minute the Welsh bowmen behind their *chevaux-de-frises* put 72,000 arrows into the air. The whole thing was over in thirty minutes. The woody defile was stacked high with dead men and dead horses. Eight thousand Frenchmen were killed, and 2,000 were taken prisoner. Their commander, the Constable d'Albret, was among the slain. As Shakespeare's Henry V exclaims: "Here was a royal fellowship of death!"

Writing almost two centuries later, Shakespeare rendered a close and accurate account of the battle, his tone of exultation testifying that even at so long a distance in time the afterglow of that "glorious and well-foughten field" had not faded. And in the person of the valiant Welsh captain Fluellen he created a character in whom the Welsh still delight to recognize a masterful portrait of themselves. (*Fluellen* was the closest an Elizabethan Englishman could come to pronouncing the Welsh *Llewellyn*, with its devilish *ll*, a sound unique to Welsh, or indeed to any other language, a tongue-twister comparable to such phenomena as the Zulu click.) As a prototypical Englishman, of course, Shakespeare necessarily found Llewellyn, as the English find all foreigners, very droll, but it is a loving and admiring portrait, for all that. Shakespeare clearly had an affection for the Welsh, as we can tell from such other Welsh characters as Owen Glendower and his daughter in *Henry IV*, or the parson Hugh Evans in *The Merry Wives of Windsor*. He captured the likeness of us Welshmen marvelously, if a shade mercilessly. But then, he knew us well; he was born and brought up a few miles from the Welsh border and must have had many Welsh friends, in Warwickshire and later in London. His father had had a prominent Welsh Stratfordian serving with him on the town council.

There is another Welsh character in *Henry V* who is as important as Fluellen: Michael Williams, the soldier who has a brush with the king on the night before the battle. He is not designated specifically as Welsh, but, after all, four-fifths of

Henry's army were Welsh and Williams is one of the very commonest of Welsh surnames. Williams is a totally different Welsh type from Fluellen: the introverted Welshman, quiet, grave, courteous, given to melancholy and morbidity. Henry is so impressed with him that he delivers to Williams the longest prose speeches that Shakespeare ever wrote. Yet it is the fiery, extroverted Fluellen, surely a son of Glamorgan, the very pattern of a South Walian, who seizes our attention and tickles our sense of humor. Shakespeare was also aware that, to an even greater extent than at Crécy and Poitiers, Fluellen and his fellow Welshmen felt that they had a personal reason to identify with their leader and to make his cause their own. Henry V, who as Prince of Wales had been the mischievous Prince Hal, had been born in Wales, in Gwent, in the heartland of the Welsh longbowman. He was known to them as Harry of Monmouth, the pretty county town where his statue stands in the main square.

Here is part of the exchange between King Harry and Captain Fluellen after the battle. Shakespeare possesses an acute ear for the inflections of the Welshman speaking English.

> KING HENRY: Then call we this the field of Agincourt,
> Fought on the day of Crispin Crispianus.

> FLUELLEN: Your grandfather of famous memory, an't please your Majesty, and your great-uncle Edward the Plack Prince of Wales, as I have read in the chronicles, fought a most prave battle here in France.

> KING HENRY: They did, Fluellen.

> FLUELLEN: Your Majesty says very true; if your Majesties is rememb'red of it, the Welshmen did good service in a garden where leeks did grow, wearing leeks in their Monmouth caps; which your Majesty know to this hour is an honourable badge of the service; and I do believe

your Majesty takes no scorn to wear the leek upon Saint
Tavy's day.

KING HENRY: I wear it for a memorable honour;
For I am Welsh, you know, good countryman.

FLUELLEN: All the water in the Wye cannot wash your
Majesty's Welsh plood out of your pody, I can tell you
that. Got pless it and preserve it as long as it pleases his
Grace and his Majesty too!

KING HENRY: Thanks, good my countryman.

FLUELLEN: By Jeshu, I am your Majesty's countryman, I
care not who knows it; I will confess it to all the 'orld:
I need not be ashamed of your Majesty, praised be Got,
so long as your Majesty is an honest man.

The "prave pattle" fought by the "Plack Prince" was presumably Poitiers, though no one knows now exactly where the
"garden where leeks did grow" was situated. Presumably it was
a place where the fighting was so hot that the Welshmen stuck
leeks in their caps as a badge to distinguish them from the enemy
in the thick of the action. Wherever it was, Fluellen's forebears
had worn the leek there, and would wear it again at Agincourt.
And when the Welsh Guards were first raised, for the Battle of
Loos in 1915, it was with the leek as their cap badge that they
received their baptism of fire. I too as a very young man wore
the leek in my cap when I transferred from the Royal Navy to
serve in the Welsh Guards. I have it now, properly polished and
shining, on the table in front of me as I write. Some authorities
hold that Fluellen's story about the garden with the leeks is
apocryphal, and that the leek was adopted as one of the three
principal Welsh emblems (the daffodil and the red dragon are the
others) because green and white happened to be colors of the
House of Valois and figured in the coat of arms of a later English

king with powerful Welsh associations, Henry VII. Certainly when Henry VII landed in Wales on his way to conquer England, in 1485, the Welshmen who accompanied him on his march to the battlefield of Bosworth adopted as their favor the green-and-white leek, which grows freely in South Wales. And whatever its emblematic origin, the Welsh are almost as fond of eating leeks as they are of eating Welsh rarebit; leeks are the main ingredients of such dishes as *pasteiod cennin* or leek pasties, *tarten gennin* or leek tarts, and *cawl Cymreig* or Welsh broth.

By the reign of Henry of Monmouth, then, the Welsh were beginning to develop an attitude toward the English of "if you can't beat 'em, join 'em." Obviously Shakespeare himself, if we can judge from the passage just quoted, was an advocate of Anglo-Welsh rapprochement—and not just Anglo-Welsh, since *Henry V* also contains flattering portraits of Fluellen's fellow captains, an Irishman and a Scotsman.

Shakespeare, however, was writing with hindsight. During the reigns of Edward III, Henry IV, and even Henry V, the rapport between England and Wales was far from complete. Whatever the willingness of large numbers of Welshmen to earn their sixpence a day on the Continent, their brothers at home had been chafing under the heavy-handed domestic policy of that same Edward III and his Black Prince. Although their last legitimate king had been killed, and the Treaty of Rhuddlan had relegated them to the status of second-class citizens, the Welsh kept up a drumfire of sporadic unrest and seething revolt. In the first year of the fifteenth century, matters came to a head: Welsh resentment and discontent boiled over, bursting out into what was destined to be Wales's last and most spectacular attempt to assert its independence.

It began because, with their endearing capacity to pick losers, the Welsh had become attached to the unlucky Richard II,

Edward III's mild-mannered successor, in the same way that earlier they had become attached to the equally unfortunate Edward II. If, as Borges remarks, "for a gentleman, only lost causes should be attractive," then there have always been a lot of gentlemen in Wales. When Richard II's kingship was threatened, they rallied to his cause, and when he was imprisoned and then murdered in Pontefract Castle, in 1400, they were outraged. And at this same time one of the English Marcher barons in North Wales had begun to act with an unexampled rapacity that combined with the brutal removal of Richard to provoke the Welsh into rebellion—a rebellion that would plunge Wales into a full ten years of perhaps the most violent and continuous strife that that obdurate little country would ever know.

They had found their leader, their Caratacus and Cadwaladr, their reincarnation of Arthur, their once and future king prophesied by Merlin. He was not in the line of direct descent of the house of Gwynedd, though he was a North Walian with royal blood in his veins, but at the outset of this most nationalistic of all their wars his countrymen had no hesitation in hailing him as their emancipator and as their own Prince of Wales. His appeal and personality were so electric that they credited him with supernatural powers, powers he was not above claiming for himself. He was one of that long succession of Welsh wizards who periodically vault onto the stage of British history.

Owain Glyndŵr, or Owen Glendower as the English called him, was no provincial moss-trooper. In breeding and education he was more than the equal of the English princes he challenged. Shakespeare, in the magnificent scene which he devotes to him in *Henry IV*, represents him as expressing himself not in the music-hall manner of a Fluellen or a Hugh Evans, but in the fluent accents of one who, as his son-in-law Earl Mortimer puts it, is "a worthy gentleman, exceedingly well-read." As Glendower explains to Hotspur:

> *I can speak English, lord, as well as you,*
> *For I was trained up in the English court.*

At no ordinary court, either, for Glyndŵr would have been the contemporary there, and possibly the friend, of Geoffrey Chaucer.

What began as a territorial squabble between two North Welsh magnates, Glyndŵr and Lord Grey of Ruthin, quickly blossomed into full-scale war. When Glyndŵr, already forty and a sedate country gentleman, was suddenly roused to seize and burn Grey's castle at Ruthin in 1400, it was the spark that touched off an extraordinary explosion of anti-English feeling. The Welsh artisans in London and the Welsh students at Oxford and at universities abroad joined the Welsh citizens of the English border towns in flocking back to their native land to join the insurrection. At times Glyndŵr was able to put an army of eight to ten thousand men into the field, a huge number for the Wales of that period. In two years Glyndŵr had cleared out the southern lowlands, taken many English castles (including Cardiff), and won two pitched battles, one at Vyrnwy, where he captured Lord Grey, and one at Pilleth, where he captured two thousand of the enemy and took Earl Mortimer, then an adherent of the English, prisoner.

He went from strength to strength. As he could boast to Hotspur:

> *Three times hath Henry Bolingbroke made head*
> *Against my power: thrice from the banks of Wye*
> *And sandy-bottomed Severn have I sent him*
> *Bootless home and weather-beaten back.*

He was now a kingmaker. Hotspur, who had until recently been one of Henry IV's generals, became an ally of Glyndŵr when his father, the Earl of Northumberland, and his fellow

Percy the Earl of Worcester went against the king. Mortimer married Glyndŵr's daughter and joined them. And, since Mortimer had a legitimate claim to the English throne, Glyndŵr saw himself as the father of England's future queen. Wales, the north of England, and Scotland had all declared themselves enemies of Henry IV, and the prospects of the rebels looked bright, despite the fact that Glyndŵr could not reach Hotspur in time to save the latter from defeat and death at the Battle of Shrewsbury in 1403. In 1404 Glyndŵr was riding sufficiently high to plan with the Percies and with Mortimer the parceling out of Henry's dominions, with himself taking over the whole of the Marches and a great chunk of western England.

It was in this *annus mirabilis*, with the castles of Harlech, Conway, and Aberystwyth in his hands, with firm control over the whole of Wales, and with an efficient structure of government staffed with the most gifted and able men available, that Glyndŵr had himself formally crowned as one of the recognized princes of Christendom. His coronation was witnessed and confirmed by envoys from France, Castile, Scotland, and Rome, in all of whose courts now resided Welsh ambassadors. He adopted a privy seal and a great seal on which he was depicted as sitting in state, crowned, and bearing the orb and the scepter. He gave orders for a Welsh parliament to be established and presided over its deliberations at Machynlleth and Dolgellau. He recodified Welsh law, levied taxes, sanctioned treaties, and decreed the creation—more than four hundred years ahead of their actual founding—of Welsh universities, one for the north of Wales and one for the south.

Intellectually as well as physically, Glyndŵr was a bold man, a visionary, surely possessed of more than a touch of that supernatural faculty with which he was said to be endowed. He was a meteor, flashing across the Welsh sky, and even today his countrymen are conscious of its brilliance and its afterglow. For another year or so his fortunes continued to surge. The French king augmented his army with a contingent of two thousand soldiers. The Pope at Avignon assented to the sundering of the Welsh church from Canterbury and the elevation of St. David's as a metropolitan see, with its authority extending deep into England, thus fulfilling for a brief moment the old dream of Gerald the Welshman.

Then, as quickly as it had blazed, the meteor burned out. In 1405 Prince Henry, the future Henry V, defeated Glyndŵr twice in rapid succession, at Grosmont and at Pwll Melyn. Glyndŵr had never succeeded in the crucial task of capturing Caernarvon, and his attempted invasion of England was turned back at Worcester. Henry IV captured the Scottish king, then defeated the Percies at Bramham Moor, and managed to patch up a peace with France. After a two-year siege Glyndŵr's capital, Harlech, was taken and his wife, daughter, and grandchildren all made prisoner. The English, as the English always do, had pulled themselves together and reasserted themselves. By 1410 Glyndŵr's grand design was in ruins.

Like so many Welsh leaders before him, Glyndŵr took to the hills. Until 1412 he carried on desultory guerrilla operations, but gradually his capacity to resist was worn down. With an appropriate touch of mystery for a man who had worked such marvels, he literally faded from sight. Some say he perished, frozen and hungry, in a mountain cave. Some say he lived out the rest of his life as a fugitive, residing incognito as a pensioner in the houses of his former adherents. He had an enormous bounty placed on his head: a huge temptation for the Welshmen of that age. But he was never betrayed. His head was never stuck up on an iron spike, as Llewellyn ap Gruffydd's had been. The Welsh have never forgotten nor ever will forget him. Like Arthur and Cadwaladr, he merely sleeps and will one day wake again. His struggle and travail are summed up for his countrymen in a famous story. Some years after his downfall, he was wandering anonymously around his former estate in northeast Wales when, at dawn, the abbot of the nearby abbey of Valle Crucis came riding by. "Good morning, Your Reverence," said Glyndŵr. "Surely you are up very early?" "No, Your Majesty," replied the abbot, "I am afraid that it is you who were up too soon."

And so, nearly six hundred years later, we Welsh are still awaiting the dawn of our independence and the return of one or other of our legendary heroes. In the meantime, after the eclipse of Owain Glyndŵr, the Welsh archers trooped off to Flanders to win the Battle of Agincourt. But Henry V, twenty-eight at Agincourt, died suddenly at thirty-five, throwing England, and Wales with it, once again into dynastic and political turmoil. Like England, Wales was split in its support of the House of York or the House of Lancaster, the east and south declaring for the Yorkists, the north and west for the Lancastrians. There were Welshmen engaged on both sides at the battles of Wakefield, Mortimer's Cross, Banbury, Edgecote, and Tewkesbury, and at Harlech Castle the Welsh garrison under Sir Dafydd ap Jevon held out against the Yorkists for seven years before starvation eventually forced them to surrender. In old age Sir Dafydd was wont to say that he had once held a castle in France until every old woman in Wales had heard of it, and a castle in Wales until every old woman in France had heard of it.

All the same, Welsh aspirations for nationhood, or at least for a measure of generous treatment at the hands of the English, had still not been quite extinguished with Glyndŵr. For this, in a curious fashion, the unexpected death of Henry V was responsible. Henry himself, it will be remembered, had been born in Wales and had exercised a strong appeal for the Welsh. And after his death his widow, Katherine of Valois (who is seen being wooed by the king in a charming scene in Shakespeare's play), fell violently in love with and married a handsome Welsh noble-man whom she saw bathing naked in a river. Owain Tudwr (Owen Tudor, in English) belonged to an Anglesey family which had served Gwynedd and Glyndŵr, and was evidently a lively and engaging young man. Sadly, he came to a sticky end. In 1461, after the Lancastrians were routed at Mortimer's Cross, he fell into Yorkist hands and was taken to Hereford to be executed. As he lowered his head to put it on the block, he remarked with black Welsh humor that he had once been used to "put it on Queen Katherine's lap." A romantic fellow. However, before the early death of his queen they had produced an heir, Edmund Tudor, Earl of Richmond, who, although he himself died young, produced Henry Tudor, the future king Henry VII. Thus the Welsh association of Henry V was powerfully underscored by the actual Welsh blood of his widow's progeny.

Inevitably, with the victory of the twenty-eight-year-old Henry Tudor at the Battle of Bosworth, the Welsh were jubilant. When he had sailed from France to Britain to challenge Richard III for the crown of England, Henry had landed in West Wales, at Milford Haven, expressly to solicit Welsh support. They had not failed him. They banded together and accompanied him into England, and helped him to win the day at Bosworth, where he bore on his banner the red dragon of Cadwaladr. The Welsh could hardly be blamed for assuming that, with one of their own now seated on the English throne, their hour had come, but again they were doomed to be disappointed. Henry Tudor soon showed himself (and it was fortunate for war-torn and distracted England that he did) to be not a dashing prince in the mold of Henry of Monmouth but a dour and cautious bureaucrat and paper shuffler. In this he is said to have resembled his Anglesey forebears, who in the tradition of the north Welsh were also reputed to be close men with a groat. Like the Tudors who came after him, he was efficient, hardheaded, totally unsentimental, a canny politician and a shrewd picker of royal servants. By marrying Elizabeth of York, he healed the wounds of the civil war and set Britain on the relatively stable and prosperous course it would enjoy throughout the sixteenth century. Recognizing the expectations of the Welsh, he catered to them by providing them with a certain amount of the spoils, ordered St. David's Day to be officially celebrated at court, and made available to Welshmen the higher positions in his administration. The Tudors had the egalitarian instincts of the Welsh, and would always encourage able and ambitious men, however humble or misprized their origins. On the other hand, they also knew the Welsh far too well to give their quarrelsome and contentious fellow countrymen their heads, Welsh blood or no Welsh blood, dynastic debt or no dynastic debt. As the sixteenth century progressed, the Welsh were to find themselves treated with an increasing stringency.

With both his Welsh and his English subjects, Henry VII had been firm but fair. His son Henry VIII, however, seems seldom to have been capable of understanding anything more than the crudest application of force. It is difficult to understand why the English regard this gross, sodden man with such affection. For his policies of coercion, in Wales as well as England, he would find in Thomas Cromwell his perfect instrument. In the end, of course, Cromwell would join the bloody procession to the block; gratitude was an emotion not known to his coldhearted master. The atmosphere of Henry's palace at Lambeth must have had a lot in common with the atmosphere of Stalin's Kremlin and Hitler's Berchtesgaden: anyone could be killed or destroyed at will, or as the result of a whim. "To be close to the czar," as the Russians say, "is to be close to death." The Welsh were not likely to receive points for Poitiers, Agincourt, or Bosworth at the hand of a man who murdered his retainers, terrorized his family, robbed and ruined his own church, and finished his life with a body so bloated and ulcerated that it had to be raised and lowered from the dining table by means of a crane. Cromwell was instructed to take the Welsh in hand. He did so. Appointed Lord President of the Council of the Marches, he dispatched to Wales a fellow gangster named Rowland Lee, a Judge Jeffreys born before his time, with orders to carry out what Himmler's S.S. in France used to call a *ratissage*, a rat hunt or raking over, as a prelude to "pacification."

Once the Welsh were softened up, the king and Cromwell were ready to come forward with what they were pleased to call an Act of Union, though the "Union" was all on the English side. It was in fact an Act of Annexation. Edward I's Statute of Rhuddlan had at least been a kind of treaty, an agreement supposedly drawn up between two contracting parties. Henry VIII's Act of Union, promulgated in 1536 and enlarged and made even more restrictive in 1543, was totally one-sided, an outright diktat in which one of the parties had not been consulted. Wales was now reduced to the condition of a dependency of England. Its distinctive code of laws, reaching back to the laws of Hywel Dda, was abolished and replaced by the legal system of England, a system that was to be strictly applied in the English language. The official business of the country was also to be conducted in English, though Welsh was still tolerated as the language of religion, perhaps because Henry VIII was reluctant to add to the religious troubles with which he had already saddled himself. Henceforward the Welsh tongue, whose literary achievements to that date were immeasurably greater than the English, was to be regarded as no more than a local patois.

Under the Statute of Rhuddlan, Edward I had sought, without a great deal of success in the light of later events, to introduce the English shire system into Wales and had established the counties of Anglesey, Caernarvon, Merioneth, Cardigan, and Carmarthen. The Act of Union brought thirteen counties into existence, although Gwent, in the southeastern corner, was hived off and attached, under an administrative pretext, to England. For four hundred years Gwent would occupy this anomalous position, existing as a kind of no-man's-land between the two countries and owing an uncertain allegiance to both. Otherwise the Tudor pattern of shires, in both England and Wales, would persist until the redrawing and reduction of the counties in 1974, a testament to the thoroughness of Tudor management. Each Welsh county was required to send two representatives to the parliament at Westminster, while the English counties each sent four.

The Tudor enactments did not stop at the rearrangement of the Welsh counties. As part of the rationalization process so dear to the hearts of bureaucrats, the Welsh were commanded to adopt last names or surnames in the English style. The old and cozy method of using the name of the father as a second name (e.g., Dafydd ap Jevon, David the son of John) was indicative of the intimate nature of Welsh life, the sense that all Welshmen were members of one large family. This did not suit the impersonal nature of English law, English taxation, and English record keeping. Therefore the Welsh were compelled to adopt the English usage of assuming a distinctive last name or else have one issued to them by a government clerk, rather in the way that many immigrant Americans were arbitrarily assigned a name on Staten Island. Hitherto a Welshman had simply been content to tack his father's name onto his own with the connective *ap*, "son of." This was also the Scandinavian and Icelandic method.

English bureaucracy decided that the easiest way to cope with the matter was to make the Welsh drop the *ap* and squeeze the two names together. So Ioan ap Dafydd would become Ioan Dafydd, and, if his name were later Englished, he would become John David or John Davidson. Ivor ap Hywel would become Ivor Hywel, and later on Ivor Howell or Ivor Howells. This explains the preponderance of Welsh surnames that were originally first names: Jones (Ioan), Evans (Ifan, Ieuan, Iwan), Williams (Gwilym), Davis or Davies (Dafydd), Griffith or Griffiths (Gruffydd), Rees, Reese, or Rice (Rhys), Jenkins (Siencyn), Meredith (Meredydd), Thomas (Tomos), Morris (Morus), Owen (Owain), Vaughan (Fychan), not to mention Peters, Phillips, Walters,

Llewellyn, Cadwaladr, and so on. Sometimes the *p* of the *ap* would collide with the last name, giving Price (ap Rhys), Parry (ap Harri), Probert (ap Robert), Pritchard (ap Richard). As an alternative, a Welshman of the period could prefer to follow the common English practice of calling himself after the trade or profession he followed: Farmer, Miller, Shepherd, Painter, Carter, Fletcher, Mason, Collier, et cetera. The disadvantage of employing the relatively small number of first names as last names is that Wales has become overstocked with people called Jones, Jenkins, Williams, Davies, Rees, Morris, and Griffiths. In Welsh schools, the profusion of Joneses leads to them being referred to as Jones One, Jones Two, Jones Three, Jones Four, and so on down the line. Often the Welsh get around the same difficulty in an original and amusing way, by affixing to somebody's name the name of the place where he or she lives or works, or some obvious distinguishing mark: Mr. or Mrs. Evans Ty-Gwyn (the White House), Jones Corner-Shop, Roberts King's-Arms (or some other public house), Walters Cross-Foxes (a village), Parry Post-Office. The Welsh also have a great fondness for nicknames: Dick Davies Four-Eyes (he wears spectacles), Dick Dot-and-Carry-One (he limps or has a wooden leg), Tommy Elbow (he drinks), Williams the Hearse (the undertaker), James the Spike (the policeman). When I was in the Guards, one of my friends was a Scotsman who had got pushed in among us Welsh, got used to us, and settled down to stay. We called him Dai Bagpipes.

Tinkering about with names like this may sound like only a minor matter. True, it simplified the labors of Tudor judges and tax collectors, but it may also have inflicted a deeper wound on the Welsh psyche than was immediately apparent. As another move in the English strategy to unbalance and unnerve the Welsh, it may have had more importance than one might assume. One's name is a very intimate thing, perhaps the most personal thing that one possesses, and Welsh names were peculiarly personal. Now at one stroke the Welshman was sundered from himself, from his immediate sense of ancestry, from the feeling of close kinship that was so natural to him.

It has always seemed to me that it is from the Tudor settlement, following the debacle of Owain Glyndŵr, that one can date a certain uneasiness and lack of confidence in the Welsh that has been characteristic of them until the most recent times. When I was a boy, returning to Cardiff from school in England, I was always half aware that the atmosphere of Cardiff, big and busy city though it was, was tinged with an anxious, apologetic taint not present in London. Since the Welsh were already in a helpless condition, the Tudors had no difficulty convincing them that somehow, after all the thrashings they had received at the hands of their neighbor, they must be innately inferior to the English. In the days of the Empire the English went on to become very good at that, not only where the Welsh were concerned. The terrible irony is that it was the Tudors, their own flesh and blood, who inflicted on the Welsh a sense of weakness and subservience which it would take them four centuries to begin to shake off.

The Tudors also dealt the Welsh a second and perhaps an even more serious wound. The Tudors took away their leaders; they skimmed off the cream of Welsh society, removing almost the entire top layer of Welsh life. Because Wales was now shattered and poverty stricken, there was no incentive for an energetic and ambitious young Welshman to try to make a career at home. He had to head for England. If the Welsh had lost their confidence, there was no lack of confidence in Tudor England. England was becoming conscious of its destiny, flexing its muscles. After the setbacks of the Black Death and the Wars of the Roses, the population was increasing by leaps and bounds, and the economy was flourishing. England was as prosperous as Wales was impoverished. Young Welshmen could be forgiven for leaving the country in droves to be educated at Oxford and Cambridge and afterward to take part in the good life of London and the other booming English cities. This was the England of the

Renaissance: vibrant, exuberant, exciting. It was in England, not in the stagnant backwater of Wales, that a man's opportunities lay. The Tudor monarchs were encouraging; they found it was easier to keep an eye on their clever young Welshmen if they lured them to the Inns of Court or to Jesus College, Oxford, which had been founded especially for Welsh students in 1571. If the Welsh upper classes were provided with sinecures at court, they were not home in their own country fomenting trouble. The English have always been clever at absorbing bright and potentially bothersome young men into their Establishment. It was a technique which in course of time they would also employ in Scotland and Ireland, and in their possessions overseas.

Few of these Welsh émigrés to England would ever be tempted to return to their native country. Their defection, or their seduction by England, resulted in a devastating social and intellectual loss to their homeland. It would change the whole complexion of Welsh life. For fifteen hundred years the Welsh had been royally led. From the tribal days of the Celts right up to Owain Glyndŵr and, as they thought, to Henry VII, they had looked to the leadership of homegrown kings and princes. Now their aristocracy had forsaken them and gone off to England to join the cause of the English kings. Actually, one could see its point: why continue to live in a cold and crumbling castle on a rainy Welsh hillside, with only sheep and cattle for company, when you could live in warm and well-furnished quarters in Cheapside or Bankside? Thereafter, as a result of its defection, Wales ceased willy-nilly to be a country whose life was based on an idea of royalty or hierarchy and became instead a populist and democratic one. Of course, it had always been democratic in a larger sense: egalitarian, with a shared familial feeling that was foreign to the English. But now the Welsh would have to become truly democratic, searching for their leaders among the humble folk who had stayed behind, the common people, the farmers, preachers, and artisans, everywhere except among the class that they had once looked to for guidance. And indeed, when the Welsh aristocracy sold out their countrymen, they sold them out not only figuratively but literally; many of them sold off their lands and property to acquisitive English entrepreneurs, often at absurd prices. Henceforward very few of the aristocrats and great landowners in Wales would be Welsh; they would be alien.

It was a collapse, a surrender. What rendered it more horrible, over the next three centuries, was the relish rather than the regret with which so many of the Welsh performed their act of apostasy. Many Welshmen left their homeland because they were driven to it, reluctantly and with tears, but many of them not only threw in their lot with the English with unbecoming glee but actively took to blaming and blackguarding the nation they had forsaken. It became fashionable among English-educated Welshmen to run down Wales. They had grown ashamed of it. They found a queer pleasure in being able to shrug off what they regarded as Wales's sempiternal role as a loser. It was a pleasure to embrace and identify themselves with a winner.

However, that gallant Welsh passion for losing was only dormant and was to manifest itself yet again in the succeeding century, during the Great Civil War that began in 1642 and dragged itself on until 1651. Needless to say, the Welsh were overwhelmingly on the side of Charles I, who was to meet the same sad end as Edward II, Richard II, and other members of the English royal family supported by the Welsh down the ages. The Welsh were heavily involved, as usual, in many calamitous defeats. There were five thousand of them at Edgehill and as many more in the Royalist ranks at the equally hard-fought Battle of Naseby. Seven thousand Welshmen accompanied the Marquis of Hartford on a march from Cardiff to Tewkesbury, where the Roundheads killed twenty-five hundred of them and took another twelve hundred prisoner after one of the bloodiest and most desperate encounters of the entire war.

From the beginning, Wales served as a fertile recruiting ground for the Royalist cause, and Wales itself was the stage for a continuous series of lively scrimmages and sieges. The major battle on Welsh soil took place at St. Fagans, near Cardiff, in May 1648, when Colonel Horton, in charge of a small Round-head force, outmaneuvered a much larger Welsh army under Major General Laugharne and captured three thousand of them, after killing one thousand more. In the main, however, the action in Wales was concentrated on sieges, as befitted a country top-heavy with castles. Harlech, Chester, Chirk, Chepstow, Carew, Picton, and a host of other castles were all the scenes of violent contests.

The siege of Pembroke Castle constituted a minor epic. It was held for the Royalists by Laugharne, still suffering from the wounds he had received at St. Fagans, until long after Charles I had surrendered and the war was over (we Welsh never seem to get important news until everyone else has received it). Oliver Cromwell had to travel to West Wales to attend to the reduction of Pembroke in person. He confidently predicted its early fall. It held out. The siege became the centerpiece of what became known as the Second Civil War. It presented Cromwell with a critical problem: while he was pinned down in Wales, the Scots had invaded England with a substantial army. Cromwell launched furious assaults on the castle, but they were beaten back, and Laugharne replied with sorties of his own. Cromwell had to detach precious troops to hurry north to face the Scots and was compelled to cool his heels until his heavy siege guns could be trundled into Wales from Gloucester. It was only after his supplies were exhausted, and the Puritan artillery had breached the walls, that Laugharne gave up.

The episode had done nothing to improve the future Lord Protector's temper, which in fact was so uncertain that several historians have suggested that he was clinically mad. Subsequently he went off to Ireland and behaved in such a totally cruel and irrational fashion, at the sieges of Wexford and Drogheda, that the English have been burdened with the consequences ever since. In their baffling fashion, they have nonetheless erected a statue of Cromwell outside those very Houses of Parliament that he treated with a more sustained show of contempt than any other character in their history. Who can fathom the ways of the English? May heaven protect them from another such Protector.

With the ending of its Royalist hopes and sympathies in the Civil War, Wales had no alternative but to resign itself to its future role of poor relation to England, grateful for any crumbs that fell from the English table. And poor the Welsh were. Apart from the thriving non-Welsh landowners and a handful of wealthy native sons, the Welsh settled into a rut of poor farming and poor fishing, with a scattering of poor manufacturing. Nature, while endowing Wales with magnificent perspectives and panoramas, had not bestowed on her more than a minimum of fertile soil and grazing. The towns and the countryside of Wales were poverty-stricken versions of the towns and the countryside of England. English tourists began to visit Wales as an alternative to visiting Turkey or Albania, finding it all delightfully backward and primitive. The Welsh became picturesque. Most of them were cottagers, running a few sheep and goats on hardscrabble hillside farms, or earning a meager living fishing the shores and streams. The more venturesome element took to the high seas and established that seafaring tradition for which Wales was already well-known. Although the Welsh enjoyed their compensations, particularly the close contact with natural things, Wales was a comfortless country, and the majority of its people eked out a beggarly kind of existence.

Yet, if there were few physical comforts and compensations,

the Welsh discovered and seized upon other, spiritual ones. Deprived of earthly outlets and delights, they turned their eyes heavenward. The eighteenth and nineteenth centuries were to witness one of the most astounding religious outbursts known to the history of any nation, large or small.

The seedbed had already been sown in Tudor times. Henry VIII and his daughter Elizabeth I had wished to extend the liturgy and practices of their new Anglican church into Wales. But as the majority of their Welsh subjects, with the exception of those living in Glamorgan and the south coast, spoke only their own language, it was obvious that this could only be done in the Welsh tongue. Thus the Anglican Prayer Book and the New Testament were issued in a Welsh translation in 1567, to be followed in 1588 by Bishop Morgan's magisterial translation of the entire Bible. Printing in Wales had begun as early as 1546 and became largely devoted to feeding the increasingly avid religious appetite of its readers.

Anglicanism, organized around the four traditional bishop-rics, would maintain the upper hand in Wales until the mid-eighteenth century, though small but stubborn sects of Puritans, Quakers, and Dissenters would cause constant friction, and there were still a few lingering pockets of Roman Catholicism. Then came the change. In the earlier part of the eighteenth century, John Wesley and his coadjutor George Whitefield brought Meth-odism to Wales in a succession of missionary forays that proved even more dizzying and galvanic, if that were possible, than their tours in England. They struck a spark in the Welsh character that astonished even themselves.

The Welsh, from the days of the Druids and even earlier, had always been a markedly religious people. The Celtic church had struck deep roots in Wales, and even if the saintliness of the army of Welsh saints was exaggerated, they were at least a phalanx of holy men. We know from the writings of such men as Gerald the Welshman that the Welshmen of the Norman Conquest and

the Middle Ages were singularly devout, but with the death of
their princes, the onset of the Tudors, and the Reformation, the
compelling force that had once inspired the Celtic church and
Roman Catholicism had dwindled and died, leaving them spiritually bereft. They needed something to fill the void. They had
never taken enthusiastically to Anglicanism, first because it was
the religion of England, the religion of their masters and oppres-
sors, and second because it was in essence, thanks to its English
origin, a cool and standoffish religion, very tepid to the Welsh
taste. The Welsh, with their centuries-old grounding in poetry
and heightened language, with their love of rhetoric and drama,
craved something more florid and fiery. In Methodism they
found it. But Methodism possessed a deeper appeal than its fervor
alone. It was not, like Anglicanism, an official, state religion but
a religion that questioned authority. In its extreme form (and the
Welsh are nothing if not extreme) it was the creed of the outcast,
the rejected, the dispossessed, of everything the Welsh now felt
themselves to be. Moreover, whereas Anglicanism was the religion of the upper classes, Methodism was the religion of
the proletariat, and Wales, since the Tudor settlement and the
decimation of its own upper classes, had become a proletarian
country.

History can point to precisely where and when the spiritual
tinder was ignited. It was in May 1735, when Hywel Harris was
inspired by a sermon he heard in the village of Talgarth, in the
county of Brecon, to go and spread the word of God. He quickly
became the leader of the Welsh Wesleyans, gathering around him
a group of associates that included Daniel Rowlands and William
Williams of Pantycelyn, a preacher-poet whom the Welsh regard
as incontestably the greatest of their hymn writers. Harris received Whitefield's apostolic blessing, as it were, when the latter
took him to America on a missionary campaign, and, when the
Calvinist Whitefield eventually split with the Arminian Wesley,
it was inevitable that Harris would take his own following into

the Calvinist fold with Whitefield. Henceforward Whitefield and Harris took to themselves the lion's share of the Welsh Methodists, while Wesley was reduced to visiting the chapels of the English-speaking regions of Glamorgan and the south coast. Whitefield, with his frantic style of preaching, would necessarily exert a greater influence over the susceptible Welsh character than the more temperate Wesley. It was said of Whitefield that he only had to enunciate the word *Mesopotamia* to make members of his audience faint clean away, in the way that Paganini was reputed to be able to do by slowly playing the scale of C major. Once, when Whitefield was describing the rush of the Gadarene swine toward the abyss, the effect was so electric that Horace Walpole, of all people, found himself leaping to his feet and shouting, "My God—they're gone!"

Whitefield and Harris had touched the vatic nerve that tingles just beneath the skin of all Welshmen. When the religious blaze began to take hold and spread, which it did with astounding speed, every Welsh denomination came to possess its own outstanding orators and "exhorters." The Calvinists had Harris, while Daniel Rowlands aroused the crowds in West Wales to such a frenzy that they were nicknamed the Holy Rollers. The Baptists had the quaintly named Christmas Evans, with his sinister single eye, while the Congregationalists and Independents had Joshua Jones, David Lloyd, and Williams of Wern. Preaching became a growth industry. Moving around the country, performing on hillsides, makeshift platforms, and farm carts, they were the pop stars and show-business luminaries of the age. They were rated and included in the Top Twenty according to the pitch of hysteria to which they could stir their listeners and by their ability to achieve a trancelike state called the *hwyl*, a word that signifies a heightened, manic mood and a singsong delivery, like that of an Eskimo shaman or an African witch doctor when the spirit enters into him.

No one can question, of course, the seriousness and sincerity

of the vast majority of these men, whatever their spiritual shenanigans, or the demonstrable need that the physically and
spiritually downtrodden Welshmen of the time had for their
services. Between 1785 and 1905 there would be sixteen major
revivals, an average of one every seven to eight years, and Welsh
revivals were no milk-and-water affairs. They could sweep the
entire country into a frenzy. I can remember the Cardiff tent
revivals of my youth, along Crwys Road and the Newport Road,
the canvas taut and bulging with the singing, the shouting, the
sobbing, and the wailing. Most of the preachers were honest men,
occasionally even men of real intellectual and scholarly distinction. In course of time, however, it was inevitable that the
opportunities for personal gain and notoriety would produce a
proportion of frauds and charlatans who would eventually bring
the entire movement into disrepute. It would be tempting to
compare some of the worst of the eighteenth- and nineteenth-
century preachers to Elmer Gantry, or to those contemporary
American religious gangsters, the televangelists. Indeed, with the
outflow of Welshmen to America during these centuries, and
especially to its southern states (Wesley himself undertook a brief
and unfortunate mission to Georgia), it is possible that Wales
must bear a good deal of the responsibility for the unsavory
creatures who froth and bellow on American television on Sunday mornings. What their viewers are seeing and hearing is a
caricature of the *hwyl,* introduced into America by the English
and especially the Welsh dissenters. Nor is it an accident that this
style of preaching and worship is predominant in the South,
which with its history of poverty, defeat, and despair bears such
a close resemblance to Wales. Few members of the Welsh ministries have ever been as blatant and insolent as the televangelists,
but there are many interesting parallels between them, not only
in tone and style but also in the incidence of juicy scandals,
sexual or financial, and often both.

There were other unpleasant concomitants of the religious

revival, quite apart from the confessions and the convulsions and the whole apparatus of tawdry delirium. One of its most obvious and most baneful results was purely visible and architectural, the smearing of the beautiful Welsh landscape with a rash of hideous conventicles and God boxes. Some of the earlier Methodist chapels are chaste and seemly enough, though few of the Welsh chapels have ever possessed the virtue of being able to blend in harmoniously with their surroundings. But almost without exception the chapels of the Primitive Methodists, Calvinists, Baptists, Congregationalists, and the rest are graceless, if not outright barbarous. Apart from their atrocious design, or rather lack of it, a large proportion of them were executed in Ruabon brick, a brick manufactured in North Wales that became the standard for Victorian and Edwardian schools and chapels. Ruabon brick is a very nasty shade of purplish crimson, the color of a ripe carbuncle. Indeed, the Welsh schools and chapels of the period were interchangeable, the schools looking like large chapels and the chapels like small schools, and what went on inside them was very similar, as I can testify from the Cadoxton, Marlborough Road, and Roath Park schools that I attended in my infancy.

The ugly chapels were too often presided over by ugly clerics. Some of them were amiable mediocrities, of the Billy Graham persuasion, but others were bullies and ignoramuses. The tendency of all the dissenting denominations was to throw up religious autocrats, often on the grand scale of a Hywel Harris, or of John Elias of Anglesey, the "Methodist Pope," whose pronouncements were known as the Bulls of Bala. Local ministries too were ruled with rods of iron. In his own tight little community, agricultural or industrial, it was all too easy for a preacher to assume the role of a miniature Calvin or John Knox. The chapel on Sunday became a place of trepidation or outright terror, replete with hellfire sermons, denunciations, warnings, expulsions, and sendings to Coventry. In a small community such treatment was a social death sentence. The preachers encouraged their favorites and sycophants to indulge in all manner of sneaking, spying, and whispered innuendo and accusation. Life could be made very uncomfortable and even intolerable for those who refused to conform. For some, the Rule of the Saints may have been a blessing, but for many more it was a curse. It was bad enough for the Welsh to have been at the mercy of the English; it was twice as bad to be at the mercy of a flint-faced Sanhedrin of their own people. More unfortunate still, it seems likely that it was during this period that many Welshmen began, under the influence of religion, to develop that reputation for being sly, soapy, and hypocritical that has clung to them even into our own century. Religion and humbug are natural companions.

So powerful and overbearing, in fact, did the Welsh Calvinists and their dissenting allies become that in 1881 they prevailed upon the House of Commons to pass the Welsh Sunday Closing Act—significantly, the first piece of British legislation to possess a specifically Welsh application. Mercifully, it has now been repealed, but the horrors of the Welsh Sunday during the time I was growing up had to be experienced to be appreciated. Teetotalism and Sabbatarianism had united: Mr. Stiggins had married Mrs. Grundy. Public houses, restaurants, shops, and cinemas were all closed, and cricket and football were forbidden. The only places open for business were the churches and the chapels. The atmosphere in the streets of Cardiff was as dismal and oppressive as the atmosphere in the cities of Eastern Europe under Communism. Indeed, it is easy to see the similarities between the domineering regime of the nonconformists (than whom no one exacted a more rigid conformity) and the regime of the Socialists who were soon to succeed them. Both would spring up in response to a genuine craving, would satisfy it for a while, and would then grow overweening, succumb to moral vanity, and be rejected. Both creeds would offer their devotees much the same inducement—a promissory note to be redeemed, in the case of religion, at the Millennium, in the case of Socialism at the Great Red Dawn. In both cases the Welsh would eventually come to see that the promises were specious and the premiums excessive.

Religion ruled supreme during the era when the social organization of Wales was predominantly rural. It would be displaced by the secular religion of Socialism when Wales became industrialized. Both systems of belief had commingled and overlapped during the Victorian epoch, when Welsh political loyalties were almost entirely commanded by the Liberal Party.

In point of fact, the mineral resources of Wales had begun to be systematically exploited several centuries before the onset of the Industrial Revolution. The oldest coal mine in Glamorgan is dated before 1400, and by 1600 Wales was exporting coal to France from its southern ports. A brass and wire foundry was in operation in Gwent as early as 1570, and copper, lead, silver, and limestone were all extracted and processed on a small scale in Tudor times. The sixteenth century also saw the birth of what was to become the great Welsh iron industry, after English ironmasters from the Sussex Weald moved into Glamorgan and began to practice their craft there. Before the end of the eighteenth century the classic foci of the industry at Merthyr Tydfil, Neath, Swansea, and Llanelli were all in operation. However, before 1800 the most important Welsh industrial undertaking was the production of slate from the quarries of North Wales, principally in Merionethshire and Caernarvonshire (now combined in the county of Gwynedd). Even before the end of the seventeenth century, a million slates a year were being exported from Merioneth and Caernarvon, and by 1800, 60 percent of the roofs of England were furnished with Welsh slate.

Slate would become a giant enterprise, lapsing only with the onset of World War I, being gradually overshadowed only by the growth of another Welsh industry: coal. No one could have foreseen, at the beginning of the Industrial Revolution, that in a few decades coal would sprout not merely into an activity to rival slate but into a colossus. To begin with, it was regarded purely as an ancillary to iron, a local product conveniently situated to feed the furnaces of the nearby ironworks. Iron was king. Here, for example, is the impression made on George Borrow in 1854 by the famous Cyfarthfa Works at Merthyr:

What shall I say about Cyfarthfa? I had best say but very little. I saw enormous furnaces. I saw streams of molten metal. I saw a long ductile piece of molten metal being operated upon. I saw millions of sparks flying about. I saw an immense wheel impelled around with frightful velocity by a steam-engine of two hundred and forty horse power. I heard all kinds of dreadful sounds. The general effect was stunning. Afterwards I roamed about making general observations. The mountain of dross that had startled me on the previous night with its terrific glare, and which stands to the north-west of the town, looked now nothing more than an immense dark heap of cinders. It is only when the shades of night have settled down that the fire within manifests itself, making the hill appear an immense glowing mass. All the hills around the town, some of which are very high, have a scorched and blackened look. Moreover Merthyr can show several other remarkable edifices of a gloomy horrid Satanic character. There is the Hall of Iron, with its arches, from whence proceeds incessantly a thundering noise of hammers. Then there is an edifice at the foot of a mountain, half-way up the side of which is a blasted forest and on the top an enormous crag. A truly wonderful edifice it is, the palace of Satan. There it stands: a house of reddish brick with a slate roof—four horrid black towers behind, two of them belching forth smoke and flame from their tops—holes like pigeonholes here and there—two immense white chimneys standing by themselves. What edifice can that be of such strange mad details? I ought to have put that question to some one in Merthyr, but did not, though I stood staring at the diabolical structure with my mouth open.

Born and brought up as a countryman, Borrow was dismayed by the spectacle of the newborn iron industry. And if he considered iron working as diabolical, an alien excrescence on the life and land of Wales, what would he have thought of the business of coal mining? What, he might have asked himself, could a land of modest cultivators and herdsmen have done to deserve the monstrous curse of coal? With the coming of coal, the history of Wales, and most particularly of my own South Wales, was suddenly and hideously transformed.

Until the 1850s the demand for Welsh coal had been local and domestic, an appendage of the iron industry, which required 3 tons of coal to smelt 1 ton of iron ore. But in the 1850s the Welsh coal industry tore itself loose, as it began to feed the demand for coal of the factories, railways, and hearths of England, then of the world. The new steamships of the British merchant marine and the ever-growing British Navy developed an insatiable appetite for Welsh steam coal, and long before the outbreak of the First World War most of the other leading navies of the world were bunkering on coal from the blackened valleys of Glamorgan and western Gwent. Glamorgan contained every type of coal—steam, dry steam, bituminous, anthracite, semianthracite—and for a century its bowels would be systematically and pitilessly burrowed into and hacked out. Glamorgan was gored and gutted. It may be too much to say that the scars and welts her body now bears will never heal, for patient and much-afflicted Nature can absorb and obliterate many of the wounds inflicted on her by the hand of man. But it seems safe to guess that it may be a thousand years before the evidence of the huge crime that was committed against the soil and culture of Wales will begin to be forgotten. And Glamorgan will bear, to the end of time, many a rent and many a gaping hole, many a gash and many a cicatrix, many a mountainous tumor of slag and shale, the filthy legacy of a hundred years of greed and exploitation.

How is it possible to write temperately of an activity like coal mining? We may not know much about humankind, but it seems safe to say that one of the things we do know is that human beings were not meant to grunt, sweat, and grub about like half-blind animals in the depths of the earth. They were not meant to be crushed, suffocated, killed, maimed, or afflicted with lung diseases as a result of inhaling coal dust 700 or 800 yards under the ground. Nor are we speaking of men alone, since until well into the nineteenth century women and small children worked underground, and it was not until the 1870s, when the whole devilish undertaking was in full swing, that it was considered advisable to restrict boys of under sixteen to ten-hour shifts at the coal face.

I have only been down a Welsh coal mine three times in my life. The first time was when I was about eleven, when I used to keep my Uncle Arthur company on his rounds as an accident assessor. The second was when I was sixteen and was filling in time between leaving school and a first brief wartime year at Cambridge by working as a reporter on the *South Wales Echo*. The last time was a few years later, when I was staying in a mining village after playing rugby football against the local team. Today the Welsh Tourist Board has sanitized some of the disused pits and offers guided tours, but I found my visits to those working pits very unnerving experiences, from the moment the cage dropped me with sickening suddenness out of the sweet sunlight until an hour or so later, when I groped and stumbled my way back along the warren of tunnels. I am not by nature unduly claustrophobic; I took the Navy course for divers and firefighting, and made a trip in a submarine. But for someone unprepared and precipitated into it, even someone young and of a strong constitution, the world of the miner is eerie and intimidating. It is not just the alternation of shadows and lurid lights that is frightening, or the patches of devouring darkness; it is the noise, the heat, the stink, the sense of lurking violence. One of the things I remember about my first visit in the 1930s was the smell of the ponies, condemned to spend the whole of their lives in that hellish place. As for the noise, there was the racket of the trams, the conveyor belts, the ventilators, the hammers, mandrels, picks, and shovels, the shot firing, the creaking and groaning of the props and trusses, the incessant shouts and calls.

You have to be a real man to stand all that. You have to be a real man to be a miner. That is why miners take such pride in their strength and skill, in their ability to do a job which would quickly kill someone not used to it, someone not brought up to it. As well as physical strength, you need knowledge and instinct; you have to know when to trust and when to be wary of those subtle dips and shiftings of the seams. You have to be alert for the whiff of gas, the glimmer of flame, the serpentine hiss and trickle of dust. Mining today, with all its safety refinements, is still the most dangerous job in the world. The list of disasters since the inception of mining in Glamorgan is chilling—not to mention the equally terrible disasters in the pits of Scotland, the north of England, and the English Midlands. At the height of coal-mining activity, somewhere in Britain a miner was killed every six hours. In Wales, 65 men and boys were killed at Middle Dyffryn (1852), 114 at Cymmer (1856), 81 at Mardy (1885), 439 at the Universal Colliery at Senghenydd (1939), 45 at the Six Bells Colliery at Abertillery (1960). One of the worst Welsh disasters occurred in 1934, when 265 miners were killed at the Gresford Colliery near Wrexham in northeast Wales (there were collieries, if not so numerous or productive, in North Wales as well). Between 1850 and 1900 there was a disaster which killed 10 men or more almost every year. And these were only the major explosions, cave-ins, or floodings. There was also the daily toll of individual injuries, often mortal: skulls cracked open, spines broken, limbs crushed, fingers lopped off. For these, during most of the history of the mines, there was pitiful compensation, often no compensation at all.

When I was a boy and the miners came down to Cardiff for a spree on their day off, I would gaze curiously at the scars on their gnarled hands and pallid faces, scars that were a vivid dark blue because of the coal dust that had got into the cuts and become ingrained there. Many of the men were queerly bent and hunched over, where shoulders, ribs, and hips had been smashed, and I would watch with surprise as they would suddenly stop dead to retch their lungs up, becoming dark in the face with breathlessness, leaning against a wall or clinging to the railings to keep themselves upright, spitting into the gutter thick gobs of phlegm of an intense and sparkling black.

And for all this, for their pain, struggle, and risk, what did they receive? Precious little. For some twenty years, round about the turn of the century, if he wasn't killed, mangled, or stricken with pneumoconiosis, the Welsh miner may have done relatively well, according to his own very modest idea of doing well, and for a few years after World War II he enjoyed improved pay and conditions. But in the final analysis mining brought no benefit to the Welsh miner, the Welsh landscape, the Welsh people. Most of the coal owners were English, and few of them chose to involve themselves in the distasteful business of running the mines. Their chief concern lay in garnering the profits and removing them as speedily as possible from the country. As John Paul Getty once observed, "The meek shall inherit the earth, but they can forget about the mineral rights." Where the small group of Welsh coal owners was concerned, if the Welsh people expected to be treated preferentially by their own kind, as with the Tudors, they were doomed to disappointment. The Thomases of the Cambrian Combine, the Powells of Powell Dyffryn, the Lewises of Lewis

Merthyr, the Davieses of the Ocean Coal Company were as tight-fisted as their English counterparts.

All mining brought Wales was muck and misery. It represents the saddest episode in the country's sad history. The mining villages of Wales, huddled rows of jerry-built back-to-back houses, interspersed with gaunt schools and forbidding chapels and cowering beneath the shadow of monstrous slag heaps, are among the most desolate dwelling places ever devised by man. Yet, even in these mournful surroundings, in the most adverse circumstances that could possibly be imagined, there bloomed a culture notable for its vigor, its generosity, its individuality. Even there the Welsh continued to indulge their enduring love of poetry and music. In the worst of times, through the strikes and the slumps, the sullied villages and sooty towns rang with the voices of their bards and their singers. More, they continued to praise the God who had condemned them to pass their lives in this squalid corner of the world. In 1869 the miners of the Mynydd Newydd Colliery near Swansea hacked out, in the Six-Foot Seam, more than 700 feet below the ground, a subterranean chapel from the solid coal. There, every week for the next sixty years, until the pit closed in 1932, they worshiped their God.

The mining towns, which still strike a chill into the heart as you walk or drive into them, were remarkable places. When I visited them with my uncle, at the height of the Depression, when half the men were out of work and many of their families were close to starvation, it was felt to be a thing of shame not to be able to offer a guest a cup of tea, a Welsh cake, a slice of apple tart. Many of them were too poor to be able to do so. I can see those women still, hugging their shawls around their shoulders, their faces gray and drawn, their necks often swollen with the grotesque goiters that were the result of undernourishment and bad water, standing in their open doorways, trying to raise a smile for us as we came down the street. In the Valleys no door was ever closed during the daytime, no door was ever locked.

*       *       *

The growth of the South Wales coal industry, during the scant century of its baleful existence, was phenomenal, a sinister mushroom expansion.

In 1851, when the Scots-English family of the Butes, lords of Cardiff Castle and proprietors of what were turning out to be 22,000 acres of priceless land in Glamorgan, sank their first pit in the Rhondda Valley, the Welsh coalfield was producing 8 million tons of coal a year, largely for the steelworks of Dowlais, Cyfarthfa, Blaenavon, Rhymney, and Ebbw Vale. In 1856 the discovery of the Bessemer process and the subsequent conversion of the iron industry into the steel industry created an attendant surge in the demand for coal. Welsh rails began to carry the growing railway traffic of many of the major industrializing countries of the world, including the United States. The production of coal began to increase exponentially. By 1870 it had doubled, and by 1900 it had trebled. By the outbreak of World War I, South Wales was producing a third of all the coal exports in the world. In 1914 there were 485 collieries in Wales, of which 323 were in Glamorgan, employing over 230,000 men and yielding 57 million tons of coal.

In half a century Wales had become one of the world's most intensive industrial centers. Needless to say, the mechanics of exporting such a mass of coal, iron, steel, and tinplate led to gigantic problems. The earliest method of shifting it from its point of origin to the seaports of South Glamorgan was by canal. By the end of the eighteenth century, a system of canals embracing Cardiff, Swansea, Neath, and Newport was already in place, making a neat fortune for the local toll owners, and it continued to function efficiently and at full capacity for more than a hundred years. However, when the railway boom of the 1830s and 1840s seized Britain, the canals were first supplanted, then superseded. As the small maritime outlets grew glutted, the Butes and the other magnates hurriedly recruited whole armies of work-hungry laborers from the growing slums of industrial England and the fields of potato-famine Ireland to gouge out the new dock cities of Cardiff and its neighborhood. Nor were the waves of immigration totally from outside Wales, since Welsh families from all quarters of rural Wales were flocking to the south, where there were promises of lucrative work to be had and fortunes to be made. This flight from the land was to render the already poverty-stricken agricultural regions of Wales even poorer and to make the economic structure of Wales, always fragile, even more precarious.

In 1820 my native city of Cardiff was a glorified fishing-cum-marketing village of under four thousand people. By the end of the century its population was 160,000 and climbing. It had become by far the largest city in Wales. Even so, it was unable to cope with the flood of exports and with the increasing volume of imports attracted by its ever-expanding dock facilities. It had become one of the busiest ports in Great Britain, for a time outstripping London and Liverpool. *Bound East for Cardiff* became not just the title of a Eugene O'Neill play but the destination of a large slice of the world's shipping. Soon Cardiff overflowed, and two nearby harbors had to be pressed into service. Penarth, a mile away by water, had a hundred people when work began on its dock in the 1860s; by 1914 it had a population of 20,000. Barry, 9 miles to the southwest, had 85 people in 1880 and, after David Davies opened his dock there, 40,000 people a quarter of a century later. In a few decades the South Welsh ports, which had come to include Swansea, Port Talbot, and Llanelli, as well as Cardiff, Penarth, and Barry, had become as swollen and congested as the mining towns a short distance inland which they had been created to serve.

The story of Cardiff became the story of the opening of its succession of docks. Brought up in Cardiff, with a family attachment to the sea reaching back several centuries, I know the dates by heart. My uncles were christened, married, even named in relation to the opening of those docks. My Uncle Jack, the black sheep of the family, was born in the year of the opening of the Mount Stuart Dry Dock, so he became John Stuart White. (This was a common Welsh practice. My father's lawyer was Mr. Matabele Davies, who had taken part in the Matabeleland Campaign of 1893. There was also a Ulundi Jenkins and an Atbara Phillips, similarly named for African battles and campaigns. One of my mother's maids, Vicky, rejoiced in the full name of Victoria Regina Diamond Jubilee Hughes.)

> *Bute West Dock*—1839
> *Bute East Dock*—1859
> *Roath Basin*—1874
> *Roath Dock*—1887
> *Alexandra Dock*—1907

When I was a boy in the Cathedral Road, a photograph of the opening of the Alexandra Dock hung on my bedroom wall. The ships are dressed overall, a forest of masts vibrant with flags and bunting. Dear, sweet, deaf, long-suffering Queen Alexandra, the beautiful Danish princess whom the British so much loved, is about to cut the inaugural ribbon. Somewhere among all those captains and commodores, the shipowners and the civic dignitaries, top-hatted, bemedaled, gold-watch-chained, stands my father, shortly to become a shipowner himself. My sailor uncles and granduncles are among the crowd. Everyone is smiling and confident. All is well with Cardiff and the Empire.

This is the world into which, not too many years distant, I am destined to be born: the world of docks, shipping, and the ocean. That, and the wider world of Wales beyond. I would be the heir—though it would take many years before I would understand how I belonged to it and fitted into it—of all our helter-skelter history: Bronze Age and Iron Age, Caratacus and

Arthur, the High Kings and the Normans, Fluellen and Glyndŵr, the Tudors, the Cavaliers and Roundheads, the pirates, the poets, the preachers. Whether I understood it or not, whether I wanted to be or not, I was bound into it by blood and would have to play my part in the procession. "Each age unwinds the skein another age has wound."

Snip-snip go the silver scissors in the fingers of the queen. Snip-snap go the shears in the fingers of the Fates.

The Alexandra Dock. Fifty-two acres. The largest masonry dock ever built anywhere in the world.

No one in the photograph on my bedroom wall could know, could guess, could ever believe, that that bright day is the high-water mark, that the tide is already poised to turn. Once more the fabled and fearful Seventh Wave of Welsh history is about to topple and crash, bearing us all out onto an uncharted sea. The memory of my earliest years, after a brief burst of glory, of riding high in the water, will be of being swirled and buffeted about with the other bits of flotsam from the giant wreck.

*In those days I loved a ship as a man loves daybreak or burgundy!*

I have woken this morning with those words of Stevenson—a man whose boyhood, like mine, was spent close to the sea—running through my head. I throw off the covers and jump out of bed. Today I am going down to the docks.

I part the curtains and look out. A fine day—fine for Wales, that is. The Cathedral Road is bathed in a brittle, blustery sunshine. I glance at the house across the way. Slightly sleepy still, I feel a little shiver. Yes—very odd indeed that the taxi driver should have brought me to a hotel exactly opposite my old home. Buttoning my shirt, I am conscious of the creepy sensation I felt the previous evening. What if a childish little face—*my* face—should appear at the window over the way and stare back at me? . . .

There comes into my mind a disturbing tale by Nathaniel Hawthorne. A middle-aged man called Wakefield (this is how I remember the story) is a citizen of a small Massachusetts town. Perhaps it is a port town like Salem, where I have visited the Custom House, looking out on the long quay, where Hawthorne worked—not too energetically—for many years. Wakefield is a successful businessman, with a wife and family. One morning he wakes up and gets out of bed (just as I am doing now), and after breakfast he walks out of the house—as he has done every day for years—and vanishes. He is never seen again. He utterly disappears. Actually, what he does is simply go directly across the street, where there is a lodging house, and take a room there under an assumed name. He lives in that room for years, without anyone suspecting that he is there, spending his days peeping through his window at his former home. He watches all the comings and goings. He watches the hue and cry that follow his disappearance erupt and die away. He watches his distracted wife in her widow's weeds. He watches as in due course a stranger courts her and marries her. He watches his own children and his stepchildren grow up and get married and have children of their own. Eventually he dies, and his coffin is taken out of the lodging house and is driven off to the cemetery. Nobody realizes whose funeral it is or that the dead man is—or at least once was—Wakefield.

Knotting my tie, looking across the road, I wonder—am I, in some sense, Wakefield? Was Hawthorne trying to convey—and for once he didn't ruin his story by spelling it out—that we are all Wakefields, watching ourselves living our lives as well as living them? Staring through the curtains at the tall stone porch of the Victorian mansion over the way, I seem to glimpse a ghostly vision of my early selves, like a parade of ghosts in Shakespeare. I see myself as a schoolboy, yawning, blinking, stretching after a night spent with my family down in the cellar, translating Villon and Leconte de Lisle by the light of an oil lamp as the bombs come down and the antiaircraft batteries keep up a rolling fire and aboveground the air is filled with the smell of soot and ash and the sound of ambulance bells and fire truck sirens.

Night after winter night, after the Luftwaffe had been defeated in the Battle of Britain and had shifted its targets to the ports and the industrial cities, we would spend ten or twelve hours down in that cellar. Cardiff, Newport, Swansea, Llanelli, together with Portsmouth, Plymouth, Bristol, Liverpool, were under regular and heavy attack. The air-raid warning would rout us out of our warm beds after one or two hours' sleep, and we would shuffle downstairs to the cellar with our eiderdowns clutched around our shoulders. There we sat in deck chairs, half a dozen members of the family, with boxes, lumber, furniture piled up around us. The bare bulb overhead flickered constantly on and off, sometimes staying off for hours at a time or even for the whole night, if the power station was hit, at which times the electric radiators went off too. We were well supplied with candles and oil lamps, with blankets, cakes, and sandwiches, thermos bottles of tea and coffee. Provisions were always readied long before nightfall. The house was substantial, and the walls and roof were thick, but every time a bomb fell on the docks, a mile or two away, the place shook and a fine rain of plaster and whitewash sifted down from the ceiling. There was always the fear that we might receive a direct hit from a random bomb, as the German planes flew high and often dumped their bomb loads hurriedly, in which case we might be killed or buried alive.

My mother was by nature a timid woman, very frightened all her life by the idea of death. When things grew lively my cousin Maude, who was waiting to be called up by the Women's Royal Naval Service, and I would hitch our deck chairs close beside hers and hold her hands. Thirty years later I was holding her hand when she died, not in a dusty cellar but peacefully in her own bed. She was very brave, but with every detonation she would jump, utter a sound somewhere between a squeak and a giggle, and gasp out, "O dear—O dear—O dear—O dear—O dear! . . ."

Then, after each bomb, we would all sing one of her favorite songs. "Overhead the Moon is Beaming!" . . . *BOOM* . . . "O dear—O dear—O dear—O dear—O dear! . . ." *BOOM* . . . "Deep in My Heart, Dear!" . . . *BOOM* . . . "O dear—O dear— O dear—O dear—O dear! . . ." "Lilac Time" or "The Merry Widow" or "The Belle of New York." Some of the bombs merely belched and growled and pounded on the earth like surly animals, but others, particularly the land mines that floated down by parachute and exploded in midair, sounded like a herd of elephants crashing through a tin roof, or like the gods dropping a load of gigantic saucepans or trays of cutlery.

Three feet away my Aunt Ness, my mother's elder sister, sat hunched forward in her corner of the cellar, totally impervious, puffing away on her cigarette. She knitted the most terrible socks ever to come off a pair of knitting needles. She was a tough old bird, a former hospital matron, and had served under fire in Flanders in the First World War. She took personally Hermann Goering's attempts to kill her and treated them with complete disdain. Nevertheless the puffs did seem to come a little quicker and the stitches drop a little faster as the bombs fell, so she and my mother kept up a constant duet of *Clickety-clickety-clickety-click!* "O dear—O dear—O dear—O dear!" *Clickety-clickety-clickety-click!* "O dear—O dear—O dear—O dear!" *Clickety-clickety-clickety-click!* And I was the one who was eventually compelled to wear those awful socks.

But next, after the yawning, blinking schoolboy, comes the youngster on his way to work on the *Western Mail & South Wales Echo,* his ear still cocked for the air-raid sirens. And after him a young man in a blue serge jersey, bell-bottomed trousers, round cap tilted over his ear, white lanyard, broad collar with its four stripes commemorating Admiral Nelson's four victories. And finally the young Welsh Guardsman, belt, buckles, and buttons gleaming brightly, black-and-silver flashes on the shoulders, cap with Fluellen's leek, its "hard-hitting" peak resting on the bridge of his nose. Such a bold and trim and straight-backed and raven-haired young man. Where on earth has he marched off to?

When I leave the hotel and set off, an hour later, I pause and look across again at Number 169, half-expecting to see the four of them standing together there, beneath the porch. No sign of them. They have long since gone their separate ways. I shiver a little and button up my topcoat. I am wearing my Texas hat and carrying Admiral Pickard, the silver-mounted walking stick that once belonged to the captain who sailed the first ship through the Suez Canal. It seems appropriate for exploring the docks. I step out smartly, so as not to disgrace that dead young Guardsman, then cut left into Sophia Gardens.

I have been looking forward to this little outing for weeks. In bed at night, in Tennessee, before I drop off to sleep I often take a stroll around Cardiff Docks. Yet I know there is bound to be a certain amount of pain, real pain involved. As Katherine Mansfield put it: "How hard it is to escape from places! However carefully you go, they hold you—you leave little bits of yourself fluttering on the fences, little rags and shreds of your very life."

Take these Sophia Gardens, for instance—plenty of rags and shreds caught on the bushes here, plenty of blood sprinkled on the grass. Here I played cricket and touch football, and foraged beneath the chestnut trees for the fat, shiny, toffee-colored conkers. Conkers, a game unknown to American children, consists of taking a horse chestnut, boring a hole through it, suspending it on a string (a good long one, otherwise you will get your thumb smashed), and whacking it in turns as hard as you can against the similarly prepared conker of your opponent. The conker that survives then takes on the tally of the one that has been shattered; thus, if your conker is a "three-er" and the loser's was a "six-er," you become the proud possessor of a "nine-er." Many a tough and knobbly "sixty-er" and "seventy-er" did I own as a boy.

I poke around for a minute or two with Admiral Pickard, select a couple of the juicier looking horse chestnuts, and slip them in my pocket for luck. And, as I am scouting around, I can't help recalling that it was lolling with my back against the trunks of these ancient trees that I read, as a schoolboy, some of those books that helped to determine the course of my life—George Moore's *Confessions of a Young Man,* Aldous Huxley's *Antic Hay,* Richard Aldington's *Death of a Hero*—books written by young men, and for young men, callow enough in their way, but devastating stuff for a schoolboy reader in the 1930s.

I give the chestnut trees an affectionate thwack with Admiral Pickard, take a deep breath, and scramble up onto the towpath beside the river Taff. Schoolboys and sailors and Guardsmen come and go, but "still glides the stream and will forever glide." The Taff has the same sinister gunmetal hue it had when the miners upstream were tipping their shoals of slag into it; it will take a century or two to purify those fouled waters. Sheer and solid on the other bank rise the towers and battlements of Cardiff Castle, and it is with a certain feeling of release that I leave the quiet towpath and the sheltered gardens, with their freight of memories, and emerge on the broad and busy expanse of Canton Bridge. From here, beyond the sweep of the castle wall surmounted with its carvings of heraldic animals, I get a good view of the center of the city. Cardiff does not seem to have changed much; if anything, it looks at first blush more clean, spacious, and prosperous than I was prepared to remember it. Large signs tell me CANOLFAN DINESIG (City Center), CANOLFAN SIOPA (Shopping Center). The sight of the words written in that old and stubborn language lifts my spirits.

Here, in the open, the Welsh wind is unforgiving, despite the fitful blaze of the September sun. It suddenly occurs to me how far it is to that other bridge, at the bottom of St. Mary's Street, where the docks begin, and how much farther beyond that is my ultimate destination, the Pier Head. Shall I hop aboard one of those passing buses, at least for a part of the journey? No. I have promised myself to complete as much as I can of this journey on foot. How else can I get the proper bittersweet flavor of it? I square my shoulders and grasp Admiral Pickard tighter and launch out into the stream of people in Castle Street.

Past the Angel Hotel (many good glasses of wine and much merriment there in the old days, with such Welsh worthies as Emyr Humphreys, Clifford Evans, Saunders Lewis, Alun Hoddinott). Through the Castle Arcade, which I note is being lovingly restored (a great feature of the Victorian boomtowns of England and Wales, these arcades). Past the entrance to St. John's Street, dominated by the church outside which my ancestor Rawlins White was burned alive in 1555. In its little churchyard, between the church and the public library and opposite the city market, my great-grandfather William White lies buried. He was buried in his seaboots, and my uncle Captain Evan Evans, a fierce and litigious little man, was continually badgering the city council to exhume him because it was sinful to waste such a good pair of seaboots. I can hear Evan now, filling my mother's drawing room with his loud complaints; and in fact a few years later I came to appreciate his grievance, when I was demobilized from the Royal Navy and the only article of official clothing I was required to surrender were my seaboots. Oiled and supple, superlatively comfortable, they were old friends in whom I'd sailed and slept for many months, watch and watch about, and it was a wrench to be made to give them up. It would not surprise me if William White's seaboots aren't as snug and serviceable as the day he was buried in them. Not bad gear to wear while you are waiting for the Last Trump.

Let's see—surely that's the spot where the old Dorothy Café used to be? Those cafés—the places where my friends and I constituted ourselves the flower and chivalry and avant garde of the principality. Here we would forgather to linger over our cups of coffee—and we had to make each cup last a long time, in those days—Dannie Abse and Bernice Rubens and the rest of us, as we argued, philosophized, declaimed our poems, handed round the sketches of our sonatas and symphonies, boasted of the novels we were going to write. *Vie de bohème:* Cardiff style. I can still smell the coffee and see Dannie, slender, pale, handsome, a dark lock falling over his forehead, his eyes burning as he leans forward across the table, and Bernice, with her vivid, brown, triangular face beneath its jet black fringe, her full, satiny lips parted, the beautiful reigning Cleopatra of our little South Welsh café society.

But—wait. . . . A few steps farther on there is a ghostly aroma even more evocative than that of the fancied smell of coffee: the dampish, sweetish, clinging aroma of newsprint. Here used to be the premises and printing shop of the old *Western Mail*. One of those fizzy, fissile young men who used to be me walked in here one spring morning, bluffed his way into the office of the managing director, Sir Robert Webber, and demanded a job as a reporter. I suppose I had just turned sixteen. I got the job, too, partly because Sir Robert was amused by my cheek, but partly because I was the son of Gwilym White, who was not long dead. Being the son of Gwilym White really counted for something in the Cardiff of that day.

Sir Robert paid me a princely two pounds a week. I gave a pound of it to my mother and lorded it around town on the rest. A ticket to the theater cost one and six, a ticket to the cinema a shilling, a pint of beer eightpence. I seldom had to shell out money for the theater or the cinema because I was "Our Theatrical Correspondent" and "Our Cinema Correspondent." I also doubled as "Our Literary Correspondent," "Our Sporting Correspondent," and even at a pinch "Our Fashion Correspondent" and "Our Agricultural Correspondent." For a few heady months, while almost all the regular reporters were in the army or doing war work, I covered the coroner's court and the stipendiary magistrate's court, interviewed ladies and gentlemen who had been born in the 1840s and had witnessed astonishing things, dodged the bombs, and had an altogether marvelous time.

"Our Theatrical Correspondent." I think that that was the hat I wore with the most pleasure. And here—only a hundred yards farther down St. Mary's Street, in the direction of the docks—is the little Prince of Wales's Theatre. It was here that I saw my first plays as a boy before the war and as an adolescent reporter at the beginning of it, working out my reviews in my head as I ran toward the office during the air raids. In one of the lumpy seats in that hot, narrow, gilt-and-red-plush interior I saw Emlyn Williams play Danny in his *Night Must Fall*, I saw John Gielgud in Josephine Tey's *Richard of Bordeaux*, I saw Michael Redgrave and Mervyn Johns in Patrick Hamilton's *Duke in Darkness,* an allegory of the Occupation that France was suffering under at the time. I saw Barbara Everest and Allan Jeayes in what I think is Priestley's most effective Time Play, *Time and the Conways*. I saw Robert Donat in Clemence Dane's *The Man from Stratford*. I include the names of the playwrights because even then, though I would never be destined to write for the theater, I had an inkling that I would grow up to be a writer, and that some portion of my work would be in dramatic form.

I am not certain, now, whether the first play I ever saw was *Much Ado about Nothing,* with Cathleen Nesbitt and D. A. Clarke-Smith, on a trip from school to the Open Air Theatre in Regent's Park, or whether it was James Bridie's *The Man from Nowhere*, with Laurence Olivier, at the Old Vic, on a visit to London with my mother. My mother would take me on outings to the Prince of Wales's Theatre almost every week, as a much-needed break from nursing my father. We would sit in the dark, clutching each other's hand, gasping and clapping and exclaiming and laughing and weeping immoderately, as is the Welsh way. We loved everything we saw. We loved the plays at the Prince of Wales's, the variety shows at the New Theatre (now the home of the Welsh National Opera), the movies at the Continental, the Queens, the Park Hall, the Empire, the Gaiety, the Globe. Even today, at the end of a particularly affecting play, I sometimes have to be led weeping from the theater, sniveling into my handkerchief, by embarrassed friends or relations. My mother liked to go to the theater and the cinema for what was known in those days as "a good cry." Her factitious grief somehow mitigated her real grief for my father, and I think a good deal of my own heightened reaction to plays, movies, and books stems from the fact that I was first exposed to them at a time of long-drawn-out family agony and drama. But such a reaction was by no means confined to my family. A great deal of weeping and manic laughter was heard in the theaters, music halls, and cinemas of England and Wales during the Depression and World War II. They were places of escape, and most of the audience had a great deal, then, that they needed to escape from, at least for a blessed hour or two. There was a real edge, a real urgency about theater- and moviegoing in the 1920s, 1930s, and 1940s that I haven't quite experienced since. Nor was it altogether a question of self-pity or wallowing in misery: people at that time, like the ancient Greeks, did not find the spectacle of suffering and tragedy depressing but found it reassuring, even ennobling, and left the theater or the cinema feeling fortified and more able to face the troubles that awaited them on the cold and dreary streets outside.

At any rate, whether it was a matter of escaping from sad conditions at home, the spirit of the times, the novelty of the talkies, or a personal predisposition toward literature and the drama, I was hooked very early on the stage and the movies. As a small boy, when pocket money was tight or nonexistent, I knew how to climb through the lavatory windows of most of the cinemas in Cardiff, and the lavatory windows of the Prince of Wales's too. I sat through every movie program twice. Some films, forgotten now, made a profound and lasting impression on me: Ronald Colman in *If I Were King* (with Basil Rathbone giving one of his virtuoso performances as Louis XI, the Spider King), Bette Davis and Leslie Howard in *The Petrified Forest*, Nova Pilbeam and Cedric Hardwicke in *The Tudor Rose,* Conrad Veidt and Joseph Schildkraut in *Jew Süss,* and so on, and so on. I make a point of not seeing those films again, if they are ever rerun; I don't want to risk spoiling that early impression.

I must say this tendency to overenthusiasm stood me in good stead in my juvenile role as Our Cinema Correspondent and Our Theatrical Correspondent. I never had to be urged by our chief reporter not to write the kind of harsh reviews that make managements withdraw their advertising. As I say, I loved everything I saw, and got the best seats free, and was paid two pounds a week into the bargain.

Therefore it hurts me, standing outside the old Prince of Wales's today, on this brightening and chilly morning—it really hurts me to see how woebegone and dilapidated it is. This was the home of Welsh acting. This was where Richard Burton and Stanley Baker started their careers together, as apprentices and extras. This was where I saw the greatest King Lear of my life: Hugh Griffith, acting the part in Welsh, a rich, passionate, nervous, majestic, heightened language that lent a special resonance to the Celtic background of the play. Today, trash is piled up against the entrance gates. The pretty front, with its pillars and classical statues, is chipped, peeling, boarded up. Torn and grimy posters reveal that toward the end of its long run it fell on evil times, serving as a bingo parlor and a place for showing blue movies. The shops and pubs opposite it and on either side of it are painted up and well cared for. Why has the Prince of Wales's been excepted from the general prosperity? Surely a theater where Emlyn Williams, John Gielgud, Robert Donat, and Michael Redgrave once performed deserves better care? Perhaps it had passed the point of no return. Perhaps all that passion had exhausted it. More merciful to have pulled it down and razed it, rather than let it stand here, blank and dumb.

I shift Admiral Pickard to my left hand and lay my right hand for a moment on the cheek of one of the caryatids who once invited me to participate in the mysterious rites within. Her hands lopped off, her tongue cut out, she resembles poor ravished Lavinia in *Titus Andronicus*.

No point in lamenting: Our Theatrical Correspondent has disappeared down the same road as the schoolboy, the Cambridge undergraduate, the sailor, the jaunty Guardsman with the leek in his cap. Turning, I can see the Custom House a hundred yards or so away, at the top of Bute Street, with the cloaked and coroneted statue of the second Marquess of Bute beside it. I head toward it, my pulse quickening. There, on the other side of the Custom House, I can see the dark square hole where the road takes a sudden dip and swerve, then plunges down under the old Taff Vale railway bridge into Bute Street. That dark square hole is the entrance to Dockland.

When I was a child, the slope beneath the bridge was the mouth of a cavern that led to magic regions. Above the bridge was respectable, residential Cardiff; below it was Tiger Bay. The division was absolute. Respectable Cardiff was ashamed of Tiger Bay. It was ashamed of the Rhondda and the coal pits. Though both of them were the source of its wealth, respectable Cardiff tried to pretend they did not exist. Most of the people who lived in respectable Cardiff passed all their lives there without ever paying a single visit to Tiger Bay, doing their best not to think about it. Yet there was a time when the shipowners of Butetown, my own father among them, could rival the merchants of Ragusa, Venice, and the Hanseatic League, and sent out on the world's oceans a fleet of five hundred vessels.

The chill band of shadow under the bridge makes me shiver slightly, but I step out eagerly, thumping along with Admiral Pickard. Bute Street was always cold and windy, a funnel for the icy breezes off the Bristol Channel. In the old days I used to rattle down to the Pier Head on the tramcar, lurching and swaying as it tilted down the incline and cleared the bottom of the bridge by inches. The clatter and bang of those Cardiff trams was the music of my youth. They were magnificent vehicles, tall and stately as dignified old dowagers, shining and elegant in brown and yellow, in polished brass and gleaming mahogany, bearing on their flanks the municipal coat of arms. They had presence. The drab and utilitarian buses and trolleybuses that took their place could never match them, in appearance, comfort, speed, or efficiency. It was with a real pang that I read some years ago that my Cardiff trams had been sold off to some city in Brazil. *Brazil.* There they plod along, I imagine, like weary old cart horses, shabby and overworked, remembering the days of their pride and grandeur in a country across the sea. Well—at least they are ending their career in the warmth and sunshine, two commodities they seldom enjoyed in their prime in Glamorganshire.

My heart is beginning to beat hard now, walking down Bute Street, leaning into the wind. I am approaching family ground. This was where I had my origin. I have been away a long time. I have lived for many years in England, France, Spain, America. But now the words of a wise American come back to me. In one of her novels Willa Cather wrote: "As we grow old we become more and more the stuff our forebears put into us. We think we are so individual and so misunderstood when we are young: but the nature our strain of blood carries inside there is waiting, like our skeleton."

The stuff that my forebears have put into me has certainly become more apparent and real to me as I myself have grown older. It seems even more close and insistent now, as I penetrate more deeply into Dockland. This is where, centuries before the Bute West Dock and the Bute East Dock were thought of, my forefathers lived and worked, or died in their beds looking out on the Channel, or were brought back dead in their cabins to be buried in Wales. Joshua White put out from here in his ship *Tryton,* like a host of other God-fearing or God-forsaken Whites and Manchips. Here old Rawlins White, in the 1550s, moored his little flotilla of fishing boats. And I suppose that, of all my relatives and forebears, it is Rawlins who has meant the most to me, whom I have most thought about and pondered on.

\*     \*     \*

Rawlins's story is a remarkable one, and is related at length in Foxe's *Book of Martyrs,* a powerful and influential piece of late Tudor Protestant propaganda that could still be seen in my own time lying side by side with the Bible on Welsh parlor tables. Rawlins was a pious old widower. The Cardiff town records show him to have been prosperous both as a fishing captain and as a landowner. However, he was unable to read, and, having developed a passionate interest in the Bible, he sent his son to school so that the boy could read the Bible to him. Unfortunately, what the old man heard in his son's Bible readings dismayed him. He found that it was impossible for him to square his Bible studies with his Roman Catholic religion, and this at a time when Mary Tudor and her husband, Philip of Spain, were busily reimposing Catholicism by means of the rack and the bonfire.

In the radio and television play I wrote about him, directed by one of Wales's leading writers and directors, Emyr Humphreys, Rawlins was played by one of Wales's leading actors, Clifford Evans. In it the old man is portrayed as questioning not only the literal content of the Bible but by extension the tenets of Catholicism. All his life he has possessed a special reverence for the Holy Bible; now he discovers that it is filled with a lot of nonsense no sensible man, let alone an opinionated old Welshman, could possibly believe in for a moment. Take all that business about the Prophet Elijah being whisked up to heaven by a fiery chariot. Could any practical man, any down-to-earth old fisherman, honestly believe that the clouds could open and a great wooden contraption, pulled by a team of horses, could come crashing and bumping down from the sky and snatch up an elderly prophet and whirl him up to heaven? The thing is against all common sense. And so, when the old man persists in shouting out protests and sarcastic comments during the sermons in Llandaff Cathedral, the Bishop, an old friend, but afraid of his ecclesiastical superiors, feels compelled to have Rawlins arrested.

Rawlins is given a week to think the matter over. At the end of the week, during which he will be lodged comfortably in the bishop's palace, he will be brought before a tribunal and asked, "Do you now believe that the Prophet Elijah was taken up to heaven in a fiery chariot?" If he answers "Yes," all well and good. If he answers "No," then his friend the Bishop will be forced to sentence him to death for heresy and have him burned at the stake.

Naturally, everyone—friends, family, the Bishop himself—tries to persuade the pigheaded old fellow to conform. What possible harm could it do to utter the few simple words that the tribunal will require? And besides, it is already apparent that Queen Mary is sick, that her reign of terror is already coming to an end. What is the point of being willful and stubborn? But needless to say, being a White, and obstinate through and through, Rawlins holds out and gives the wrong answer at his trial. Foxe, a rabid Catholic baiter, is not altogether a reliable witness, but the answer that he puts into Rawlins's mouth in reply to the Bishop's question: "Now, Rawlins, will you revoke your opinions or not?" has such a ring of truth that I naturally included it in my play. "Surely, my Lord," he said, "Rawlins you left me, and Rawlins you find me, and by God's grace Rawlins I will remain."

Whereupon the old man was taken off and put in the Cockmarel, "a dark, loathsome, and vile dungeon." He sent to his home for a clean shirt, which he called his "wedding garment" (and you can be sure that, for the sake of dramatic pathos, I chose to interpret this as the actual shirt in which he had been married to his dead wife forty years before). This he wore the next morning, when he was led out to execution on the open ground outside St. John's Church, a stone's throw from Cardiff Castle and the nearby river Taff. He would die almost within sight of the sea. "In going towards the stake," we are told, he fell down upon his knees and kissed the ground. In rising again, he noticed a little piece of mud sticking to his nose, upon which he said: "Earth to earth and dust to dust: you are my mother, and to you I must return." He then went and placed himself with his back to the stake, and a smith came with a great chain of iron and fastened him to it. A temporary pulpit had been erected, and a priest mounted it and addressed the people and denounced the pernicious opinions of Rawlins White. Then some of those who surrounded Rawlins said: "Set fire to him! Set fire to him!" which being done White bathed his hands in the flames until the sinews shrunk and the fat dropped away. All this while he cried with a loud voice: "O Lord, receive my spirit." The extremity of the fire was so vehement against his legs that they were consumed almost before the rest of his body was hurt, which made the whole of the body fall over into the fire sooner than it would have done.

It was often the practice to fasten a small bag of gunpowder around the neck of a man condemned to be burned, to terminate his sufferings quickly. Evidently this mercy was not accorded to Rawlins: like the Savior in whom he believed, he had to endure the agony of a long-drawn-out and agonizing death.

Whenever I reread *Moby-Dick* and come to Father Mapple's sermon, it always puts me in mind of Rawlins: "Delight,—topgallant delight to him who acknowledges no law or lord, but the Lord his God, and is only a patriot to heaven!" That is what old Rawlins was: a patriot to heaven. And there was a good deal of Captain Ahab in him, too, as there has been in all the Whites. They were always great ones for nailing the doubloon to the mast. "From storm to storm! So be it, then. Born in throes, 'tis fit that man should live in pains and die in pangs! So be it, then!"

\* \* \*

"Rawlins you left me, and Rawlins you find me, and by God's grace Rawlins I will remain." A fit rejoinder for a man and for a Welshman. Nothing servile or apologetic there, nothing of the latter-day notion of an "identity crisis" or of "trying to find oneself." Not that anyone, of course, can ever really know himself; the Delphic injunction of *Nosce teipsum* is incapable of realization. But insofar as it is possible to have a secure sense of oneself, that those old Whites had. And, because of it, they had no difficulty in recognizing what the Greeks called their *kairos,* the one thing which they were called into the world to do. They sailed ships, and they owned them, and when necessary they died in them. Their motto was the motto of the old Nantucket whalemen: "A dead whale or a stove boat." They were a high-tempered lot, a curious mixture of the extremely practical and the slightly mad. You can see it in the faded portraits of my grandfather Moses and my great-grandfather William (he who was drowned at sea, off Nash Point, and brought back to be buried in his seaboots beside St. John's Church). William was sufficiently practical, however, to build and own one of the biggest ships ever built in Cardiff, at Hodges Yard. She was an iron steamer of 1,195 tons, the *Cathorne,* launched in 1873. Moses was a famous "deep-ocean man" in his day, finally retiring to his house on the Windsor Esplanade, looking out on the Channel, and ending his days as Cardiff's harbormaster. Their eyes gaze out at you from their pictures, fierce and arrogant and direct, the eyes of sea eagles.

The eyes are also what I remember most vividly about my Uncle Evan and my Uncle Isaac. Both of them possessed their master's certificates in sail as well as in steam, both had been notorious "hard-case" mates and skippers, and in their later years they both left the ocean trade and became Bristol Channel pilots and successive chairmen of the Bristol Channel pilotage board. Evan in particular was an unforgettable character: short and swarthy, a little blue-serge-suited dynamo of a man, thick across the shoulders and thick through the chest like a Rhondda collier. Even when he was in his eighties, he did not have a single white hair. I remember those small, keen, bleached gray eyes with their sharp, triangular lids looking down at me out of the knobby brown face as I trotted with him around the docks on a Saturday afternoon or accompanied him on the pilot boat. He tugged me too fast and hauled me aboard too roughly, but that was his way, and I didn't mind. The rough skin of his palms scraped like the skin of a shark. There was a bright blue star tattooed at the base of his thumb, and a white ragged scar at the corner of his mouth. He had very small feet in highly polished boots, which may have been one of the reasons for his exceptional quickness and agility. It was said that sailors applying for berths at company offices were so aware of his reputation for rough justice that they would drop on their knees and beseech God not to send them to sea with Captain Evans.

He never had less than half a dozen lawsuits against neighbors and associates going at the same time, all of which he lost, and, like a typical Jack Ashore, he was full of get-rich-quick schemes that cost him most of his money. He was perpetually seeking my father's financial advice and promptly ignoring it. On one occasion, when his neighbors had called the police, he knocked a policeman's hat off, and it was only his reputation as a local character that got him a fine and an injunction to keep the peace instead of a term in the pokey. His constant appearances in court to plead his own cases were so hilarious that barristers and solicitors would drop their own cases and come from miles around to attend. He had a wonderful dotty eloquence and an awesome command of indignation and invective.

He had the compulsion that many Welshmen have to play the clown. He was forever painting, plastering, and spiffing up his house, shoving his ladders through the upstairs windows, upsetting pots of paint on passersby (accidentally on purpose, in the case of people he disliked), cutting down trees so that they fell the wrong way onto his greenhouse, driving 6-inch nails through his gas pipes instead of the floorboards. He was a tiny terror. One day, when I was playing with my toy soldiers on the floor in his hall, I heard him trip on the carpet at the top of the stairs—he was arguing loudly with my Aunt Minnie and wasn't looking where he was going—and I saw him fall down the entire flight of stairs and land on the doormat. He had a glass of whiskey in his hand at the time, and did not spill a drop, no doubt because he was used to stormy conditions at sea. He simply picked himself up and went on arguing with my Aunt Minnie as if nothing had happened. I was enormously impressed.

By all accounts, Evan had been an outstanding sailor. He had commanded every kind of ship and had carried every kind of cargo, though his specialty had been the ore trade which Conrad describes in *The Mirror of the Sea:* "The copper-ore trade, the famous copper-ore trade out of the Bristol Channel, coal out and ore in, deep-loaded both ways, as if in wanton defiance of the great Cape Horn seas—a work, this, for staunch ships, and a great school of staunchness for seamen. A whole fleet of copper-bottomed barques, as strong in rib and planking, as well found in gear, as ever was sent upon the seas, manned by hardy crews and commanded by young masters."

Joseph Conrad—we may note in passing—often sailed in and out of Cardiff. He finished his first really ambitious story, *The Nigger of the Narcissus,* in a house in the Cathedral Road only a few doors away from the hotel that I left forty or fifty minutes ago, where he was staying with his friends the Spiridions. He also spent several weeks with them some years later, when he became afraid that he would be unable to support himself ashore by writing, and was trying without success to return to sea. On one of those visits he made use of the public library, where his strong, upright signature can be seen in the guest book. The Spiridions, incidentally, were oculists, of Greek origin. They had a string of shops in Cardiff, outside of which hung signs that fascinated me in my childhood: enormous staring eyes surrounded by thick black spectacles, like the sign of Dr. T. J. Eckleburg that dominates the New York wasteland in Fitzgerald's *Great Gatsby*.

My Uncle Isaac was a totally different proposition from Evan. Like Moses White, he had got his Old Testamentary name from a fit of Calvinistic Methodism that must have assailed the family in the middle of the nineteenth century, though he was always known as Ike. He and Evan were deeply attached to each other, and respected each other, but whereas Evan was short and wiry and hurtled his way through the world, Ike was large, pale, meaty, and slow moving. He had presence. Evan had appropriated Ike's ration of humor, and Ike was solemn, gloomy, taciturn; he seldom smiled. He too was a fine sailor; in World War I he was drafted into the Royal Navy with the rank of commander and took charge of a group of minesweepers in the Indian Ocean. In spite of his aloof manner, he was a kind man, devoted to my dippy, fluttery Aunt Sybil, the worst housekeeper and cook in Cardiff, though she made delicious custards in tall glasses, which she kept in a cool cupboard under the stairs.

Like Evan, Ike was devoted to my mother, who was going through such a troubled period at this time. One New Year's morning, when my mother and I were walking together to pay a call on him and Sybil, I was given an extraordinary proof of it. I was about nine or ten, and my father was not with us because he was already confined to his bed, suffering from the tuberculosis that would, with cat-and-mouse slowness, kill him. It was a bright, cold day, and my mother was carrying a big bunch of yellow chrysanthemums that blazed in the sunshine.

We were drawing level with the gate of Ike's house when there was a shout. We stopped and turned to see my Uncle Jack weaving up the road behind us. Jack was the ne'er-do-well of the family. In World War I he had served in France with some distinction, whereupon he decided to rest on his laurels and take things easily. My father, who had made four attempts to enlist and been turned down, felt guilty about not having been on active service, and Jack played the role of war hero to the hilt and took up permanent residence in our household. My father was wealthy and could indulge him, giving him money to spend all his time in pubs and at the racetrack. My father, in fact, had a weakness for playing the paterfamilias, and our house when I was young resembled one of those country houses in Chekhov where bores and deadbeats and obscure relations are always dropping in and lounging about. Heaven knows why my mother put up with it, except that she was exceptionally softhearted and, like my father, a pushover for any hard-luck story. She had loved and looked after my Uncle Hubert, the baby of the family, who had early contracted tuberculosis and had died in her arms at the age of twenty. She also loved and looked after Jack, which was not difficult, since he was exceptionally handsome and loaded with charm.

That New Year's morning Jack had evidently been following us. He was very drunk. Something had annoyed him; perhaps his running feud with my formidable Aunt Ness, who also lived with us. He swayed to a halt in front of us and began pawing and pestering my mother, shouting incoherently. I stepped in front of her, giving him a push or two to keep him off. I felt no fear or anger, because I had seen him that way often, and I loved him too. That was his trouble: he was too lovable. He caught hold of me and shook me and threw me against the railings.

The front door of the house opened, and Ike appeared. He came slowly down the garden path. Slowly he opened the gate. Slowly he walked down the pavement toward us. There was no expression on his fleshy, lardy face. He came up to us, halted, and hit Jack a short, sudden blow that knocked him flat on the pavement.

Lovableness was Jack's stock-in-trade. It wasn't Ike's. Jack lay on the ground like a sack of coals. He stayed there.

There was no animus in the blow. It was delivered in an almost matter-of-fact way. Ike had simply done what he would have done at sea. Hearing a disturbance on the deck, he would have come up unhurriedly from his cabin, settled the matter with a sock on the jaw, and gone back below again. He and Evan had gone to sea at the age of twelve, in sailing ships, and this was the swift and casual fashion in which these minor affairs were dealt with in those arduous days. Conrad, a gentleman, may have given rather too civilized an account of what a seaman's life was like in Victorian times; perhaps Richard Henry Dana had been closer to the mark. The way in which Ike dealt with Jack was an indication of what it took to rise to the rank of captain in the era of sail.

I stared with round eyes at my Uncle Jack, stretched out there on the cold pavement at our feet. Happy New Year, Uncle Jack. It had been a knockout punch straight from the repertoire of Cardiff's greatest fighter, Jimmy Wilde, the world flyweight champion, the famous "Ghost with the Hammer in His Hand." Ike could only have delivered a blow like that as the result of plenty of practice in quays and pubs all around the world. My mother went white and nearly dropped her flowers. Her knees buckled, not because she was going to faint but because she wanted to tend to Jack. Ike stopped her. He took her arm and steered her firmly and deliberately up the garden path and into the house. I followed. Ike closed the front door. Jack remained outside, unconscious, on the paving stones.

After Evan and Ike and others of my seafaring relatives had finished ranging the oceans, they finally settled into another profession, closer to home but no less demanding. This was the profession of Bristol Channel pilot. William White too had taken up that trade in his later years, building for the purpose one of the most famous pilot cutters of the time, *The Maid of Sker*. When she was lost at sea, off Ireland, he felt the same sense of grief that Conrad experienced all the rest of his life after the loss of his beautiful brig, the *Tremolino*.

Pilots were free lances in those early days. They went out "seeking," as they called it, far beyond the southern coast of Ireland and out into the Atlantic. It was a fiercely competitive business, where first come was first served. Possibly the most fearless and renowned of all the Bristol Channel pilots was my stepgrandfather, Captain Frank Trott.

Old Trotty, as my father and his brothers called him, had the thickest eyebrows and the blackest and bushiest mustache of any man who ever sat for a photograph. He commissioned and launched his marvelous cutter, the *Marguerite*, in April 1893. He not only earned his livelihood with her but also was a passionate racer. With her he won the Cardiff regatta in 1895, 1896, 1897, 1905, and 1907, the year in which the Alexandra Dock was opened. The next year he fitted her with an auxiliary engine, though he refused to use the engine when he was out "seeking" because it would have been unsporting. In writing about "the redoubtable Captain Trott" in his *Sailing Pilots of the Bristol Channel*, Peter J. Stucky says, "Trott took racing so seriously that he took several weeks off during the regatta season in order to take part in as many races as possible. The *Marguerite* was put on the sand at Ilfracombe, scrubbed clean and her hull painted grey instead of the obligatory working black. Racing sails and spars were rigged and she then proceeded to win a string of victories all along the coast. Until recent years a brass plate was still mounted inside her main companion hatch, listing all her successes—including even some events which Trott considered she had won but 'lost on a technicality'!" And Stucky comments, "It is generally acknowledged that the Bristol Channel pilot cutter was the most advanced fore-and-aft sailing craft of her time and had she been granted a few more years in commercial service it would have been interesting to see how she would have evolved. For *evolve* is the word, rather than *design*, since in common with all other small commercial sailing craft she was built, almost literally, by rule of thumb—the product of the intuition and instinct of men whose very existence relied upon keeping the seas, winter and summer, in the harsh conditions of the Bristol Channel and the Atlantic."

The *Marguerite,* which was still sailing the seas when Mr. Stucky was writing in the 1970s, was named after Frank Trott's first wife, a French woman. He was besotted about her, and after her death went on mourning her for the rest of his life. Not only the cutter itself but his house on the Windsor Esplanade were lavishly embellished with representations of marguerites. There were marguerites in the stained glass, marguerites on the banisters, marguerites on the wooden panels in the dining room, marguerites on the bedroom wallpaper, and marguerites growing in the garden. Small wonder my grandmother came to detest the flower and its dead namesake. I gather that, although those were times when families were very closemouthed about their secrets, there were some piercing disputes and conflicts, in the Welsh way. Certainly, to the best of my recollection, I never heard my own father speak of his stepfather. But my grandmother was a bold, warm, and handsome woman, and my father had a good deal of the Welsh Hamlet in his character.

My grandmother had seven sons. One was drowned as a child when he fell into the Bute West Dock, two others lost their lives at sea while still in their twenties. Ortega y Gasset remarks in an essay that "man always lives with the water at his throat," and this was literally as well as figuratively true of my family. Still, although my father did not take to the sea, he remained in Dockland all his life and earned his living from it. He was a first-class man of business, and when he was scarcely out of his teens he was active in the building and breaking of ships, and in his early thirties became the managing director of his own shipping company. Admittedly, at that date, just after World War I, Cardiff could show 122 such companies, controlling a million and a half gross tons of shipping between them, making it the greatest single shipowning port in the world.

I really believe that my father was a remarkable man. Unlike many of his fellow shipowners, he was a man of taste and style. The majority of them were a coarse and breezy lot, boozers and backslappers. In those exuberant days my father was something of an odd man out. He was tall, lean, dignified, with an uncomfortably sharp sense of humor, friendly but not at all a man to take liberties with. Most Cardiff businessmen only knew how to make money, a knack that is commonplace enough. My father possessed the much rarer gift of knowing how to spend it. He amassed a comprehensive library and acquired some excellent pictures. He raised orchids, was a capable photographer in that tripod-and-black-cloth era, and had a dahlia named after him by the head of the Seyle-Hayne College of Agriculture. He drove a big blue Bugatti. He was always beautifully turned out and liked good wine and good food.

His prosperous years, again like those of the majority of Cardiff shipowners, were fated to be few. But just as he had shown that he could make money with panache, he now showed that he could lose it with good grace. He fought a long and determined battle to save his company, in order to soften the blow to his employees, when most of the owners were simply turning them off and doing what they could to save their own skins. It was during the course of this hard-fought rearguard action that he contracted the consumption that would rack him for the last six years of his life, killing him at the age of forty-nine. And as he had known how to live, so, like Rawlins White, he knew how to die. He spent three years in a sanatorium in one of the bleakest valleys in Glamorgan—not at all the sort of luxurious institution described in *The Magic Mountain*—undergoing the gruesome and agonizing treatments that were current at that time, before the introduction of penicillin. First his lungs were collapsed, and when that failed one of his lungs was cut out, then half the other. Finally he was released and sent home to spend the last two years of his life in bed. I remember him propped up on his pillows, reading Pepys or John Evelyn, Fielding or Smollett. Occasionally I was allowed to scramble up on the bed beside him, though not for very long, because of the risk of infection. We would conduct our conversations through the medium of his notebook. He was not allowed to talk—in fact he was unable to, except in a low, slow, rasping whisper which it hurt him to use. I would take the notebook and scribble my childish question, and he would take it back and write his answer. I was interested to find out, later, that this was the method that Kafka was forced to use, during his own terminal battle with phthisis. My father's long silence, together with his patience, endurance, and total lack of self-pity, have always reminded me of de Vigny's wolf: *Souffre et meurs sans parler*. His final years were rendered even harder, in addition to the strain and unhappiness which his illness was causing my mother, by the fact that, again because of the fear of infection, I had to be sent away from home at the age of eight to school in England. However, I understood the reason for it, that it was done out of love and concern for me, and I never felt that it was an act of betrayal, of cold convenience to get me out of the way, as many of the English children did. Consequently my emotional link with my father and mother, and with home and Wales, was never diminished or severed.

It would be foolish to exaggerate my father into something greater than he was. He was essentially a regional businessman, a provincial autodidact, though one of real discrimination and quality. He would certainly have gone far if he had received more than a Bute Town upbringing and education. I am sure I idolize him because he died young, when I was thirteen, before his failings became apparent to me. I saw only his kindness, his courage, the humorous stoicism with which he endured his long illness and death. Likewise, he died before my own character was formed and my own failings emerged. I am sure that had he lived we would have engaged in many battles and disagreements, in the normal manner of fathers and sons, and my view of him would have become a good deal less rosy. As it was, he died before our relationship could become clouded by arguments and misunderstandings. On the other hand, there were plenty of occasions in my younger years when I wish I had had a wise-headed father to turn to for advice and guidance. Perhaps I might have avoided at least some of the more egregious mistakes and bad choices that I have made along the way. However, if I have made mistakes, they were nonetheless my own; I have lived my own life. Even so, in all those years since he died, I have heard, just behind my shoulder, that soft, phthisical cough, and have been convinced that if I suddenly turned around I would catch a glimpse of that beloved face.

I never spoke to my father, to the best of my knowledge, about his not going to sea as his brothers had. Still, to all intents and purposes Tiger Bay *was* the sea, so in effect he never ceased to live in continuous contact with it.

I too was familiar with the sea from childhood, not just because of my father's profession and his fondness for taking me down to his office at the Pier Head, but because Evan and Ike used to take me out nearly every weekend on the pilot boat. I am sure they assumed that when I grew up I would follow the same trade. Some of my earliest memories consist of long sessions of fishing aboard the pilot boat, yanking skate and outsize conger eels from the heaving waters around Steep Holme and Flat Holme. They would thrash and slither round the deck, and my uncles would yell for a deckhand or an engineer to come running with a spike or a wrench to put the things out of their misery with a few brisk chops. The conger eels, which are bottom feeders (and God knows what gruesome debris rolled along on the bottom of the Bristol Channel), we would present to the crew of one of the numerous Paris-Lyons-Marseilles coal boats that were constantly going in and out, and the Frenchmen would line the rails and acknowledge the delicacy with much kissing of the fingers. I remember too how, with my heart thumping, I would watch Evan or Ike or one of the other pilots, none of them young men, leaping in their heavy oilskins from the lurching deck of the pilot boat to a rope ladder scraping and swaying along the side of some mountainous steamer.

Of course, I sensed even then, as a child, that my *daimon* or *kairos,* or whatever you want to call it, would lead me along paths far different from those of my family. Yet I have always maintained some contact with the sea. As a young man I would join the Royal Navy and take part in the Atlantic convoys. I would marry a girl whose father was a chief engineer who had been killed and buried at sea and whose brother was a radio operator in the Merchant Service. Many of my peacetime crossings of the Atlantic were done on ocean liners, or aboard tramp steamers. And I am still obliged to spend at least a few days of every year beside the sea. Landlocked in Texas, I would feel compelled to drive many hundreds of miles to San Diego or Corpus Christi, and in Tennessee I am seized with an annual impulse to pass a couple of summer weeks at Savannah, or on Jekyll Island, or on the Outer Banks of the Carolinas. It makes me physically uneasy to be deprived of the sea for too long, even though there was a period directly after the war when I hated the ocean so much that when I saw it I would turn and stand with my back to it. I saw it then for what it really was: an indifferent waste of water that had swallowed up too many of my shipmates and school friends. I would repeat the lines that Virgil put into the mouth of the ill-fated pilot Palinurus:

*Mene salis placidi vultum fluctusque quietos*
*Ignorare iubes? Mene huic confidere monstro?*

What? Are you asking me to forget what lies behind the
pacific face of the sea and its sleeping waves? Are you asking
me to trust this devil?

Yet I had to go down there, to the shore, to the ocean—if only
to stand with my back to it.

At intervals in my life I have been given to wild speculation
about how much more exhilarating it might have been if I had
taken to the sea rather than plodded along on dry land. Sailors
have something in their lives that landlubbers never know. I still
feel the tug of that moment on the pilot boat, or a destroyer or
corvette or ocean liner, when the gear is stowed, the engines
rumble, the deck quivers, the anchor chains rattle, the hawsers
are cast off, the bows swing to the sea, the salt breeze blows in
your face. It must be marvelous to be an astronaut and sail
through space: but I wonder if those smooth and silent voyages
can ever rival the lurch and slap of the sea, the embrace of the
element itself?

And so, this morning, halfway down Bute Street, I feel a
twinge of melancholy and hear myself murmuring, with the
drunken sailors in *The Tempest:*

> *I shall no more to sea, to sea,*
> *Here shall I die ashore.*

It is definitely blowing colder. And the nearer I get to the
Pier Head, the more obvious it is that something is very wrong.
The people. Where are the people? My memories of Tiger Bay
are of throngs of people: seamen swaggering along with their
women, hordes of children pelting down the pavements, trades-

men in straw hats and striped aprons pushing their carts, trams bucketing past bulging with passengers, cart horses slipping and straining under the weight of the barrels on the brewers' drays, vans and lorries stacked high with produce. In those days Tiger Bay was a place with a spice of drama and danger to it, an incessant sense of arrival and departure, as if the docks were a vast open-air version of the old Paddington Station with the same smoky, sulfurous reek to them. Today . . . nothing. A few dispirited-looking stragglers. A passing car or two. The whole straight street practically empty. It is as if the population of Dockland was skulking indoors, hiding, or had gone to a funeral.

And what about the smells? No stink of fish, or stale beer, or rank tobacco, or cheap perfume. No rancid smell of sweat, garbage, tallow, or tarpaulin. Not even much of a smell of salt in the wind, as if the sea breeze can't be bothered with Bute Street anymore.

No noises, either. Once, when you passsed Louisa Street, you would hear the sound of Spanish, and when you passed George Street the sound of Arabic, Somali, Malay, Chinese. You could hear the language of every maritime nation in the world: Greek, Norwegian, Finnish, Russian, French, Portuguese, Italian, Dutch, Indian, West Indian. You would hear the hymns from the chapels, the chanting from the mosque. You would hear the clang of metal from the foundries, the grind and grate of the coal trucks, the thunder of the Lewis Hunter tips as the avalanches of coal and ore shot into the holds. You would hear the ceaseless stream of chatter and the click of dice from the coffeehouses, the screams and laughter and thumps and jeers from the pubs. You would hear the harangues of the Labour and Trades Union speakers booming out of the Corey Hall.

I can remember, as a small child, being wedged in beside my father in one of the big oaken booths in one or other of the score of high-ceilinged cafés, where the din was so loud that even ship's bosuns with lungs of leather couldn't make themselves heard. My feet didn't reach the floor. The booth was packed. Everyone was pounding on the table, arguing, bargaining, laying bets, gambling. They gambled on everything: ships, cargoes, the tides, the weather. They gambled about who would pay for the coffee. My father had a little eight-sided silver spinner. Everyone took a number, he spun it, and the loser paid the score. My childish eyes were hypnotized by that bright silver spinner, buzzing and bumping around between the spilled coffee and the empty cups; it was fate itself, fortune's wheel. I kept it in my pocket for years, but in the light of what happened to my father, who picked the wrong number, I never much liked to use it.

My father was an upright man. But he was tolerant of crooks, and they amused him, and in any case they constituted a fair proportion of the people he had to do business with. Among the men squeezed in around that rowdy table would be a couple of rank bad hats, even a jailbird or two. Several of my honorary "uncles" in the docks were decidedly off-color characters, while one of my real uncles (I won't give his name) was widely respected in Tiger Bay as a gifted sinker of ships. During the Depression, when hundreds of ships were laid up and there was no profit in buying or selling them, the only value a vessel had was its insurance. My uncle was an artist at staging wrecks. He could take a ship to sea, sail it to an out-of-the-way spot, open the sea cocks, and down she went in a way that would satisfy the underwriters, or that at least they were unable to question. It had to be done adroitly. One skipper sank a ship on a sunny day, on a sea as calm as a millpond, in plain view of Cardiff Docks. He got ten years.

But today—this morning—where is all that cheerful noise? Where is the ringing, raucous bustle of Tiger Bay? Today—nothing. Nothing but silence. Nothing but grayness. Nothing but vacancy. No crowds milling around the Sailors' Union on "Windy Corner," or round Lloyd's Bank on "Poverty Point." Yet the real shock is to discover not just that Bute Town is deserted but that so much of it has totally vanished. Loudon Square, the Imperial Buildings, Gloucester Chambers, most of Mount Street Square: all the old landmarks—gone. A disaster area. Worse than the Blitz. Weeds and rubble. Whole blocks abandoned, blackened, crudely boarded up.

I am walking slowly—really slowly—now. This is worse than anything I could have imagined. Bute Town was hardly humming with activity last time I came down here, but today I can't take in the swiftness and scale of the collapse. It is—truly—like wandering through the bombed-out ruins of Coventry, Rotterdam, Berlin, Dresden, Hiroshima.

I move steadily forward in the direction of the Pier Head. There seem to be practically no shops left in Lower Bute Street. To my surprise, The Packet is still open—once one of the most famous pubs in the world, talked about by sailors in every port on the seven seas. It is past eleven o'clock, but the only occupant of the cavernous interior is the barman, listlessly polishing a glass. There were dozens of famous pubs in Bute Town once: The Anglesey, The North and South Wales, The Dowlais, The White Swan. Most of them seem to have disappeared, along with every-thing else.

Of course, when I think of it, the beginning of the end, not just for Cardiff Docks but for Barry, Penarth, and Newport, had been signaled more than half a century before, round about the time I was born.

In the years immediately following World War I, there had been a tremendous surge of prosperity. But the Depression began to bite in Europe as early as 1923 or 1924, four or five years before it started in America with the Wall Street Crash. My father and the other Cardiff shipowners managed to struggle along for a while by carrying general cargo, but essentially the fortunes of Cardiff and the other Glamorgan ports depended on the export of coal and steel, and when that failed it took Cardiff down with it.

The collapse of coal was an inevitable result of the rise of oil. Coal-burning ships were replaced by oil-burning ships. Oil was increasingly used for heating and industrial purposes. The bare figures for the decline of the coal industry were as startling as the figures for its rise had been. In 1920 there were over six hundred mines in the South Wales coalfields, employing over a quarter of a million men. By 1975 there were forty mines, employing thirty thousand men. And not only was the coal industry played out, but the coal seams themselves were either exhausted or increasingly inaccessible and uneconomic to work. Welsh pits could no longer compete with their rivals in Europe and America.

The interwar period was murderous. Virtually half the population of South Wales was unemployed and on the dole, a terrible situation for proud, active, hard-muscled men. To make their condition worse, they were poorly led by their unions and by the Labour party—"lions led by donkeys," as someone put it. Some of their trade union leaders and Labour representatives were astute and honest, but others were Marxists, fellow travelers or out-and-out Stalinist fanatics, as bigoted in their own way as the Calvinistic Methodist preachers. Many of them were opportunists, "the profiteers of the class war," as somebody called them, willing to jump on any political bandwagon that promised them advancement.

The shrinkage of coal was compounded by the shrinkage of steel. British steel, like British coal, could not compete with that of the steelmakers abroad. The great Welsh steelworks shut down one after the other: Cyfarthfa, which Borrow had visited at the outset of its skyrocket career, closed in the 1920s. Blaenavon, Ebbw Vale, Dowlais followed suit. A body blow to Cardiff Docks was the closure of East Moors in the 1950s. Though the industry, like coal, shows some signs of recovery, it will never regain its former importance, nor ever again employ such large numbers of workers.

The effect of the Depression on Wales as a whole was devastating. The country's population actually declined as industrial workers, teachers, and members of other professions emigrated to England or went overseas. The effects of the Depression are apparent in Wales even today, both in a physical and demographic fashion and in its nightmarish folk memory, like the memory of the Black Death or of the Great Purge in Russia.

Yet who is willing to lament the passing of the coal-mining era in Wales? Old King Coal was *not* a merry old soul; he was a dirty old brute. Still, it is saddening, nonetheless, to witness the almost total collapse of a way of life to which, however deadly it was, several generations of men had become fiercely attached. The end of coal mining was certainly a release for Wales. It was always an anomaly, an aberration, an excrescence. Wales was not a country meant for activities like coal mining, or designed by Nature to bear the full rigors of an industrial revolution. Perhaps it can now revert to what it was originally meant to be: a beautiful and pastoral corner of the earth. And yet there is pathos in the image of all those magnificent and mistreated men, men who had once taken pride in a terrific, satanic calling, now being "retrained" for namby-pamby jobs on industrial estates. Think of those big fists that broke the coal trying to adapt themselves to assembling thermos flasks, vacuum cleaners, push-bikes, toasters, teakettles, and other such piddling stuff.

And so, when coal mining subsided, like the subsidence of one of its old and used-up coal pits, it took its ports, its docks, its shipping down with it. As with coal, however, the downward slide of the Docklands was not continuous; there were brief and deceptive periods of remission. After the dispiriting years of the Depression, the Cardiff docks revived during World War II, when 80 percent of the troops and supplies for the American forces in Britain were brought in through the port. Today, in America, I often run across American veterans whose faces light up when I tell them I am from Cardiff. And after 1945 there was the usual postwar boomlet, raising false hopes that it might after all be possible to stave off the major collapse that was in the offing.

Already, in the late 1940s, the mark of death was on Cardiff docks, and on Penarth, and Barry, and Newport. Without coal and steel, there was no incentive for ships to make the long trip beating up the Bristol Channel, with its tricky approaches for which the men of my family had served as expert navigators. It was easier to sail into Glasgow or Liverpool, or head for one of the ports on the English east coast. Moreover, the trend was toward larger, specialized ships. The small, handy general-cargo ships that could go anywhere and carry anything, the classic tramp steamers of Evan, Ike, and my father, were disappearing. In comparison the ships of today are huge, and are built for a single purpose, as dry bulk carriers, liquid bulk carriers, or container carriers. The days of Conrad's "coal out and ore in" were over. Ports were becoming specialized too: special ports for special ships. The most important port in South Wales today is Milford Haven, in West Wales, which is not really a port at all; it is an offshore pipeline terminal, where the giant tankers of today discharge their oil without ever coming into harbor. There was no point in, and no money for, trying to transform Cardiff into such a port, or seeking to make it one of the great new hub ports which are now coming into existence.

Modern ports are not ports in any case: not in the way I remember Cardiff between the wars. Modern ports are sterile, clinical installations, employing technicians rather than dockers, and not even many of those. The ships slide in, and the robot equipment plucks out the containers and pallets and swivels them smoothly onto the electric trains waiting with their obedient *tick-tick-tick* on the adjacent sidings. Nowadays it is all RORO: "Roll On, Roll Off." All very efficient, very tidy, very time-and-motion. But can I really grow enthusiastic about docks that are less like docks than like airports? Or about white-coated attendants and computer operators instead of real stevedores and real sailors? Or about gigantic floating barges, impersonal leviathans, instead of the tough, battered, rusty little terriers that rode the oceans in the days of my father, my grandfather, my great-grandfather? I can still remember the days when I saw the wharves and quays of the Bute Dock, the Roath Dock, and the Alexandra Dock crammed with ships that bore the blazon of the Cardiff shipowners on their flags and funnels: Morel, Lovering, Tatum, Reardon Smith, Instone, Radcliffe, Turnbull, Jones, Jenkins, Emlyn, Hain, Sanger, Hansen, Williams, and all their proud companions.

And now, as I reach the Pier Head itself, I discover that not only are the ships and the companies that owned them gone, gone too is the Gothic bulk of the Pier Head Chambers, one of the line of lofty buildings that once dominated the waterfront. The old Pilotage House still stands, thank heavens, a short distance away. It seems to be in good condition, and its doors and windows have been freshly painted, but it appears to be deserted, and the clock over the front door has stopped, and there is no stream of people continuously passing in and out as there was in the days when Evan and Ike used to bring me down here. No ships, no pilots. Yet the Windsor Hotel, next door to it, has a well-tended look, even though both the hotel and the Pilotage House are stranded together in a Sargasso Sea of weed and rubble.

The front door of the Windsor is shuttered, but the side door into the bar is open. I enter—though only after a moment's hesitation. Haven't I been disillusioned enough already, during my stroll through Tiger Bay? And there are too many of my personal ghosts in the Windsor—including the ghost of that confident boy who once lived in the Cathedral Road. The party for my twenty-first birthday was held here, in the Windsor. However, since it is one of the few landmarks in Bute Town still standing, and apparently still in commission, I can scarcely refuse to step inside. I tuck Admiral Pickard under my arm and straighten my shoulders.

The interior is still handsome, the ceilings high, the proportions generous. It seems in good enough repair. But I am immediately struck by its apathetic atmosphere. In the big room where we used to dance, the chairs are piled up higgledy-piggledy. There has evidently been no dancing here for a long time. The tables in the dining room are laid as if for lunch, but the tablecloths are creased and the cutlery is cheap and tinny. There is a sour smell of vinegar, chips, and pickles. At the time of my birthday party, and for a dozen years thereafter, this was a notable eating place. It was owned by a Frenchman called Abel Magneron, who worked diligently and cunningly throughout the years of rationing to make the kitchens of the Windsor the most inviting in South Wales. Tiger Bay had scores of exotic cafés and restaurants, but the haute cuisine of Monsieur Magneron's establishment was unique in the Glamorgan of forty-five years ago. Peace be to his genial and ample shade.

It is getting on for twelve o'clock. I am the only customer. No wonder the barman seems indifferent and glum. As he serves me with my Glenfiddich, he barely looks at me and is obviously disinclined to chat—an unusual thing in a Welshman, and an index of the general gloom that has settled over what little remains of Dockland. I take my scotch and retire to a distant corner of what used to be a cheerful and is now a distinctly dreary bar.

I am glad to have an opportunity to sort out my thoughts. Above all, I shall be leaving the Pier Head with one overriding personal impression. In the mid–twentieth century, in this, my own part of Wales, there have been three industrial and cultural disasters, all of them interlinked. Coal has collapsed, the steel and tinplate industries have largely collapsed, the maritime industry has totally collapsed. Of these disasters, the failures of coal and steel have been palpable enough to me, since the abandoned works and mines press around Cardiff in a ring whose radius is no more than 20 or 30 miles away. But the processes of making steel and mining coal strike me as hazy and peripheral, whereas the extinction of the docks and of shipping is a wholly personal kind of debacle. Most people in South Wales, in this century, have lived through their own upheavals and nightmares; the death of Cardiff Docks is mine, as it was my father's. It also represents in some degree the actual death of my family, since what had been for so long its occupation has now gone. "We shall no more to sea, to sea, here shall we die ashore." There are no more Whites, now, answering the call of the tides.

I suppose most people in Britain would consider the decline of the coal, steel, and heavy industries in general to be much graver matters than the expiration of ships and sailing. I wonder if they are right. Of course, the maritime phase of British history is still not quite over; there is still plenty of yachting and amateur sailing, the ferries still ply between Britain and the Continent and Ireland, there is still a British Navy, capable of mounting the kind of daring campaign we saw in the Falklands. On the other hand, the Navy, like the Merchant Service, is a shadow of the Grand Fleet of 1914 or 1939. In "Recessional," Kipling had warned:

> Far-called, our navies melt away—
> On dune and headland sinks the fire—
> Lo, all our pomp of yesterday
> Is one with Nineveh and Tyre!

Kipling could scarcely have foreseen, however, that the fire on dune and headland would have been doused so swiftly and abruptly, within two decades of his death.

No Briton lives more than a short day's drive away from the sea, and British families are still accustomed to spending their holidays beside it. But very few British families now, unlike those of earlier years, can boast of having a son, a nephew, a cousin, or even a second cousin in the Royal Navy or the Merchant Service. The sight of a sailor on the streets is an uncommon one. Not many British children nowadays know the excitement of having an uncle come rolling in from foreign ports and extracting strange and marvelous gifts from his ditty bag. Mass-produced toys from the duty-free shop at the airport are hardly the same thing. Few modern Britons any longer have any intimate acquaintance with the sea, though until recently it was the distinctive consciousness of the sea that saturated and lent salt to British history. The vocabulary of the sea was an important element in the language itself. Think of the number of nautical expressions that are still in use, although most of the people who use them have long since forgotten their origin: *On the rocks, three sheets in the wind, full steam ahead, sheet anchor, anchor to windward, anchor man, dead calm, steady as she goes, copper-bottomed certainty, mate* (which comes from *shipmate*), and so on and so on. Think of the accumulation of nautical words and nautical images in Shakespeare, quite apart from the number of scenes in his plays that are set on shipboard or along the coast. Scholars have speculated whether he might not have made a voyage or two, so frequently and confidently does he use nautical terms. He must at least have been used to being rowed up and down the river Thames, like all the inhabitants of London at that time. Country boy from Warwickshire though he was, his plays reveal that he regarded a knowledge and awareness of the sea as a natural part of his endowment as an Englishman.

There were writers in English about the sea long before Shakespeare. Shakespeare himself was an avid reader of stories about the sea, drawing heavily on Hakluyt, Purchas, and other chroniclers. Until very recently the literature of the sea constituted a separate and respected category of British literature, an accepted genre for British writers. With the possible exception of America, no other country has produced so many writers of sea stories as Britain. Smollett and Captain Marryat were among the pioneers, and from later years one can instance Conrad, Masefield, H. M. Tomlinson, W. W. Jacobs, James Hanley, Nicholas Monsarrat, Hammond Innes, C. S. Forester. The fact that there are now few authors who specialize in the subject is indicative, I think, of one of two great blows to the psyche that Britain has sustained in the twentieth century. The first was the loss of the Empire—for though its critics have argued that the imperial idea was a bad one, and that shedding the Empire was a positive act, there is no doubt that its loss robbed Britons of an exciting dimension, an adventurous extension to their lives. Young Britons who felt cramped and confined at home could always tear themselves loose and carve out a career in India, Kenya, Rhodesia, Nigeria. Now Britain has become diminutive and parochial. And with the dismantling of the Empire came a second blow: the disappearance of the great Empire trading system and the carrying trade on which it depended.

The loss of the Empire was the loss of the sea. At one time to think of Britain was simultaneously to think of the sea, to think of the tankers and tramp steamers and the Royal Navy that guarded and sustained it. It was to think of the defeat of the Armada, of the Glorious First of June, of Trafalgar, of Jutland, of Matapan. The British were the Island Race. Britain was "This precious stone, set in a silver sea." The first eight notes of "Rule, Britannia," said Wagner, were a complete summing-up of the British character. Now it is only on the last night of the Promenade Concerts that Britons sing "Rule, Britannia." And though they sing it fervently they know that Britain no longer rules the waves, just as when they go on to "Land of Hope and Glory" they know that there is really no point any longer in singing "Wider yet and wider shall thy bounds be set: God who made thee mighty, make thee mightier yet." The tide has gone out for Britain, as it has gone out for Cardiff Docks, washing away with it much of the ancient feeling of separateness, the sense of a singular and special destiny. The very conception of Britain as an island is evaporating. Britain is yoked to the European Community. The Channel Tunnel is under construction. There will be no more defeats of the Armada, no more Dunkirks.

Such sad thoughts are making me thirsty. I could do with another Glenfiddich, but for some reason the barman has disappeared into the dim internal regions of the hotel. I am alone in the bar, staring through an open door at the dusty dining room, where Monsieur Magneron once stood with the other guests to raise a glass to a black-haired, twenty-one-year-old youngster in his Guardsman's uniform.

Nothing to do, now, but finish my whiskey and retrieve Admiral Pickard, then make my way out to the weedy street for my last stop on this morning's little pilgrimage.

The Windsor Esplanade. Fifteen or twenty houses at the farthest seamark of Tiger Bay, facing out to sea. Here lived my grandfather, the "deep ocean man" turned harbormaster. Here my father was born.

I was afraid, turning the corner from the Pilotage House and the Windsor Hotel, of what might confront me. Once upon a time the houses of the Windsor Esplanade rivaled the shipmasters' mansions of Loudon Square as the most desirable residences in Dockland; but when I passed Loudon Square an hour ago I saw that it had long since been demolished. I am therefore immensely relieved to find that the Windsor Esplanade still stands in its old Victorian dignity, intact in the bright autumn sunlight. At least one small portion of this blighted region has survived the general shipwreck. And not only survived; it gleams with fresh paint and fresh plaster and with repointed brickwork. Well-tended roses and hydrangeas bloom in the front gardens. Across the road, beside the seawall, the pavements have been neatly relaid and a line of young trees has been planted. The seawall itself has been strengthened and recapped with white stone. In short, the Esplanade has been "gentrified," and though I would be willing to guess that none of its present occupants are seafaring folk, whereas during my boyhood none of them would have been anything else, it is still satisfying to note that the houses are as smartly turned out as in the days when Captain Trott decorated his front door with glass panels depicting marguerites.

I stand there gazing lovingly along its length. I am more grateful than I can say to have stumbled on this little oasis of elegance and sanity among all these mad wastes of trash and ruin. No doubt time will overwhelm the Esplanade in the end, as it must overwhelm everything else, but not for a while yet—and at least not in the lifetime of the last of the seagoing Whites, if I may presume to put my own brief years as a matelot into the scale.

But then, crossing the road and looking over the seawall, I get another of those unpleasant shocks that have been shaking me all morning. Where is the sea? Where is the smooth, shining expanse of water, silver under the sharp September sun?

I find myself staring out at mud. Mud, mud, and more mud. Mud as gray as the flanks of a dead whale. On one side of the rim of the undredged and lifeless harbor is a quay with a couple of motionless cranes canted at careless angles. On the other side are the cliffs and the town of Penarth, its own docks derelict and rotting.

A gangrenous vista. Tiger Bay—a great ship beached—a stinking carcass stranded on a glutinous and putrid shore.

A rueful muddy smell is in the wind, a sad iodine taste in my mouth. I know what Joyce meant when he spoke of "the cold infrahuman odour of the sea."

Was it from here that old Rawlins White put out with his

fishing boats, and Joshua White in his *Tryton*, and Maurice White on his way to be hanged, and Ike toward the Indian Ocean, and Evan bound for Callao and Valparaiso?

Was it really from here that King Arthur took ship, in pursuit of Sir Lancelot?

From time to time I have supplied the Welsh composer Alun Hoddinott with words for music. Among them is a cycle of poems for soloist with chorus and orchestra called *Voyagers*. One of the poems comes into my mind now as I stand on the Windsor Esplanade, watching the cold clouds sailing away from the land like the vanished ships of the Cardiff fleets:

> *Morgan Rees lies deep at rest,*
> *Where the tides rip wild and fast,*
> *Where the sullen breakers roar*
> *Down along the Labrador.*

> *Billy Powell tries to sleep,*
> *Where the tempests howl and weep,*
> *Round about the misty shape*
> *Of Africa's last lonely Cape.*

> *And there below the cloudy straight,*
> *Where steep Gibraltar guards the gate,*
> *Rolls old Walter Williams' bones,*
> *And all that's left of young Jim Jones.*

> *God make the weight of water light*
> *On Evan Hughes and William White,*
> *Whose coffin is the ocean broad,*
> *Whose bodies have the wave for shroud.*

God grant your peace to men like these,
Who went from Wales to sail the seas,
And never made the voyage home,
But took the whole world for their tomb.

Of course, I told myself, as I walked slowly through Llandaff Fields, I was only going there this morning for the singing. Just for the singing, nothing else.

Cardiff owes much of its beauty to the number and size of its parks: Sophia Gardens, Gorsedd Gardens, Roath Park, Victoria Park, Waterloo Gardens. Its central area, around the castle, the city hall, the law courts, the National Museum, the university, is one continuous park, lovingly and elaborately tended. And of all the parks Llandaff Fields, extending from the top of the Cathedral Road across to the cathedral and the village of Llandaff, is the largest and most handsome, a wide expanse of rolling parkland.

Pleasant to be walking here on a Sunday morning. Good to be breathing in the untainted air after the deliquescent reek of Tiger Bay. Sky a pure cornflower blue. Grass a ripe jade green. No hint of a breeze to ruffle the leaves of the ancient oaks, still innocent of any touch of decay. All nature rapt and motionless. A Sabbath calm. The summer still held as though in suspension inside a glowing piece of amber.

Few people. An elderly man walking his elderly dog, the *Sunday Times* tucked under his arm. When I lived in the Cathedral Road, I sometimes came here to do my stuff as a leg-spin bowler, during the school holidays. Roald Dahl, I remember, was at Llandaff School, his father a Norwegian who came to Cardiff with a host of other energetic young men from abroad to seek his fortune in shipping. The school was a posh prep school run on English lines, and the headmaster was an Englishman, so in accordance with English practice young Dahl was soundly thrashed. In *Boy* he describes at length the lifelong hurt and humiliation of it. Not a nice thing to dwell on, on this perfect September morning, so crisp and clear.

Oh yes—I am only going there for the singing. I can't leave Wales, surely, without a spot of song? Breakfasting beneath a portrait of Lincoln, with his sardonic and knowing smile, I had asked myself: And where shall I go today? Oh! I know—it's a lovely day, so why not take a stroll in Llandaff Fields? And then, as if the thought had just occurred to me: And while I'm about it, why don't I just drop into the cathedral for a moment or two and listen to the singing?

Naturally, I am fooling myself. As the slim spire begins to rise above the trees, I have to admit that this was a rendezvous toward which I have secretly been moving for many months past. The idea must have started to insert itself into my mind weeks ago, in Tennessee, when I began to make preparations for the present trip, and it certainly floated to the surface during my journey down from Paddington. In the course of these last three angry years, ever since Valerie's terrible illness and incapacity, I have been very deliberately avoiding churches and chapels and cathedrals. I have turned my back on everything they claim to represent. All the same—am I really compromising, or even conceding very much, if I just step inside for a while, in order to listen to the music? Besides, my quarrel is hardly with the cathedral itself. What is a cathedral, after all, but a heap of stone and glass? In any case, I have always had a particular fondness for Llandaff Cathedral, quite apart from its religious connotations. At least one of my forebears, Isabella White, was interred inside it, with a memorial tablet, and several of the numerous brood of John Whites lie buried in its churchyard. There would be something lacking in a visit to my own small corner of Wales if I went away without seeing Llandaff.

So it is with complicated emotions that I crest the rise and climb the hill on which the cathedral stands among its ring of ancient trees, its walls gleaming in the sunshine, its stones still warm with the heat of summer. In spite of myself, I feel my heart beat a little faster. My step quickens. I have always felt that there was something particularly intimate and welcoming about Llandaff. Like all the Welsh cathedrals, it is of modest dimensions, though not actually diminutive like St. David's, the tiniest of all the British cathedrals. Llandaff is not grandiose or awe inspiring, like many of the cathedrals of England; it has the reassuring proportions of an English abbey. Also, without conveying any sense of being lopsided or half finished, it has a pleasing asymmetry, an attractive agglomeration of styles: Romanesque, Gothic, Early English, Decorated, Perpendicular. Originally it was a Celtic foundation, associated with such Welsh saints as Teilo, Dyfrig, and Euddogwy, and was raised to episcopal status and brought under the rule of Canterbury and the Western Church by the Normans. Its first bishop was the energetic Urban, active between 1107 and 1133. In the succeeding centuries it has had a tempestuous history, its towers falling down, its fabric neglected, its treasures stolen and looted. Several times it was in such a state of disrepair that it was virtually abandoned and its religious reponsibilities transferred elsewhere.

In short, the history of Llandaff is as distracted and dislocated as the history of Wales itself. Yet, like Wales, it has always managed to pull through. It even survived almost total destruction when a German parachute mine went off beside the south wall during an air raid in 1941. As it happens, I remember that particular raid well, as I was home in Cardiff at the time and had been to a dance at the Queens's Hotel. I was walking back along the Cathedral Road in the small hours, and the bombs were coming down, and the ack-ack guns were thumping, and the searchlights were combing the sky frantically. The plate-glass windows of the shops were being blown out all around me. I longed to lie down in the gutter, but I was wearing a brand-new overcoat I had borrowed for the evening and was afraid of getting it dirty, so I put my head down and kept on walking. That land mine, meant for the docks, practically demolished the cathedral. But like Coventry Cathedral, Llandaff rose again, and with the aid of the original plans was successfully restored.

Its setting, on the outskirts of its own pretty village, is exceptionally beguiling. It is surrounded by thick greenery. Up there on the slope is the tall stone cross that marks the approximate spot where, eight hundred years ago, Archbishop Baldwin of Canterbury, with Gerald the Welshman beside him, preached to a crowd of Welshmen and Englishmen: "the Welsh standing on one side and the English on the other."

The archbishop was in the early stages of a strenuous seven-week circumambulation of Wales, urging all young men of military age to take up the Cross and participate in the Third Crusade. He and Gerald, then in his early forties and a canon of St. David's and archdeacon of Brecon, were at the start of a journey in which they would visit all four Welsh cathedrals and enlist three thousand men in the cause of wresting back the Holy Cross, which had been captured by Saladin. Of these three thousand volunteers, most never reached the Holy Land, and many of those who did would prove useless, since they were highwaymen, thieves, and murderers who were eluding justice by entering military service. Baldwin himself was early signed with the Cross, and also, in a fit of enthusiasm, was Gerald. Gerald, however, never saw the Holy Land. His patron, Henry II, released him from his vows when he was about to embark for Palestine, evidently considering him more valuable as a scholar and a diplomat than as a fighting priest. But the aging Baldwin held to his word and went to the Holy Land. He perished heroically under the walls of Acre, personally leading the Christian forces to the assault.

In common with too many of the enterprises in which the

Welsh have involved themselves, the Third Crusade turned out to be pretty much of a fiasco. Richard I managed to recapture Acre and twice defeated Saladin in battle, but the closest he came to pagan-held Jerusalem was a distant glimpse of it from the heights of Mt. Joy. The only benefits Wales ultimately acquired from Baldwin's journey in that spring of 1188 were some architectural additions to the Cathedral of St. David's, where backsliders from their vows were required to donate their labor, and Gerald's own incomparable *Itinerarium Cambriae* and *Cambriae descriptio, The Journey Through Wales* and *The Description of Wales*, which he worked up later from what was evidently a full set of notes. Both books, or rather joint books—shrewd, vivid, profound, superstitious, witty—have been a constant source of amusement and instruction to me from my boyhood onward. In addition, Gerald seems to have borne a strong resemblance to my own father: a man of insatiable intellectual curiosity, quarrelsome and unforgiving in a grand way, something of a social misfit, a resolute fighter in a lost cause, unflinching in defeat. Gerald was quixotic, fearless, part scholar and part man of action, magnificently right on some occasions and magnificently wrong on others. Viewed in some ways, he was a splendid failure; viewed in other ways he was a splendid success. He was by turns arrogant and humble, a celebrated horseman, restless, a compulsive traveler, tormented all his life by his ambivalent love of and loyalty to both Wales and England (a sensation with which I too have been painfully familiar).

I am thinking of Gerald and Baldwin now as I move toward the cathedral, past the cross on its mound. They must have made a striking pair, standing up there with the gaping crowd around them: the swarthy, tubby, elderly archbishop of middling height beside the tall, vigorous, red-haired, handsome Gerald (who had no qualms about telling us just how handsome he was). I am thinking of Gerald as I make my way between the ancient graves toward the Norman side entrance, through which he himself must many times have passed. I am thinking of him so fondly and intensively that I am totally unprepared—totally amazed— by what I encounter when I swing back the heavy oaken door and step inside the cathedral.

I had noticed, in a desultory way, that there were a few cars parked outside, under the trees, though not many. Since leaving the Lincoln Hotel, I have run across fewer than a score of people. And now—suddenly—I find myself confronted with a church that is absolutely stuffed with worshipers. I wonder if the experience of dying and arriving in Heaven might be like this: an interval of solitary self-communion followed by an awakening in the midst of a silent and expectant throng?

Heads turn to look at me, though more with Welsh curiosity than with accusation. The service is about to begin. That was why I encountered no one outside. The arrival and assembly of such a large gathering, so quietly and unobtrusively, has something spectral and unnerving about it. Fortunately, a few yards down the side aisle, opposite what looks like the Lady Chapel, there is an empty chair—the last remaining empty chair. I tiptoe guiltily toward it.

How could I have anticipated that on this Sabbath morning the cathedral would be filled to overflowing? Thirty years ago, when I was trying on the role of the squire of Minsterworth Court (another of those departed young men, like the sailor, the soldier, and the student), and when I thought it was incumbent on me to attend divine service, the situation was entirely different. My wife and I would take our small daughters to sparsely attended services in the little parish church across the adjacent paddock, or else to join the notably thin congregation in Gloucester Cathedral, around the bend in the river. The Church of England, in my time, was in a threadbare condition: yet this morning, here in Cardiff, its sister Church in Wales is doing a thriving trade. What is the explanation? Is it the greater religious inclination of the Welsh? Or is the Established Church in Britain beginning to revive?

Whatever the explanation, I am impressed, impressed too by the air of confidence and well-being of the packed rows around me. Once more I am struck by the contrast I have already noted between depressed and surly England and cheerful and outgoing Wales. The people are almost all young, in their twenties and thirties. They are well dressed, and dressed with an informality that would have been frowned upon in Minsterworth Church or Gloucester Cathedral thirty years ago. The men are mostly in shirtsleeves, the women in light, summery dresses, their children—lots and lots of children—fidgeting about in casual clothes. All look as if they are on easy terms with God. They are, of course, exclusively middle class in origin—which makes the shirtsleeves, even when worn with a tie, something of a shock, though I suppose that everywhere nowadays the managerial class likes to appear with its coat off. At any rate, although I can scarcely claim to have retained any strong feeling for it, I am gratified, in a sentimental way, to discover that my good old C of E, at least in South Wales, appears to be staging something of a comeback.

There is a great swish and shuffle all about me. The congregation is rising to its feet, as if it had only been waiting for my tardy appearance before embarking on the first hymn. There is a brief and peremptory introduction on the organ, then the whole assembly bursts into song. At once I feel a prickle in my neck and jaw as I lower my head and fumble at the pages of my hymnal, trying to conceal the sting of emotion.

*Music. Welsh music.* It comes surging up all around me, enfolding me. And of all people, here in church, I think of Nietzsche: "A life without music is a mistake." Right from the beginning, here in Wales, I have never been without music. Without the spur and consolation of music, how would I have got through these past three years? My mother was an excellent pianist, and I remember her performing on the beautiful long-tailed Blüthner my father had bought for her in his affluent days. As an infant I liked to crawl underneath it and curl up when she played, exactly as D. H. Lawrence did beneath his mother's cottage upright:

> *Softly, in the dusk, a woman is singing to me;*
> *Taking me back down the vista of years, till I see*
> *A child sitting under the piano, in the boom of the tingling*
>     *strings*
> *And pressing the small, poised feet of a mother who smiles as*
>     *she sings.*
>
> *In spite of myself, the insidious mastery of song*
> *Betrays me back, till the heart of me weeps to belong*
> *To the old Sunday evenings at home, with the winter outside*
> *And hymns in the cosy parlour, the tinkling piano our guide.*
>
> *So now it is vain for the singer to burst into clamour*
> *With the great black piano appassionato. The glamour*
> *Of childish days is upon me, my manhood is cast*
> *Down in the flood of remembrance, I weep like a child for*
>     *the past.*

My father had a pleasant tenor voice. He took singing lessons from a diminutive baritone from Newport called Dai Francis, whose shining bald head, several sizes too large for his body, fascinated me. My father's taste ran to the drawing-room ballads of the period, which have recently become fashionable again. With my mother accompanying him and myself encased in the thunderous womb of the piano, he would launch out into "Nirvana," "My Lovely Celia," "Come to the Fair," "I'll Sing Thee Songs of Araby," "Love, Could I Only Tell Thee," "Have You News of My Boy Jack?" or "Shipmate o' Mine," or join Dai Francis in "Watchman, What of the Night?" Strangely, today I remember his singing voice clearly, whereas of his speaking voice I remember only the occasional strangled whisper which was all that his doctors in the sanatorium allowed him. Not long afterward I took up music myself and played in an orchestra that met once a week amid the gilt-and-marble opulence of the rotunda of the City Hall. I have often thought that playing among the splendors of all that Ionian white and gold must have been a little like playing in Haydn's orchestra at Esterházy, and certainly the grandeur of the acoustics spoiled me for playing elsewhere, though the tiled lavatory of our flat in Hamilton Terrace in London had capital acoustics too, even if using it for extended sessions as a music room was rather hard on other members of the family.

In Hamilton Terrace we had Dame Maggie Teyte as our next-door neighbor, while the conductor Alec Sherman and the pianist Gina Bachauer lived opposite and Sir Arthur Bliss and Franz Reizenstein were just around the corner. Later, at Minsterworth, Alun Hoddinott was a frequent visitor, and on his trips between Cardiff and the Cheltenham Festival and the Three Choirs Festival he would bring to see us one or other of the composers whose works were being presented: David Wynne, William Matthias, John Ogdon, Phyllis Tate, Don Banks. In due course, when I left for America, Alun became the recipient of my Broadwood baby grand.

However, undeniably the most powerful musical influence on my early life was the Rubens family, who lived a few minutes away. It was in the drawing room of old Mr. Rubens and his beautiful and stately wife that I first heard the names of such composers as Roussel, Martinu, Schönberg, and Dallapiccola—not exactly your household names in Cardiff in the late 1930s and early 1940s. The four Rubens children were outstandingly talented. The eldest son was an established piano soloist, the younger son was a member of the Hallé Orchestra, and the elder daughter was a cellist. The only one who was not an executant, Bernice, went on to make a considerable reputation as a novelist and in her *Madame Sousatzka* has painted one of the most compelling portraits of a musician in modern fiction.

> *All people that on earth do dwell,*
> *Sing to the Lord with cheerful voice.*

And it *is* a cheerful voice. I join in at the top of my lungs. I am immersed in a great wash of sound.

According to the Emperor Charles V, French is the best language in which to confer with statesmen, Italian to talk with women, English to call to birds, German to talk to horses, and Spanish to address kings, princes, and God. He might have added that Welsh and Anglo-Welsh are the best languages for singing.

The entertainers Flanders and Swann, in a song characterized by what they call "typical British understatement" ("The English, the English, the English are best—/I wouldn't give tuppence for all of the rest"), affect a deep disdain for the Welshman and his manner of singing:

> *He lives underground with a lamp in his hat,*
> *And sings far too often—too loudly . . . and FLAT!*

I think that this was to a great extent true when I was a young man in Wales ("Our Musical Correspondent"). Welsh singers and choirs did not then venture much beyond *Elijah*, *Messiah*, and Stainer's *Crucifixion*. Their repertoire was conventional and foursquare. In the past thirty years, with the emergence of such composers as Grace Williams, Daniel Jones, Arwel Hughes,

Patrick Piggott, Hoddinott, Wynne, and Matthias, and with the success of the Cardiff Festival of Modern Music and the inauguration of the Welsh National Opera Company, the picture has completely changed. Music making in Wales has become as adventurous as could be wished. Yet the ancient forms, too, such as folk song and the peculiar form of impromptu declamation called *penillion,* are also cherished and can be heard at the local and national festivals. The Welsh—as the lusty rendering of the hymn all around me testifies, with the singers freely and instinctively indulging in their own harmonies and roulades—have lost nothing of the national love of song for which they are properly famous. If God is musical, and if there is a heaven, and if there are choirs there, then we Welsh will never lack for an occupation.

There is a nice story about a time when God has decided to conduct the Heavenly Choir in a rehearsal of the *Messiah.* There are a million sopranos, a million contraltos, a million tenors, and one bass, the Welshman Dai Jones. God hitches up his gown, mounts the podium, raises his baton, and launches into the "Hallelujah Chorus." They are well into the piece, and making a glorious sound, and the vaults of heaven are ringing, when God taps with his baton on the music desk. The voices die away. God smiles and says, "Girls and boys, girls and boys"—(Welsh accent, naturally)—"Very nice, very nice indeed." He turns to the million sopranos. "Sopranos—beautiful." He turns to the million contraltos. "Contraltos—marvelous." He turns to the million tenors. "Tenors—first-class." Then he turns to the single bass, Dai Jones. "Only one thing wrong," God says. "Dai Jones—*too much bass.*"

"Let us pray."

The congregation kneels on the hassocks, the children supple and swift, their elders slow and stiff. Heads are lowered.

I do not kneel. I remain as I am, upright on my chair. I do

not incline my head. I try not to do it offensively or ostenta-tiously. I simply stay where I am, not peering about or fussing, just sitting quite quietly and staring straight ahead.

After a moment or two, I am aware of receiving some inquiring stares from people in the vicinity. Heads are discreetly swiveled. Eyes gleam at me furtively across folded hands or between latticed fingers. On the seat immediately in front of me, a little girl of five or six in a bright red frock is kneeling beside her mother. She has straight blond hair, blue eyes, freckles, a snub nose, and looks absolutely angelic. Making sure that her mother is looking the other way, she ducks her head round and sticks out her tongue at me. Also making sure that her mother is looking the other way, I stick out my tongue back.

I continue to draw anxious looks. Am I a tourist, or a foreigner, with some weird religion of my own? More alarming, am I some sort of extremist or fanatic? Am I likely at any second to jump to my feet and do a Rawlins White—shout out and try to disrupt the service with a protest against abortion, or imperi-alism, or the treatment of the Palestinians or the Jews? Am I a potential terrorist, waiting until the bishop has embarked on his sermon to roll a hand grenade down the aisle?

In fact, though I am not joining in the ceremony, I have no wish to appear or to act in any way that is provocative or disrespectful. I merely want to sit here, enjoying the music from time to time, but otherwise remaining apart and unobtrusive. Not only do I lack any kind of fanaticism but (I say it without a vestige of pride or pleasure) I am almost totally devoid of any religious conviction. Alas, I have had to live my life, as the saying goes, almost completely without invisible means of support. Despite old Rawlins White, there has never been an excess of religious enthusiasm in my family. My father (and who could blame him?) was an ironist and a skeptic, and neither my mother nor the sisters who kept house with her were churchgoers. As for me, I had enough of established religion at my school in

England, with its two attendances at chapel on Sunday and its morning and evening prayers each day in the common room. Probably my ribald and pagan English schoolmates put me off religion for life.

I have never been able to bring myself to believe in the traditional Christian version of God, reigning on high like the headmaster of an English public school. Nor can I believe in the idea of an afterlife, with or without Welsh choirs. In any case, I do not believe I should be very comfortable in Heaven, with what Nabokov calls its "appalling insecurity and lack of privacy."

On the other hand, while lacking a specifically Christian religious feeling, I do not seem to be devoid of something akin to a religious feeling itself. I simply do not believe that God gets up early on Sunday morning in order to preside in conventicles, large or small. And since it is, after all, 4.3 light-years to Alpha Centauri, our nearest star, it seems an awfully long way to come to listen to a sermon, however well preached, and a couple of hymns, however well sung.

Yet it is very pleasant sitting here among all these good Welsh folk, with the sweet September light pouring in through the windows. I only wish I could feel among us the presence of some transcendent spirit. But it seems to me that we in the congregation remain, in mood and appearance, very much the same kind of crowd we would be if we were wandering around the galleries of the National Museum. Indeed, we might be suffused with a great deal more animation if we were listening to a concert in the St. David's Hall, or watching a football match at the Arms Park. My small blond angel in front of me, for example, is so little impressed with the proceedings and so little in awe of the place that she has decided to stir things up by kicking the legs of her chair, edging it back until it makes contact with my knees. She glances back from time to time with a mischievous grin to see how I am taking it. I retaliate by gripping the back of her chair and giving it a jerk or two—whereupon her mother turns around and gives me a basilisk stare, whispering to the child to take no notice of the strange gentleman. The little imp shoots me a last glance of honeyed glee.

The Welsh have a saying, *Nesaf i'r eglwys, pellaf o Baradwys* "The nearer to church, the farther from Paradise." Fond as I have always been of popping into a handsome church or cathedral, I feel closer to God or Whoever-It-Is in the open air. I would have felt, I think, more at home with Greek religion, or with the American Indian conception of the Manitou, the Great Spirit of Nature. No one, after all, has ever seen the Christian God; he is invisible, inaudible, an abstraction, but you can see the ocean being lashed by Poseidon, or the forest being thrashed by Aeolus. The gods of Greece were tangible. You can love and fear the storm, the wind, the rain, the clouds, the lightning, the thunder; they are awesome, shifting, volatile entities that you can watch and actually feel on your skin. I can neither watch nor feel the Christian God. His priests require me to take him wholly on trust.

In consequence, in order to express my personal and primitive apprehension of the sacred and inward nature of things, I have been reduced to devising my own private religion. I have already mentioned the small ceremonial of scattering daffodils on the river Severn at Minsterworth in honor of Sabrina. And both in Gloucestershire and later in Tennessee I have carried out another, more elaborate springtime ritual. When the trilliums and the violets first begin to show, in early March, I make my way with my dog Taffy to the far end of Rebel Ridge. There is a sort of natural grove or clearing there, with a tall circle of trees, where the ridge ends and the slope suddenly tumbles into the Tennessee River a hundred feet below. On one of the Douglas firs in the clearing (always the same one, and chosen for no better reason than instinct), I pin a piece of paper on which is written in Greek characters the words *To the Unknown God.* Then, at the foot of the tree, I place four paper cups, and into them I pour water, milk, wine, and blood.

Why I should use a Greek rubric is hard to say, except that in the dense woodland around me it is easy to sense Artemis running lightly among the trees with her bow and quiver, or Pan roistering along with his companions. The Unknown God might just as easily be the Great Spirit of the Cherokee, the Shawnee, and Tuscarora, who with their predecessors roamed this territory for more than two thousand years before the coming of the Europeans. And if I were in Gloucestershire, or Wales, or pinning up my paper on a tree in the Forest of Dean, I would associate my Unknown God with Cernunnos, Lugh, the Hooded Ones, or with one of the other gods of Celtdom. There have been moments, in the woods, on the sea, beside a river, when I have felt certain that the old gods have not died.

In fact, from time to time I have toyed with the idea of inventing a brand-new religion, one in which the old gods would be assigned their proper share. Instead of a religion monopolized by one particular creed, I would put forward what might be called a triple religion, covering the three most important aspects of individual concern. Thus, if one found oneself traveling in the countryside, one would avail oneself of the old religion of nature, the pagan worship of the genius loci, adapting it to wherever those gods happened to be: Greek or Roman in the Mediterranean, Scandinavian in Scandinavia, Celtic in Celtdom, Indian in North America. On the other hand, if one found oneself living in a city or an urban environment, one would switch one's form of worship to Christianity. While the figure of Christ has always had its appeal to the peasant and the countryman, I have tended to picture him not so much as wandering through the fields, admiring the lilies, as riding into Jerusalem and functioning in an urban setting. His cult seems peculiarly suitable for the modern city dweller, overcrowded and exploited, often hungry, suffering, and desperate. And finally, after one has worshiped Apollo in the open air and Jesus Christ in a city church, when the time comes to turn one's mind toward Last Things, I would suggest that the afterlife component of the triple religion might best be adopted from the religion of ancient Egypt. The ancient Egyptians were history's most notable specialists in such things. I have qualms about whether I could exist happily in the Christian Heaven, but I have no doubt at all that I could do so in the ancient Egyptian one. For the business of our physical and spiritual preparation for death and resurrection, I would therefore propose that we seriously consider reviving an interest in the cult of Osiris, Isis, Horus, Anubis, and the other high gods of Egypt—who, after all, were actually worshiped and maintained a grip on the human imagination for longer than the Christian God.

I wriggle my shoulders and sit up straighter on the hard rush-covered chair. My little angel in front is just preparing to entrap me in another spot of mischief, but this time she collects a sharp smack on the bare arm that brings her up short. She stares at me with a look full of hurt and accusation, rubbing her arm, as if it was all my fault. Her mother nudges her father and whispers to him. He turns his head and gives me a long, serious look. I stare up innocently at the board displaying the hymn numbers.

Why, I ask myself, when the father is once more paying attention to the service and my little freckled demon is sitting still for a change, looking straight ahead, her small lower lip quivering—why am I trying to fool myself? Why am I making all this play with music, and hymn singing, and Artemis, and religious whimsy, when all this time I know very well that I have come here, to the cathedral of St. Teilo and St. Dyfrig, to my own home church, for a specific purpose?

It was not by accident that I woke up this morning in the

Lincoln Hotel, confronted by my own childhood, and decided to take a stroll across Llandaff Fields. I might have pretended it was—but that was only a pretense. I have had this visit to Llandaff Cathedral in mind (or rather, kept firmly in the back of my mind, not fully admitted to consciousness) for a long time. This trip to Wales is not just the sentimental journey of a man approaching the threshold of old age who is trying to wrest some meaning from his beginnings. The trip is more than that. I am making this pilgrimage, I have traveled 4,000 miles, because there is something that I want God, the God in whom I say I do not believe, to take notice of. I want God, or Whoever-It-Is or Whatever-It-Is, to pay attention. I have a feeling that he has not really been listening, so far.

I am, you see, in urgent need of help. I am in need of a very large favor from someone or something, from God, or Whatever-It-Is. This is rather an impertinence, I know, having lived pretty well the whole of my life in a state of indifference and agnosticism. But I am in a situation where I am forced to try everything. And it is not for me, after all. I am making this pilgrimage for the sake of my wife, who is unable to make it for herself, and who is not even in a condition to be brought here, like one of the pathetic pilgrims to Lourdes. I have come here to petition for a woman I married more than forty years ago, who cannot walk, who can hardly talk, who can barely think, who is almost totally paralyzed. She has gone beyond help in this world, and my only recourse seems to be to try to borrow some help from the next.

I said petition. That is too strong a word. I do not intend to make any direct appeal, which is why I am not kneeling and bowing my head. I just want God or Whoever-It-Is to know that I exist, and, more important, to know that my wife exists. And for some silly reason I have got it stuck in my head that this, after all, is the most likely place for it to happen: my native cathedral, in my native city, the city in which I met her and where I married her.

Sheer superstition, of course—though simply the same sort of thing, surely, that millions of other people resort to when some personal tragedy strikes them. Perhaps God does indeed pass by Llandaff on a Sunday morning. I am not in a position to neglect any possibility, however remote. Pascal's bet: Even if the existence of God is a trillion-to-one chance, it is a chance, and you might as well get your money down. I am one of those people in the lottery, scrambling to plunk down my cash, even though I know that the odds against me are astronomical. I suppose my mother may have come up here from the Cathedral Road fifty years ago on exactly the same errand, crossing Llandaff Fields and entering by the same Norman doorway. She too failed to hit a winning number and win the divine jackpot. Whoever-It-Is was deaf, or distrait, or had not bothered to turn up on that particular day. My father died a very long-drawn-out and squalid death.

I am sure my mother knelt when she addressed her prayer to the Deity. Not I. Like most of the Whites, I am stiff-necked. I don't kneel because I have never found it easy to ask anyone for anything. In any case, like the seaman in Conrad's *Victory*, "I don't hold with a man everlastingly bothering the Almighty with his troubles. It seems such cheek." It also seems "such cheek," in this particular case, to make such a fuss about the illness, however appalling, of one small elderly woman, when one compares it with the colossal amount of misery and suffering that is already going on in the world. It seems selfish and self-indulgent. Everywhere on earth, at this moment while I am sitting in this safe and quiet place, millions of men, millions of women, millions of children are dying, being maimed, or being made homeless. They are doing their feeble best to cope with fire, flood, earthquake, massacre, and epidemic. They are being starved, shot, tortured, turned out upon the roads as refugees. They are being sweated and enslaved. Somewhere in the world at this moment a man is being murdered, a woman is being raped, a child is being beaten and abused. The skies are filled with their moans and cries. The earth is one enormous insane asylum and hospital ward. So how do I have the nerve to sit here on my comfortable (well—moderately comfortable) cathedral chair, well dressed and well fed, nursing my little bourgeois injustice and trying to inflict it on a God who—God knows!—must have far more serious things on his mind?

In any case, since I have never bothered much about God, why should I expect him to bother about me? In fact, does God, even if he exists, bother himself greatly about anything to do with this world and its inhabitants? Pluto is 2.6 billion miles from Earth, and the nearest star is ten thousand times the distance from Earth to Pluto. "God," says Spinoza, "doesn't love anyone, and God doesn't hate anyone." He adds, chillingly, "Those who love God must not expect God to love them in return."

Therefore I have not dropped on my knees along with the rest. Moreover, I am not just sitting here bolt upright in order to indicate to God that I am not asking any favor for myself, or that I am ashamed of myself for being weak enough to ask him for anything in the first place. I am not kneeling because I am actually exceedingly angry with him, and I want him to know it. Ever since my wife was struck down, arbitrarily and without warning, I have had a serious quarrel with him. I regret this and do not regard it lightly. And what makes quarreling with him peculiarly painful is that one of the few fairly certain things we know about him, after all, is that he is a Welshman. Why then did the Big Welshman in the Sky behave so carelessly? So callously? If he was going to interest himself in the petty affairs of my family, and decided that the time had come to inflict a punishment on it, why did he pick on Valerie and not on me? I have led a fairly wayward life. I may have merited chastisement. But what on earth did my poor Valerie ever do? In all her life she was never anything but truthful and honest. I never knew her to commit a mean action.

For months after the thunderbolt struck her, I went about literally craning my head back and shouting abuse at the heavens. I shook my clenched fist at God like Lear on the heath. All very childish, of course, but I imagine a lot of people do this in similar circumstances, when some unexpected and unmerited disaster occurs. Life, as they say, is what happens to you when you are busy making other plans. What atrocious act could Valerie or I have committed to draw down something as disastrous as this? I suppose some priest might have tried to convince me that it was "God's plan for me," but I could only brandish my fist at the blank sky and shout, "Listen, God: Plan A isn't working! Try Plan B!" "Hatred of God," says Yeats, "can bring the soul to God," and certainly after the calamity I felt close to God in a way I never remember having done before. I could not help thinking of those tribesmen in *The Golden Bough* who, when their god misbehaved, took him out of his tabernacle, bound him with chains, and gave him a thrashing. It must have been satisfying for those so-called primitive peoples to give their lazy or naughty god a quick, hard kick in the ribs.

All around me the worshipers are on their knees, intoning the Lord's Prayer. I have often asked myself why it should be taken for granted that God should have any need of our human praise and prayers, or why he should be so avid for them. I sympathize with the Englishman who tore all the passages praising God out of his hymnbook, on the grounds that he assumed that God was a gentleman, and gentlemen dislike being praised to their face. I hear a strenuous muttering as the congregation gives glory to God and begs him, with eyes tightly shut, to forgive them their trespasses and pardon them their sins. Poor little people, what dreadful trespasses do they need to ask forgiveness for? What pardon do they need for living their humdrum, middle-class lives as doctors, dentists, lawyers, shop assistants, and insurance adjusters? I look at their bent backs and neat haircuts, at their nice clean necks, and ask myself whether it might be a question, not whether God is going to forgive them, but who is going to forgive God.

They are beginning to troop down to the altar rail to take Communion. I lean back and fold my arms and continue to sit tight. Even if I were a believer, I am not at all sure that I would be inclined to take part in it. "God," as someone said, "doesn't turn himself into a biscuit." The mother of the little blond girl, I notice, goes forward to join the queue to drink the blood and eat the flesh, but the girl herself shifts onto her mother's chair and snuggles up to her father. I wonder why he is not taking Communion, like his wife. Could he be subject to some of the same sort of doubts and distractions that I have?

I tell myself that I have never really expected any aid or respite for Valerie. Every medical resource has been exhausted. I shall never again see her walk, stand up, sit up. I accept that. But is it too much to expect that I might be accorded some small measure of insight as to why this thing should have happened? Nothing more than that. Is it really too much to ask of the All-Wise, the All-Powerful, the All-Knowing that I at least be granted some understanding of the affliction that has overtaken us? Gerald the Welshman talks repeatedly in his *Journey through Wales* of "the Judgment of God, which is sometimes hard to understand, though just." It is hard to accept that, another eight hundred years after he wrote, if he were to return to Wales he would discover that the Christian religion has not moved an inch further in giving us some inkling of the meaning of God's justice.

Of course, I should have acknowledged from the outset that my journey to Llandaff would be futile. What was the point, really, in trekking all this way from Tennessee to indulge in this charade? The supply of blood from my wife's brain to her left side has been cut off. That is the beginning and end of the matter. All Swedenborg's angels can do nothing about that. It is just that hope is so hard to extinguish. I might just as well have walked Taffy along Rebel Ridge and pinned a piece of paper to a tree.

I am visited by a terrible thought. It occurs to me that sitting in a cathedral, any cathedral, is like sitting inside a huge, stranded spaceship, cast up on the shore of some desolate planet. The cathedrals are exquisite hulks, all that remain of a once mighty fleet, rotting away like the fleets that once sailed from Cardiff. "Far-called, our navies melt away." At regular intervals the crew and the passengers still visit the abandoned shells, in order to huddle together and find what comfort and reassurance they can. They have a sense of being alone on the outer edge of a forgotten universe, on a planet that spins ever more slowly, warmed by a waning sun.

A thought strikes me that is even more terrible. What if Llandaff, like cathedrals everywhere, is not a spaceship that has made a fruitless voyage and now lies derelict. What if it is a terrestrial spaceship which has been built and which is intended to launch? What if the priests are the crew and the congregation the passengers, and we have strapped ourselves here on this Sunday morning hoping to be launched? We are sitting here in a colossal and beautiful projectile, which it has taken the ingenuity of many generations to build, with its soaring spires and towers tilted upward toward the stars. The prayers and hymns are our rocket fuel, and we are yearning for the magical, incandescent moment when ignition will take place and the whole vast, lovely contraption will lift off and whirl us all, like Elijah's chariot, up to Heaven. Every Sunday these people in the congregation flock here, take their seats, and wait eagerly for the miracle to occur. But alas, however detailed the blueprints of the designers, however much love has been lavished on them, something has gone wrong. The whole enterprise is stillborn. The ecclesiastical spaceships will never leave their launching pads. They are too unwieldy, or too heavy, or the fuel is leaking, or too thin, or the wrong octane. The crew up there on the flight deck work away frantically, and we in the congregation sing and pray our hearts out, but there is not going to be any bang and flash and the rocket is not going to be lifted off the ground by so much as a single inch. There is nothing to do except for all those present to unstrap themselves, climb out, and go home to Sunday lunch, taking whatever consolation they can from the thought, Well, at least we tried. And, after all, there is always next week. Who knows, with enough faith the miracle may eventually happen, and you will find yourself flying up through the clouds, up, up and away, on the track to Heaven, with all your dear ones about you.

The little girl's mother is returning to her place. Her face is radiant. She believes. I wish I could believe like that. Faith is a gift, a grace. I would like to have had it.

> *And my ending is despair,*
> *Unless I be relieved by prayer,*
> *Which pierces so that it assaults*
> *Mercy itself, and frees all faults.*

Directly above my head, suspended on a flying arch, is a life-size figure of Christ: the great *Majestas* which the cathedral authorities in their wisdom commissioned from Jacob Epstein when the cathedral was rebuilt after the bombing. It may be Epstein's masterpiece. Christ hovers between the congregation and the vaulted roof, between Heaven and Earth, his arms opened wide, gaunt, hollow cheeked, emaciated, his vestments a somber gray and gold. I look up at him with regret. I wish I could bring myself to pray to him.

A rustle and clearing of throats. We rise for the final hymn. There is always music.

While the organist is playing the opening bars, the imp in front of me bobs quickly around, grinning, wrinkling up her snub nose. Then, at the end of the service, she does something unexpected. As I am putting my hymnbook back in its rack, I place my hand on the rail of the chair in front of me. The girl, lingering behind her parents as they turn to join the crowd of people walking up the aisle, pauses, then lays her small hand on the back of mine. I feel the little fingers give a quick squeeze. She smiles at me, uncertain, questioning, as if troubled by what she has seen in my face, as though wanting to comfort me.

Another squeeze, a soft pat. She runs after her parents and is gone. I stand on the flagstones beneath Epstein's *Majestas* and watch the diminutive figure in its red dress run down the steps and out into the autumn sunshine, pattering away between the gray tombs on the heels of her father and mother.

Well, at least someone has forgiven me.

Perhaps I have received a blessing on this Sunday morning, after all.

Here it comes, the Cardiff team, running out from the tunnel underneath the stands.

The captain is in the lead. It is so long since I last saw a rugby match that I am astounded to see that the ball he carries is white, instead of the old familiar brown. This is a little like encountering an unexpected alteration in the church service. What else, in the next ninety minutes, am I going to find has been subtly or not so subtly changed since I last visited Cardiff Arms Park?

The captain turns and swings out a practice pass to the man trotting behind him. In a moment the field is filled with thirty men, half in the light-and-dark-blue jerseys of Cardiff, half in the sinister top-to-toe black outfits of Neath, the steel town a few miles to the west along the Glamorganshire coast, always a rugged and ruthless opponent.

I had forgotten how quickly British football matches get under way. There is none of the panoply and the building up of tension, with marching bands and cheerleaders, that marks the beginning of the American football games I have been watching for the past twenty-odd years. Here there is simply the thud and thump of a few casual dropkicks, a coin is tossed, the ball is readied, the referee blows his whistle, and the white ball is sailing up into the sunlight of the autumn afternoon.

I lean back in my seat. I am glad to be relieved for an hour or so from the sad Boethian thoughts that have been plaguing me since my visit to Llandaff. Forty years ago I left Cardiff with the illusion that I was walking away from care and trouble into a cloudless future, and here I am returning with, if anything, an even heavier burden. So much for the notion of escape.

Perhaps more than anywhere else, almost as much perhaps as the Pier Head and the docks, Cardiff Arms Park brings home to me the smell and savor of my childhood. In the most miserable Welsh winter weather, my family never missed their weekly attendance whenever the Cardiff club was playing at home. And when I say the family, I mean the whole family: children and parents, uncles and aunts, nephews and nieces. We occupied a solid block in the stands, as if we were occupying the family pews in church. It is not too fanciful to assert, in fact, that during the course of this century rugby football has waxed as Wales's religion has waned, until in point of fervor and even outright fanaticism it has become the predominant Welsh interest. The same thing has been happening with soccer, of course, in many other countries in the world.

In the 1920s my father was a director of the Cardiff Rugby Football Club. When he needed to talk to one or other of the players or officials, he would sometimes take me with him into the clubhouse and the changing rooms. I remember the awe with which I regarded the titans and demigods slumped on the benches, sloughing off their shirts, fingering their bruises, unwinding a soiled bandage from a wrist, a thigh, a knee. Among my most precious possessions as a child was a Cardiff jersey given me by Tommy Stone, the legendary Cardiff fullback, and a scarlet Welsh international jersey given me by Ossie Male, who played for Mountain Ash. A jersey that had been worn by someone who had played in the Welsh fifteen was a sacred object, and I fingered the embossed badge with its Prince of Wales's feathers with an appropriate reverence. But the Cardiff jersey was my particular favorite because it had belonged to Tommy Stone.

Week after week, month after month, it was Tommy Stone whom I went to see. He was a little man, playing in rugby's most exposed and vulnerable position. As a fullback, roughly the equivalent of an American free safety, he was the last line of defense, often called upon to take heroic action—throwing himself on the ball at the feet of a rampaging pack of forwards, catching and marking the ball in the face of men bearing down on him at full speed. He was fearless. Small as he was, he stormed around the field as if he owned it. It was a sight to see him run down and tackle a man twice his size. He was the Jack Russell of rugby players, all growl and bristle. Sadly, when it came to selecting the Welsh team, his size told against him; the selectors always played safe by choosing a heavier and taller man. I think my first serious apprehension of human injustice was the continual failure of the Welsh selectors to give Tommy Stone his Welsh cap. Eventually, at the close of his career, he was picked to play against Ireland, and that day fog in Dublin prevented the game from being played: my first serious apprehension of divine injustice.

I realize, gazing around, while the two packs are crunching down in their first scrimmage, that these are not the identical surroundings in which I used to watch Tommy Stone doing his stuff. The Arms Park has now expanded to invade and occupy the adjoining ground, which was once the playing field of the Glamorganshire cricket club, now removed to the upper reaches of Sophia Gardens. The stands, once drab and utilitarian, are glossier and smarter—like the people who occupy them. The grass on the playing field is greener and better cared for, though there is the same old cutting wind and the same gulls tumbling above the river Taff at the scoreboard end. It is still recognizably the place where the great figures of a century or almost a century ago used to perform, figures from an athletic Valhalla whose names were continually on the lips of my father and my uncles: Nicholls, Cornish, Huzzey, Driscoll, Gabe, Winfield, Bush. It is still the same place where, from the late 1920s to the late 1950s, though on an increasingly sporadic basis once I had left Cardiff for broader vistas, I witnessed the feats of the leading players of my own day, many of them now departed for that same Valhalla: T. G. M. Davies, Barry John, Wilf Wooller, Cliff Jones, Jack Matthews, Les Spence, Cliff Morgan, Haydn Tanner, Rex Willis, Billy Cleaver, Bleddyn Williams, Cliff Davies, Alun Thomas, Gareth Griffiths.

The crowd around me, whose applause was fitful at the outset, is beginning to get into the game. There are an increasing number of the time-honored exhortations: "Tackle him low!" "Pass!" "Work it!" "Hold it!" "Shove up!" A few cheers, most of them sarcastic. In the row behind me a pair of spectators have already begun to tut-tut disapprovingly every time one of the Cardiff centers gets the ball. He is obviously a regular target. "He won't pass, that Ken Reynolds!" one complains, and the other takes him up: "He won't pass, Ken Reynolds!" (Their Cardiff accent is impossible to render, but the words emerge as something like " *'E 'on't passsss!*") I don't know why they have got their knives into the poor fellow. He seemed to me to draw his opposite number and jink past him with admirable dexterity, then execute a beautiful pass to his winger.

I am starting to feel at home. The game seems much the same as it was—though something queer seems to have happened to the scrum, which looks less dense and testudolike than in my day. Forwards now seem to function less like anonymous infantrymen and more like individual skirmishers. In my time, a forward could go through an entire game, sometimes even an entire season, without actually touching the ball. Now everyone seems eager and able to get into the act.

What really engages my attention at this early, scrappy stage, is the difference in the spectators. There is the same improvement in dress and demeanor I noticed at Llandaff and in the streets. People now are better clothed and better fed. We must have looked a shabby lot back in the 1920s and 1930s. The crowds at the Arms Park during the Depression were generally undernourished, hollow cheeked, slope shouldered. They drooped, coughed, spat, and smoked terrible tobacco to excess. The people today, sitting on individual seats that are positively luxurious compared with the splintery benches of yesteryear, are well set up and ebullient. This is an improvement, of course, that has been occurring since the war years all over Western Europe, and would have gone even further than it has in Britain if British political life had been less stultifying.

Where there has been no alteration is in the enthusiasm of the crowd. True, Cardiff versus Neath is what the British call a needle match—a trial of strength between two traditional rivals— though all these matches between such leading South Welsh towns as Cardiff, Swansea, Bridgend, Neath, Llanelli, or Abertillery are considered needle matches. The spectators are watching the game develop with an absorption that is keener, in some ways, than the absorption I witnessed on the faces in Llandaff Cathedral. These games between city clubs are not occasions for singing, but if the game had been an international match it would have been a different matter, and the overwhelming outburst of song from the entire crowd, for which the Arms Park is famous, would have made the parallel between Welsh rugby football and Welsh religion even more apparent. One of the traditional songs, sung with unexampled passion by sixty thousand voices harmonizing naturally and instinctively in the Welsh way, is "Guide Me, O Thou Great Jehovah," to the tune of "Cwm Rhondda" or "Rhondda Valley." To be seated in the stands, joining in the singing of that noble melody, lapped around by it, is truly a stirring, indeed a unique experience. It also offers a stunning insight into the nature of the Welsh soul.

Why, in fact, should Welsh rugby football have developed, since its first organized beginnings in the 1870s, into a quasi-religious activity?

To an extent, of course, it came about because, as the old religious certainties weakened and orthodox religious observance fell into disfavor, something was needed to fill the spiritual vacuum—something equally dramatic and exciting, which would continue to give the Welsh scope for their natural enthusiasm. There is also the obvious explanation that rugby football, like all other contact sports, is an outlet for aggression, in which the tensions built up during the week can be given controlled and harmless expression at the end of it. Church services, particularly of the heightened Welsh kind, used to serve something of the same purpose. In the case of a race as restless and energetic as the Welsh, and with such a large component of men engaged in the hard physical labor of coal mining and steel making (Welsh rugby is almost exclusively confined to the old heavy industrial counties of Gwent and Glamorgan), rugby football was the perfect safety valve.

There is also, because of their unlucky and unfortunate history, a strain of furious resentment buried in the Welsh. For centuries they were treated as a conquered and inferior breed, and it was rugby football that enabled them to externalize much of that resentment and offered them an opportunity to conquer and be superior in their turn. Rugby is a great equalizer; the rugby field is a good place for one man to show that he is as strong, brave, and resourceful as the next. On a profounder level, I think that the more elemental sports also possess a symbolic significance: they celebrate the human capacity to overcome disaster, to defy fate. There is a triumphant and reassuring aspect to winning a hard-fought game of rugby, especially one fought against the odds, that transcends the mere act of winning. For Welsh colliers and steelworkers, in an oblique way it represented a victory over the grim and relentless condition of their lives. It showed them that adversity could be confronted and surmounted.

On a simpler plane, rugby serves the function of all such group activities, of binding the tribe together and providing it with badges, totems, and fetishes. Each tribe flaunts its identifying crest and color, and often, like a military regiment, possesses a totemic animal in the form of a mascot. The members of its international team are its champions in combat, its Achilleses and its Hectors. In a shipping precinct on Queen Street, the main thoroughfare of Cardiff, there stands a more-than-life-size statue to one of Wales's greatest modern heroes, Gareth Edwards, portrayed in the act of passing out the ball to his three-quarters. International matches are the equivalent of the old tribal battles, in which England, Wales, Scotland, and Ireland still strive to defeat one another, and although, for the Welsh, it is sweet to defeat their fellow Celts in Dublin or Edinburgh, it is a thousand times sweeter to grind the faces of the English into the dirt of Twickenham or the Arms Park. For three hundred and sixty-four days in the year, that is the moment many Welshmen live for.

Those English are a crafty lot. The English have always understood the usefulness of encouraging games as a surrogate for engaging in real battles. They either invented or played a major role in developing most of the world's most prominent games: rugby, soccer, cricket, boxing, tennis, hockey, squash, handball. Many of them evolved at the English public schools (rugby gets its name from Rugby School, where it grew out of soccer during the era of Dr. Arnold and *Tom Brown's Schooldays*) and came into existence to channel the very considerable aggressions and satisfy the psychological needs of the English themselves. During the days of the Empire the English, who since the Middle Ages had always possessed a marked mania for ball games, took their games with them to their overseas possessions. There they found them useful not only as an amusement for the expatriates themselves but as a way of diverting dangerous tendencies among their colonial subjects. Cricket took root on the Indian subcontinent, in Australia, New Zealand, South Africa, and throughout the Caribbean. In course of time rugby has achieved an even wider distribution, and is now played in over a hundred countries on six continents, including such countries as Czechoslovakia and Romania, Argentina and Uruguay, China, Japan, and Russia. However, the adoption overseas of cricket and rugby, though remarkable, was completely overshadowed, of course, by the phenomenal growth of soccer, which began as a popular pastime among the British soldiery, and for which (as for so many other games) the British codified the rules and devised the first organized teams and leagues. The English of those days happened to be very keen on rules and organizing.

American football and baseball clearly derive from British rugby and cricket. And in a fanciful mood I sometimes like to speculate as to whether, if rugby, soccer, and cricket had only been a little more advanced at the end of the eighteenth century, the American Revolution would have followed the course it did, or whether it would have happened at all. America, like cricketing Australia, might have stayed within the Empire. The leaders of the Revolution would have been too absorbed with playing cricket on the village greens of New England and the lawns of southern mansions to bother about such minor matters as rebellion and independence. Many of the Founding Fathers would have made first-rate players. I can see Washington, accompanied by Hamilton, striding majestically to the crease to open the innings, with solid Madison and cautious John Adams lower down the order. Patrick Henry would have made a fiery fast bowler, together with the rather erratic young Aaron Burr, while Jefferson would have been a wily leg spinner and a master of the googly. Benjamin Franklin, though rather ponderous and stiff in the joints, would have been an imposing wicket keeper. One could have a great deal of fun deciding on a side to represent the colonists against an English eleven, and give the Americans long odds if England is to be captained by the Earl of Sandwich.

As one of the subject peoples, the Welsh were introduced to rugby by the English. They took to it rapturously and instinctively, altering the style with which they played it to suit their own temperament and outlook. When you watch the annual England versus Wales international match (the international match is another British invention), you quickly realize that the game is approached by the two teams in a notably different manner. As they line up for the kickoff, the Welsh seem eager to seize their chance to take a crack at the representatives of a race who were once their masters, and whom even now they suspect of harboring a superior and patronizing attitude. There is even a hint, or certainly was in my time, of class war as well as racial war: the English, wealthy and aristocratic, are pitted against the impoverished and plebeian Welsh. These antagonisms are enhanced by the different physiques of the rival teams. On one side are the smaller, darker, more compact Welshmen in their hot crimson jerseys, on the other the tall, slim, blond Englishmen in their cool white. One is reminded of the chronic warfare of Celt against Saxon, cleverly diverted by the longheaded English so that it takes place on a playing field instead of a battlefield. And even we Welsh are compelled to admire, from time to time, the imperial bearing of our English antagonists. Who could forget the grace and composure of such English captains as Wakefield and Cranmer as, the red rose of England on their breast and the sun glittering on their yellow hair, they handed off tackles and flashed like greyhounds for the line? Once they played a real-life prince against us: Prince Obolensky, a Russian, but with all the fair-skinned and pink-cheeked handsomeness of his English compeers. He played for Oxford, and I saw him perform on the wing for the Harlequins against Cardiff, a year or two before World War II, in which he was destined to die.

" *'E 'on't passsss, that Ken Reynolds!*" Again the lugubrious cry from my twin experts. Hard men to satisfy. Again Ken Reynolds swings out a swift and impeccable ball.

A close game. Neither side has yet scored. The dry conditions make it fast. The two teams drive like quicksilver up and down the field. My head swivels continually this way and that. It is this speed and fluidity, I think, that distinguishes rugby football from its American counterpart, and as I watch I begin to ask myself what the differences and similarities are between the game as played by the two nations, and what they might tell us about their respective characters.

The links between American and British football result from the fact that in the nineteenth century rugby football, like cricket, was quite extensively played in America, particularly in the big cities of the east. Several of the more venerable cricket and rugby clubs, some of the latter dating back to the 1870s, still exist. Rugby is now once more catching on in America, largely under the influence of Commonwealth students at American universities, and a respectable number of colleges, states, and cities now field rugby teams. In 1990 there were 1,200 registered rugby clubs in the United States, with 75,000 active players, and under the auspices of the U.S. Rugby Football Union, founded in 1975, the United States now fields its own international team, the U.S. Eagles. Not only does the game possess snob appeal for young Americans, but they like it because its atmosphere is so much more relaxed and good-natured than the more vicious and totally commercialized American game. They can enjoy giving rein to their animal spirits without the fear of crippling themselves for life or of being humiliated by uncouth coaches, and afterward they can indulge in the boisterous camaraderie of the clubhouse, swilling beer and singing dirty songs.

Like its British parent, American football uses a ball of the same shape (a little smaller in the American game), similar goalposts, and many of the same technical terms. There is the same division of the teams into forwards and backs, and their aim is identical: to cross the opponents' line (though in America it is not necessary to touch the ball down), after which a kicker trots on to try to add to the score. The kickoffs are similar, and there are similar refinements such as marks and touchbacks. In both games the same man is the controlling factor: the quarterback in America, the scrum half in Britain. In each country it is this player who determines the form of attack.

Here, however, the resemblances end. In Britain, the ball can only be passed backward or advanced by skilled kicking, whereas in America, although the ball is on rare occasions passed, it is commonly advanced by being thrown forward by the quarterback to one of his designated receivers. In America, the term *football* is really a misnomer, since apart from sporadic kicking by specialists, who play virtually no other part in the game, the foot is only applied to the ball infrequently and by accident. American football is almost entirely a handling game, whereas British rugby has never severed its affinities with soccer. In British football, too, there is no such thing as blocking. You can only play the man who has possession of the ball. You cannot roam around the field deliberately blindsiding and knocking down members of the other team. Added to these, of course, are several more obvious differences. The British play with fifteen men on the field, the Americans with eleven. The fifteen Britons must all spend two halves of forty-five minutes on the field, with very small allowance for substitution, and with defense and offense all mixed up. In America there are four quarters of fifteen minutes, and defense and offense are entirely different squads, taking it in turns to play. Thus an American player will spend only twenty to forty minutes on the field, in comparison with the Briton's ninety minutes, but it is a wickedly punishing thirty or forty minutes, more akin to time in a boxing ring than time on a football field. One might also add that, ninety minutes or not, the British game is all over inside a couple of hours, while the American game, ostensibly shorter, drags on for three.

Which game, in point of fact, is the more punishing? Most Americans are convinced that, because the British do not wear any body armor, except for flimsy shin guards and an occasional scrum cap, British rugby is the rougher. It is no game for sissies, admittedly. Down on the field at this moment, I can see, banging away in the line-outs and hacking away in the scrimmages, a number of low-browed bruisers who could have sat to Phiz for his portrait of Bill Sykes. All the same, in point of sheer strength and stamina, if British players could be brought to share the field with their American counterparts, few of them would be able to make it much beyond the halfway mark. Every man on an American team is superlatively fit and supernaturally agile. It is awesome to see men of six-foot six, weighing 300 pounds, flinging themselves around with the speed and suppleness of ballet dancers.

American players, college or professional, begin work in the spring, in camps that are more like concentration camps than training camps, although the season does not begin until September. They train for ten to twelve hours a day. During the summer they compete for places on the team in a grueling series of practice matches and exhibition matches, before they are ready to face the regular autumn and winter program. The scheduling of matches is so tight that no game is ever canceled because of weather or the hardness of the ground. I have watched American games being played when the temperature was over a hundred degrees or below zero. I have seen them played when the players were almost unable to see each other because of the heavy rain, the snow, or the mist. The players also have to contend with artificial turf in stadiums that are domed or covered, which causes severe "burns" on their flesh and additional injuries.

By midseason, every player on an American team is injured to a degree that would prevent a British player from being permitted to appear. They play routinely with dislocated or broken ribs, wrists, fingers, shoulders, hips, knees, and ankles. If they are put on the injured list, you know that they are very seriously injured indeed. They are expected to be able "to play with pain" and are rated on their ability and willingness to do so.

They are cut from the team if they refuse. The tackling, blocking, and hitting in the American game—and basically it is a game of hitting—are so lethal that it is only the strictness of the rules and the players' superior physical conditioning that prevent them from being killed outright.

American football is not a sport, in the sense that the British understand the word. The sporting element disappeared from it decades ago. It is a circus, a spectacle, a gladiatorial contest. It is an activity dedicated to the infliction of violence, to the ability to give and take pain. The participants are bred up to it: they begin their careers in high school, then go on in college. Some of them begin even earlier, at the age of six or seven, in the so-called Peewee Leagues. At no stage is the game ever played for fun, for simple enjoyment, for if and when a man makes it through the system and becomes a fully fledged professional—and the odds against doing so are several thousand to one—he joins a band of only one to two thousand players nationwide who will be paid enormous sums of money, often running into many millions of dollars a season.

An American player is not only a gladiator but also a commodity. He has limited control over his own destiny. He is sold or traded at the will of his masters. American football is a business, a matter of cold cash, an affair involving strikes, lock-outs, owners, managers, agents, and trades unions. It is because of the cash that the players accept the pain and the risk. For the majority of them, who come from the black underclass, football, together with baseball and basketball, which are similarly com-mercialized, represents a major escape route from squalor and poverty. (Pop music and boxing are other routes.) Inevitably, it is corrupt and corrupting. This does not matter so much in the major leagues; the players there are grown-ups, big boys, who ought to be expected to take responsibility for themselves. The real social damage is done at the high-school and especially the university level, where the lopsided pursuit of football and basketball has been allowed to distort and trivialize much of America's educational effort. Athletic departments now play the role of cuckoo in the nest. They appropriate funds which ought to be devoted to more worthwhile activities, and in many instances they have become bloated enterprises that overshadow the institutions to which they nominally belong. Football and basketball coaches are paid more than college presidents, whereas the young men who play for college teams are paid nothing, officially, that is, though it is common knowledge that bribery and shamateurism are common practices. Most of the players are awarded scholarships, and the official pretense is that they are bona fide students, though many of them are illiterate or virtually illiterate. Between 70 and 80 percent of them will fail to obtain a college degree. They are essentially cannon fodder. Perhaps one in three or four hundred will achieve his dream of being drafted into the majors and turning professional, while the others will be returned to the impoverished environment from which they came, many with irksome physical disabilities that will persist for the rest of their lives. The entire business is an exercise in exploitation and cynicism.

When I was at the University of Texas, the coach of the Texas Longhorns, Darrell Royal, offered a candid definition of the college game: "Stink on stink, flesh on flesh, bone on bone." The professional game is even more arduous and destructive. While a few hoary old veterans manage to survive for twelve or fifteen seasons, the average is only four or five. After a hundred games, most men have become too slow, sore, banged up, and worn out to continue. Yet there is in American football an extraordinary and compelling beauty—a brutal beauty which has its roots partly in the game's appearance, partly in its character.

While British footballers look smart enough in their colored jerseys and stockings, American footballers are decked out in a panoply that is glamorous and eye-catching. One can regard their outfits as futuristic, as if they were an exotic breed who had just emerged from spaceships, or as some re-creation of mankind's heroic past. There is something of Arthurian legend or the Middle Ages about them, of the Crusaders or the Wars of the Roses. Their helmets, shoulder pads, and thigh pads bear a striking resemblance to the helmets, pauldrons, vambraces, and cuisses that one sees on the memorial brasses in British churches. The emblems they wear on their helmets bring to mind the emblems born into battle by Plantagenet warriors, a whole heraldry of fantastic birds and beasts: lions, bears, rams, dolphins, eagles, and falcons, as well as a rich assortment of fleurs-de-lis and skulls and crossbones. These emblems possess, like the names of the teams, a totemic significance. They bestow on their wearers a sense of mythic and primitive power, and lend identity and serve as a rallying point for the huge, amorphous cities to which the teams belong. They help to bind together a highly diverse population dispersed across an enormous continent.

It might be noted, incidentally, how very successful the Americans have been in imparting a sense of community and common purpose over the vast area of North America. Other continental peoples, such as the Russians, the Chinese, the Indians, coexist within a notably rickety and unstable framework. America, on the other hand, despite the fact that Europeans like to perceive it as violent and unpredictable, is in fact remarkably tranquil. Apart from the Civil War, the civil rights movement, and some sporadic inner-city strife, its history since independence has been a good deal more peaceful and progressive than might have been expected, and it has shown a stronger sense of continuity than most European countries over the same period. It has refused to be racked by the brutal political ideologies of the extreme right and extreme left that have devastated Europe, and its governments have succeeded one another with a decorum and sense of order that Europeans might envy. True, several of its presidents and notables have been assassinated, but the heads of state of many European countries have had an even stickier time of it in the past two centuries, let alone in the centuries that preceded them. Even Canada, so fond of comparing itself favorably with the United States, is not so closely knit a continental power as its neighbor to the south. There is no state in America as bellicose and irreconcilable as Québec. Though Americans are sometimes given grudging credit for their achievement with regard to social order and discipline, the scale and sheer geographic extent of that achievement is seldom acknowledged.

It is that sense of order and discipline which characterizes American football, and which seems to afford the spectators as much satisfaction as, if not more satisfaction than, the basic hitting and tackling. What the spectators exult in is the unexampled precision with which the players execute the several dozen plays at their disposal. Every play is described and diagramed in a player's personal playbook, which resembles a military manual. The plays are learned by heart and practiced until they become second nature.

The American game utterly eschews the spontaneity and improvising genius of British rugby. The greatest fear of the coaches and the quarterbacks is that the play which has been decided on, and which has been carried out literally hundreds of times in the team "drills," will break down, resulting in a "broken play" or a "busted play," a play that has got out of control. For every game there is a predetermined game plan, to which every attempt is made to adhere. The disruption of the game plan by the opposition is regarded as a prelude to the loss of the game. Nor are these individual plays usually decided upon in the huddle, by the quarterback. In most cases the quarterback is merely a junior executive. He carries out the plays that are conveyed to him by means of a shuttle service from the sideline, or transmitted by a signal either from his coach or from one of the subordinate coaches who are responsible for conducting the offense and the defense. Neither do the sideline coaches enjoy an absolute authority; in turn they are hooked up by telephone to a battery of advisers, who survey and often control the game from boxes high up in the stadium, sending down a continuous stream of reports and recommendations. Nor is it uncommon for the team's owner to take a hand in dictating the course of play, ordering his coaches to employ certain plays in certain situations and forbidding them to do so in others.

All this strikes devotees of the British game as bewildering, even grotesque. The essence of the British game is its amateur, spirited, free-flowing nature. The American game seems ludicrously overcontrolled. Only a referee and a couple of linesmen are needed to regulate the British game, while the American requires a crew of eleven, five officials on the field and six on the sideline. In addition, extra officials up in the boxes watch the game on closed-circuit television, conferring by walkie-talkie with the officials down on the field in the case of disputed calls. Such a system must seem positively weird and Martian to a Briton.

This overregulation is actually a reflection of a leading characteristic of the American character. American society is profoundly legalistic. Over two-thirds of the members of the American Congress are lawyers, who spend much of their time setting up tribunals to put one another on trial or attempting to impeach their president. Society in general is riven with lawsuits or the threat of lawsuits. My old Uncle Evan, he of the litigious propensities, would have loved America. The terminology of American football is permeated with legalisms. A foul is "an illegal procedure," and teams are penalized for such offenses as "illegal use of hands" and "illegal receiver downfield." Americans, who like to think that foreigners picture them as lawless freebooters and freewheeling gunslingers, are in fact the most law-bound people on the face of the earth.

Americans themselves might argue, of course, that all this tight control, with the whistle continually shrilling and halting play, is necessary because of the excessively violent nature of the game. And it *is* violent, exceedingly violent—which is another paradox, since whatever foreigners may believe, or whatever Americans believe themselves, America as a country is not outstandingly violent. The pace of life in America, a handful of cities excepted, is much more placid than the pace of life in Britain, for example. Nor, apart from the Civil War, have Americans shown themselves to be unduly warlike. They had to be coaxed into entering both the world wars, and unlike the Europeans have shown little enthusiasm for slaughtering each other by the million two or three times in every century. Their forays overseas are very small stuff compared with the buccaneering ventures of the old colonial powers. It is therefore something of a puzzle that they should have developed such a ferocious sport as American football, and should watch it so avidly on Sunday afternoons. Even so, it ought to be noted that sporting crowds in America are inordinately well behaved compared with crowds elsewhere in the world, particularly in Britain, and that they are not at all given to hooliganism and mayhem. No American parents would hesitate to take their tiniest children, or even babes in arms, to a football or baseball game.

The ritualized, carefully channeled violence of American football clearly possesses a special appeal for its spectators. Evidently they approve of its formality and its leisurely pace. The game resembles a giant game of chess, with each player, like Frederick the Great's Grenadiers at Potsdam, occupying his designated square and making his designated moves. The spectacle might be more closely likened, perhaps, to the medieval tourney. The players, in their visored helmets and their tight-fitting body armor, are knights, dismounted, ready to engage in hand-to-hand combat. And, as there was with the medieval tourney, there is a great beauty in it. There is beauty in the pantherine swiftness with which these outsize men stalk and strike at one another, and also the perverse beauty that is present in any sport in which there is the spice of danger—the Grand

Prix, the Cresta Run, downhill ski racing, mountain climbing, the *corrida de toros.* There is even the perverse beauty of genuine battle, for these men are literally fighting each other to gain every inch of ground. Like war, American football is a bitter and grinding form of territorial dispute. If it were not for the piquancy of the colors, the emblems, the uniforms, it would not resemble a tournament so much as Crécy, Agincourt, or the unremitting trench warfare of Loos or the Somme.

I am torn from these transatlantic musings by the shouts of the spectators. The Cardiff forwards have broken loose and are pouring down the field with the ball at their feet. The ball is bigger and more unwieldy than the American football, and the forwards lunge after it in a ragged, frantic wave quite unlike the sharp, tight spearhead of an American attack. Then a Neath forward scoops the ball up and boots it into touch, and the crowd subsides into their seats again.

The game is becoming increasingly tense. Too often, in my recollection, a British football game tends to deteriorate, midway through the second half, into boredom and anticlimax. The issue has long since been settled, and the players, because they have already been skipping around the field flat out for over an hour, are exhausted, struggling pathetically from one scrum and lineout to the next. American football possesses the advantage here. It never slows down; it maintains its savage pace to the end. Though one of the sides may be marginally fitter and have gained the physical ascendancy, this is barely perceptible from the stands. And because of the substitutions and the shortness of the plays, the participants have been allowed regular breathers. The conclusions of most American games are nail-bitingly close, with the coaches, players, and spectators watching the clock in a state of excruciating anxiety. The game can remain close and convulsive until the final second.

Looking at the people around me, as I sink back into my own seat, I note how amiable and even-tempered they are. Unlike the soccer crowds, rugby crowds seldom display any tendency to indulge in the "aggro" and "bovver" which have resulted in the banning of British soccer teams from foreign competition and British soccer fans from foreign countries. Rugby, after all, was a product of the English public schools, and even in Wales, where it is largely played by working men (one hesitates to speak of a working class in the case of such a class-free country as Wales), it still adheres to the code of the English gentleman. Soccer, quintessentially a proletarian game, has never established itself in Wales to any significant extent, and has always played a poor second fiddle to rugby. Cricket too has only been adopted on a small scale. Glamorganshire is the only Welsh team to figure in the County Championship. It was the last team to be admitted to the league, shortly after World War I, and, although it has won the County Championship on two occasions, it has spent most of its existence bumping around at the lower end of the table. The Welsh temperament is really too irritable and impatient to adapt itself to such a slow-moving and long-drawn-out activity as cricket.

As it happens, however, like most of my family, perhaps because of our Anglo-Welsh sympathies, I was always a partisan of that singularly beautiful and subtle game. Cricket was really the game I most loved to play at school and in the services, and later on, when I played in the village leagues in Essex and Cambridgeshire. As a boy I spent many blissful hours lounging in the sun in the old ground in the Arms Park, opposite the Angel and the *Western Mail*. Often at night, if sleep is slow to come, I bring the Glamorgan team of the 1930s out onto the steps of their small, primitive, peeling pavilion and send them strolling onto the field. There is Maurice Turnbull, the thick-set, red-faced captain (later to be killed in Belgium as an officer in the Welsh Guards); stolid, blue-chinned Dai Davies; dependable

Emrys Davies, his blue cap with its daffodil badge twisted over one ear; the wily leg spinner J. C. Clay; and the flashy batsmen Smartt and Lavis, both of them capable of regularly thumping the ball over the wall into Westgate Street for six (Smartt once held the record for the most runs scored in a six-ball over).

At the Arms Park I saw most of the leading batsmen of the day: magisterial Jack Hobbs, irrepressible Patsy Hendren, fiery Eddie Paynter, elegant Frank Woolley, patrician Herbert Sutcliffe, and above all the lordly and absolutely unforgettable Walter Hammond. In my dreams, Walter Hammond often smites a wristy and disdainful ball across the ropes. I also saw most of the great bowlers: bounding Maurice Tate, the hit-man Harold Larwood, the commanding Hedley Verity (also to be killed in the war). And later, in the early 1950s, when I lived at Hamilton Terrace, a stone's throw from Lord's Cricket Ground, home of Middlesex and the MCC, I would listen to the lunchtime cricket scores on the BBC and, if Compton and Edrich were batting and in good form, I would push aside my papers and hurry down to watch the fun.

What, I am beginning to wonder, as the scrum bumps heads for the twentieth time, do I actually possess in common with all these fellow Welshmen packed in around me? They are, after all, my own kind, almost, if the Welsh can be regarded as an extended family, my own kith and kin. Yet there must be significant differences, too; otherwise, why would I have elected, and at a relatively early age, to leave Wales and go and live in England? And then to move away farther still, to Texas and to Tennessee?

Some obvious explanations, of course, immediately suggest themselves. The first is that I may have wanted to flee from the effects of a childhood that had been spent in the shadow of my father's slide into poverty and his subsequent protracted sickness and death. Second, I suppose it was inevitable that my links with my native place would be weakened by being sent away to school in England at the age of eight, by my entrance into an English university, like those young Tudor Welshmen before me, and by my time in the services. In any case, like many another young Welshman, or young Englishman for that matter, I would surely have felt the urge to escape in order to make my way in what I fancied was a wider world. London, as it has always done, offers a young man more tantalizing opportunities than Cardiff, Edinburgh, Dublin, Leeds, or Birmingham. There is nothing new in this. Over a thousand years ago, as one of the tales in the *Mabinogion* tells us, Manawydan, son of Llŷr, and his three companions grew tired of a pastoral life of living on fish, and game, and wild honey. "God knows we cannot go on living like this," Manawydan said. "Let us go to England and there seek a trade by which we can support ourselves."

Such reasons would strike me as quite sufficient, if, that is, I did not suspect, as I sit here, that some far deeper sense of alienation must have been at work. The English, it is true, can strike someone who goes to live among them as strange or even downright peculiar, but it is equally difficult to belong to a race as high-strung and vehement as the Welsh. Perhaps it was because I had already sensed as an adolescent that life in Wales might be difficult and confusing that I determined to avoid it? And yet, although I left Wales at a fairly young age, I have continually been drawn back to it and have constantly remained conscious of my origins as a Welshman.

So here I am, once again, in the grandstand at Cardiff Arms Park, sitting very nearly in the same seat where I sat thirty years ago, still trying to sort it all out. *"I lie awake, night after night, and never get the answers right."* What do I have in common with all these people encircling me, and what is the nature of that notion of apartness that stirred in me and divided me from them at a relatively early stage in my life? Why should I have sensed in my teens that it might be difficult, not so much perhaps to *be* a Welshman, but to live as a Welshman in Wales?

The puzzling and self-contradictory nature of the Welsh has been explored by no one at greater length and with more discernment than Gerald the Welshman. In his *Description of Wales* he devotes eleven chapters to the virtues of the Welsh—and the next ten to a damning catalog of what he calls their "Less Good Points." The Welsh, like most other people, do not seem to have changed very much in the course of a millennium or two. All my life I have been teased by exactly the same painful and unresolved sense of dichotomy that Gerald was. No wonder he has always been something of an icon and a living presence for me.

For me, as for many educated young Welsh men and women, and particularly for someone who wanted to devote himself to the literary life, one of the most acute difficulties would have been the question of the language. Again, this was a problem that vexed the intellectual element in Welsh society as long ago as Gerald's day. It is doubtful if more than a thousand people among the twenty or thirty thousand in the stands this afternoon, cheering on two Welsh teams, can either speak Welsh or write it—yet the problem of the language hangs over all of them. Barely a fifth of the nation is now able to speak Welsh, but, with the exception of a small number of people who regard it as useless and superfluous, and wish it would die out as speedily as possible, the dwindling of the language arouses feelings of sorrow and guilt. I think most Welsh people would like, if circumstances had been different, to be able to talk their native tongue. It is, after all, the most distinct badge of Wales's individuality. And, since a writer regards himself as preeminently an individual, the dilemma of a writer, if he is born in Wales, is especially acute.

Ought I to have written my books in Welsh? True, I can list many excuses for not doing so. I am a native of Glamorgan, where the language lost its grip in Norman times and which for a thousand years has not been predominantly Welsh speaking. Nor, after my first eighteen or twenty years—though those years were admittedly crucial—have I lived permanently in Wales. And why, since writing is the business of communication, should I write in a tongue which so few people understand, even in Wales itself? Why inflict on myself greater handicaps than a writer has to face in the normal course of his trade? Yet somehow the sneaking feeling persists that writing in English has been an act of disloyalty, and that if I had written in Welsh I might have served the cause of Wales more faithfully. This has always been the slight but nagging wound that I have been required to live with, and naturally my friends among the Welsh Nationalists have never missed an opportunity to give it a rub in order to prevent it from healing. At least by leaving Wales I have been able to lessen its sting and learn to live with it.

Why not, now I am examining the Welsh character, emulate Gerald? Why not deal with its positive aspects first—trusting that my estimate, like his, will find more to praise than to blame?

What would be the first thing that a stranger would notice about the Welsh? Surely it would be their admirable vitality. "Energy," said William Blake, "is eternal delight." The Welsh are an active, bustling, high-strung people. Liveliness means loving life, and the Welsh are lively. In particular it is the South Walians, especially the people of Glamorgan, who are given to hustling and bustling about. In England, the displays of enthusiasm and outbursts of boisterousness that are characteristic of the Welsh are viewed with disfavor, but the Welsh pour their enthusiasm into everything they do. When you see them talking to each other in the street, there is a drama and an animation in their gestures that is positively Italian. They are not given to the coolness and constraint which are the order of the day in England. They are high-spirited and uninhibited, which often renders their company distressing to the English.

Not that anyone, of course, faced with the evidence of their literature, would accuse the English, cool or not, of being unimaginative. Nonetheless, the English imagination seems some-how different in kind from the Welsh, which possesses a vibrant and incandescent quality not at all to the ironic English taste. No English author could have written the *Mabinogion*, with its primitive appeal to the senses. There is a whiff of something barbaric about the Welsh which tends to make the English shy away. They have a tendency, repugnant to the English soul, to overdo things.

It is this zest which still gives a certain urgency to Welsh religion, even in a century like ours, when religion has ceased to be a chief interest. The service that I attended last Sunday in Llandaff Cathedral was marked by a fervor that would have been lacking in the Anglican services being celebrated that morning in the cathedrals of England. The devotions of the Welsh have always had about them the quality of Jacob wrestling with the Angel: "I will not let thee go unless thou bless me."

These habits go back to Celtic times. They point to some-thing ineradicable in the Welsh soul. Gerald has an interesting passage about the *awen*, which was akin to the *hywl*, that special Welsh manner of preaching and praying. "Among the Welsh," he says,

> there are persons known as *awenyddion*, who behave as if they are possessed by devils. If you consult them about some problem, at once they go into a trance, losing control of their senses. They do not give logical answers to the questions put to them, but words stream from their lips, garbled and apparently with no sense, yet somehow at the same time clearly expressed. If you listen carefully, you will receive the answer to your question. When they fall into their trance, they call upon the true and living God and the Holy Trinity, and pray that their sins will not prevent them from uttering the truth. Some of them say it feels as if honey or milk with sugar had been smeared on their lips, or as if a sheet of paper with words on it was being pressed against their mouths.

Can one imagine such druidical or oracular practices being encouraged in England? In Wales they have persisted, first in a pagan then in a Christian guise, for two thousand years, and have spilled over from religion into literature. *Awen* is an ancient word for the poetic gift, the muse, the divine afflatus. What they indicate, I think, is a kind of fundamental readiness in the Welsh soul to respond to spiritual promptings, an eagerness and openness to receive manifestations of the supernatural. It is surely not accidental that Wales should have given birth to such an abundance of devotional poets over the centuries or that, as I have mentioned earlier, many of the greatest religious poets writing in English should have possessed either Welsh blood or strong Welsh connections.

If *awen* denotes the muse or divine inspiration, then of course the same is true of poetry's sister art, music. When the crowds at Cardiff Arms Park break into song, what is the first thing that they sing? A hymn . . . what else? "Guide Me, O Thou Great Jehovah." It is only natural that Wales and the Marches should have produced not only great poets and hymn writers but such composers of religious music as Joseph Parry, Ralph Vaughan Williams, and Herbert Howells. Edward Elgar, though one of the sturdiest of Englishmen, was born and buried in the Malvern Hills. He wrote a secular cantata about Caratacus, and one of his finest works is based on a tune he heard a Welsh carter whistling during a country walk.

Music is pure language, a universal language. Sydney Smith called it "the last unfinished rapture upon earth." Early scientists sought to notate the music of the spheres. If there is a heaven, one might imagine that its method of communication is based on music rather than words. Nobody can define what music is, not even musicians themselves, but it is certainly an effort at transcendence and transformation, an impulse to express a spiritual aspiration. Small wonder, then, that the Welsh, with their religious yearnings, should have given themselves over to music with an extraordinary passion.

Gerald testifies to the complexity and sophistication that Welsh music making had already reached eight centuries ago. "When they gather to make music," he writes, "they do not sing their traditional songs in unison, as other nations do, but in parts, in many modes and modulations. When a choir assembles to sing, which happens very often in Wales, you will hear as many separate parts and voices as there are singers, all combining together to produce a single soft, sweet organic harmony and melody. Even small children sing in parts, and tiny babies do so from the moment they stop screaming and begin to sing." He observes, as was certainly the case, that the Welsh "must have developed this ability by age-old custom, and by a long usage that has rendered it second nature." Thus, as I have said earlier, when you hear the Welsh singing at the Arms Park, on a raw and wintry day, you are listening not to something random or casual but to something very ancient that comes from the heart of the race. And that they should choose to sing hymns before the start of a rugby match also tells you something, I think, about the Welsh attitude to rugby football. But let me tell you, if you have never heard Welsh voices at Cardiff Arms Park singing "Guide Me, O Thou Great Jehovah," or "Calon Lân," a great whelm of sound thundering out of the terraces, even the cheerful songs sounding curiously solemn and sad, then believe me, you have never heard a song sung, and you have never heard singing:

> *Calon lân yn llawn daioni*
> *Tecach yw na'r lili dlos:*
> *Dim ond calon lân all ganu,*
> *Canu'r dydd a chanu'r nos.*

> *A pure heart full of goodness*
> *Is lovelier than the fair lily:*
> *Only a pure heart can sing,*
> *Sing all day and sing all night.*

It is their vitality and their spiritual receptivity that have contributed to another attribute of the Welsh: their abundant sense of curiosity. Their curiosity about all aspects of human activity is insatiable. In intellectual matters they possess what John Donne called "an immoderate, hydroptique thirst for human learning and languages." They excel in the learned professions, in science and the arts, out of all proportion to their numbers. They pursue knowledge as terriers pursue a rat. At other times, their curiosity takes a no less intense form, a focus on their friends, their family, and their neighbors. They are a great race of nosey parkers. Hence their mania for genealogy, their obscure conviction that, if only the genetic cross-questioning is kept up with sufficient persistence, not only the Welsh but everyone in the world can be shown to be related to everyone else.

Being so outgoing, it is no wonder that the Welsh enjoy an outstanding reputation for hospitality. The *Mabinogion* is replete with feasting, carousing, and the entertainment of strangers. They love to feed their guests because their guests in turn feed their appetite for conversational tidbits. They also love any excuse for a party—which in turn is an excuse for singing. Most Welsh parties end with a singsong. There is a venerable Welsh institution known as the *noson llawen*, the cheerful or sociable evening, at which everyone is expected to perform his own personal party piece.

Welsh hospitality is a reflection of the Welsh instinct for generosity. Among the Celts, leaders who were openhanded were especially admired. During the Depression, when it seemed that whole stretches of South Wales were dying, it was the impulse to share one's meager goods with one's neighbors that brought the country through. That, and the ingrained Welsh sense of humor. Whenever I think of Wales, I hear in the background shrieks and howls of laughter. Things to laugh about were in short supply in the 1920s and 1930s. Fortunately, the Welsh never quite ran out of them.

I suppose the time has come, after flattering my fellow countrymen so unconscionably, to discuss some of what Gerald ominously referred to as the "Less Good Points."

Heaven knows, there are plenty of these, though I hasten to add that most of them can be viewed in the light of minor failings rather than outright enormities. The earlier history of Wales certainly possessed more than its share of brutality and violence, although hardly on the same scale as that of England during the same period. And compared with Scotland, whose annals are among the most blood-soaked in Europe, or Ireland, whose tale of atrocities shows no sign of abating, the later history of Wales appears positively tranquil. For over five hundred years, since the disappearance of Owain Glyndŵr and Henry VIII's Act of Union, except for the decade of the Great Civil War, the Welsh have not been given many opportunities to misbehave themselves. They have not been seriously embroiled in political affairs or involved in the type of activity that brings out the worst in a nation. They have largely been occupied in singing hymns, writing poetry, and playing rugby football. As a consequence, their shortcomings have tended to be personal, on a small scale, rather than public and monumental.

Whatever flaws and foibles the Welsh possess as individuals can be ascribed, as is frequently the case, to the defects of their virtues. Thus their vitality is admirable but can also, unless carefully monitored, lead them down the path of excess. This tendency, the urge to embroider and exaggerate, is the curse of the Welsh, particularly of my own South Walians. It obtrudes itself into every phase of their lives. It shows itself most obviously in their religion, where the *hywl* and the *awen* can quickly spill over into the worst kind of fanaticism. The result is that Welsh religiosity, as I have said earlier, can be as passionately callous and oppressive as it can be passionately tolerant and open-minded. The mood swings of the Welsh are notorious, veering wildly from one extreme to the other. Welsh religiosity can also become hatefully hypocritical, contributing largely to that tendency to be sly, smarmy, deceitful, and two-faced of which the Welsh are so often accused.

A more harmless and comical side effect of religiosity is the noted Welsh leaning toward superstition. No doubt this too has its origins in our Celtic past. We Welsh are a hopelessly superstitious lot. Members of my family were always aghast if anyone opened an umbrella inside the house or put a hat on a bed. At table we were continually throwing pinches of salt over our left shoulders, or wetting our fingers and putting them on the rim of a glass if anyone had set it ringing. This prevented a sailor from dying at sea. When we first saw the new moon, we bowed to it three times, turned our money over in our pockets, and were distressed if we had happened to catch sight of it through glass. We could not drink tea or coffee without poring over the leaves or the dregs in the bottom of the cup, and after dinner we were just as likely to push a tumbler around the bridge table as we were to play bridge, or sevens, or stop-me, or Newmarket. My Aunt Claire was remarkably gifted with the cards, and twice a year I would sit down for a solemn session with her and enter her predictions meticulously in the back of my diary. For someone who is not ostensibly religious, I have a marked penchant for not stepping on cracks in the sidewalk, and for retracing my steps if I miss touching a tree or a lamppost. I am upset if I see a magpie, and elated if I find myself driving behind a load of hay. For years I was almost rendered round-shouldered by the thick bunch of metal charms around my neck—though I took the chain off once and for all after Valerie had her stroke.

Together with superstition goes another Welsh failing: an inclination toward morbidity. You can seldom spend half an hour in the company of a Welsh man or Welsh woman without becoming immersed in a discussion of disease, death, and dissolution. They are among the staples of Welsh conversation. Like many people who have known humiliation, impoverishment, and defeat (like the people of the American South among whom I now live), the Welsh possess the authentic sense of tragedy. But, as with so much else, they delight in carrying it to excess. They revel in deathbeds and funerals. When I was a small boy in Cardiff, my friends and I sometimes had a singular way of whiling away the stupefying dullness of a Welsh Sunday. We would wander around Splott and Rhiwbina and other suburbs on the outer fringes of the city and visit the houses where someone had died in order to view the body, either laid out on the bed upstairs or in a coffin in the parlor. This was an accepted practice in the Wales of the day. You had to touch the corpse in order not to be troubled later by its ghost or spirit. There was the additional bonus in that, after the pleasure of admiring the corpse, and congratulating the bereaved relatives on its beautiful appearance, one was given, in the spirit of Welsh hospitality, a cup of tea and a large slice of cake.

Gloom and pessimism are the reverse aspects of the Welshman's vitality and buoyancy. Whereas the Englishman is habitually calm and judicious, the Welshman blows hot and cold, seeing every crisis in terms of the deepest black or the whitest white. His emotions are not buried deep, like the Englishman's, but bubble away just beneath the skin, ready at any moment to burst through. He has a seemingly boundless capacity for indignation, and is always on the point of exploding into denunciation and exhortation. His touchiness and prickliness often seem alarming, but, as with the Italians, they are seldom more than a demonstration of the national taste for drama. Down the centuries, however, the moodiness and irritability of the Welsh, culminating in outbursts of the celebrated "Welsh temper," have become legendary, prompting English people, who loathe all such outbursts, to give them a wide berth. The blind Mrs. Williams, who had lodgings in Dr. Johnson's house for over thirty years, often disconcerted his friends and guests with her "Welsh fire." Shakespeare makes the quarrelsomeness of the Welsh a principal ingredient in his portraits of Glendower and Fluellen, though in fact it had been notorious long before Shakespeare's time. There was a well-known medieval joke that explained why no Welshmen were to be found in Heaven. The Welshmen there had been kicking up such a racket with their incessant fighting and squabbling that God got fed up with them and told St. Peter to get rid of them. So St. Peter opened the pearly gates, stepped outside, and shouted, "Toasted cheese!" (i.e., "Welsh rarebit!"). Whereupon all the Welshmen rushed past him, and he stepped smartly back inside, slammed the gates, and locked them. From that day to this, no Welshman has ever set foot in Heaven.

This contentious and argumentative streak must be the symptom of some underlying psychological uneasiness and self-doubt. The Welsh, like another people among whom I have lived for a lengthy period, the Mexicans, are much given to what the Mexicans call *espantos,* sudden seizures of panic and insecurity. Thus the Welsh, as a rule so expansive and openhanded, can be prone to inexplicable fits of meanness and pettiness. One moment a Welshman is your best friend and the next, for no reason you can discern, your worst enemy. This is because of the fact that your Welshman, like a small volcano, is constantly seething and churning inside. He himself could not tell you when he is going to erupt, or why. He is moved by dark interior forces. This can be very hard on foreigners who become charmed with Wales, fall in love with its inhabitants, and buy a house or cottage there. For months or even years everything goes well; all is laughter and benevolence. And then, one fine morning, the foreigner wakes up and discovers that overnight the natives have unaccountably turned sullen and hostile. What can the poor man have done? He racks his brains to try to remember what terrible offense he could possibly have committed. All he knows is that henceforward he is condemned to live surrounded by a sea of stony faces. The Welsh can be dismayingly tribal.

No one who, like our hypothetical foreigner, spends even the briefest time in Wales can fail to notice the Welsh infatuation with gossip. Whenever you see them gathered together, in restaurants and cafés, on park benches, in the intervals of plays and concerts, or before the start of this football game, you can see the Welsh leaning forward with their dark heads drawn close together. They whisper or murmur in low tones, their eyes wide open as a result of the awfulness of their revelations. In the Vale of Glamorgan the expressive word for such gossiping is *clecking*, which nicely conveys the head bobbing and tongue clicking that accompany these rapt exchanges.

In some ways, perhaps, a love of gossip is not unhealthy. It is a testimony to the vibrant curiosity of the Welsh about the world around them, their immersion in the turbulent stream of existence. Better that than remain detached from the spectacle of human joy and suffering. A nice gossip does you a power of good. It puts you in touch with the current of life around you. Too often, however, the gossip you hear or overhear in Wales can turn sour and malicious. Gerald has some pointed remarks about this: "In Wales," he says, "the talk within the family circle and the conversation of prominent men at court is frequently very funny. This entertains their guests and bestows on them the reputation of being tremendous wits. They make the most amusing remarks, many of which are very clever. They adore sarcastic comments and scandalous innuendoes, plays on words, sly allusions, oblique and ambiguous hints. Some of this is simply joking, but at times it can become very bitter."

This gift for banter and tittle-tattle, often wounding, is another reason why the English often shun the Welsh. And in fact they are too fond of letting their tongues run away with them—another instance of their tendency to excess. They are proverbially indiscreet; you should never ask a Welshman to keep a secret. All of which once more points, I think, to something anxious in the Welsh soul. That strident laughter has a tinge of insecurity, and in Wales, particularly in South Wales, they laugh a lot. The Welsh are wonderful raconteurs, but they are always nervously scanning the faces of their listeners to see what effect they are making. They have the humor of music-hall comedians, flinging out one joke after another, more and more loudly, in case the first one falls flat. Too often they succumb to a compulsion to play the buffoon, as in Dylan Thomas's *Under Milk Wood*. Here an otherwise fine poet capers around, depicting his countrymen as a collection of yokels, playing the role of Uncle Tom for the delectation of the English, who are only too pleased to have their conviction confirmed that the Welsh are a bunch of bumpkins.

Clever and witty though they are, and so much given to joking, there is commonly an element of the destructive and self-destructive in the makeup of the Welsh. Dylan Thomas is an obvious instance of this, together with another greatly gifted Welshman of our time, Richard Burton. It would seem to be a product of something lodged in the Welsh psyche, allied to that moodiness, morbidity, and restlessness of which I have spoken. Too many Welshmen lack the "disciplines" on which Fluellen keeps harping. Drawn toward extreme and excess, eager to drain the cup of life to the lees, they take too readily to such aids to the *awen* and the *hwyl* as alcohol. Their attitude toward language itself—think again of Thomas and Burton—is intoxicated. Whereas the English are an Apollonian people, the Welsh are Dionysiac. There is always the desire for the dramatic gesture. They have had so much tragedy in their history that they have become addicted to it.

I have no intention of claiming anything more than a casual acquaintance with either of them, but I did meet Dylan Thomas on perhaps a dozen occasions in the early 1950s, and Richard

Burton on three or four occasions in the early 1960s. My first reason for meeting Thomas was personal: we both had a close mutual friend, the South African poet Roy Campbell. Campbell and I hobnobbed frequently, since we were temperamentally in tune and had an overriding passion for Spain and for the Spanish and Spanish-American poetry and drama that Campbell translated so well. Campbell was by no means everybody's cup of *maté*. He was burly, boastful, with the widest shoulders I have ever seen on a man and the biggest and baldest head, crowned by a huge, black, flat-brimmed *cordobés*. He looked exactly what he claimed to have been: a picador, with an additional touch of one of the enormous bad-tempered bulls that the men who fight them call *catedrales*, or cathedrals. He claimed to have won the Trois Cocardes at Arles, but, though he was built like a Dallas Cowboys linebacker, I can't believe that he was fast enough or sufficiently agile (in French-style bullfighting the bulls are fought on foot). He was a prodigious fantasist, which is what endeared him to Thomas and to me as well; it is well known that Baron Munchausen had Welsh ancestors. Campbell and Thomas were an incongruous and unlikely-looking pair: Campbell, bulging eyed and with his massive, shining, square skull, standing at the bar beside Thomas, small, rumpled, plump, puffy, wet lipped, the skin of his face puckered and slack, but with wonderfully expressive eyes and a magnificent head of hair. I think their poetic styles, apparently so different, actually possessed interesting points of similarity. The tone of their work was high-flown and rhetorical, its rhythms incantatory, it metrics subtly shaded. I am sure they recognized this themselves.

The second reason I had for meeting Thomas was professional, in that as a story editor for a British film company I was keen on acquiring his *The Doctor and the Devils*, the splendid Stevensonian screenplay he had written years before and sold for his usual suicidal sum. I thought that if I could get him to do some additional work on it, it might be possible to rescue it and get it into production. In this I failed. Anyway, whatever the reason, we indulged in several pub crawls together, or with Roy Campbell. But though we liked each other well enough, we never managed to become unduly close. Young Welshmen meeting in London, away from their native turf, tend to be suspicious of each other, and we always remained a bit standoffish, sniffing at each other, to Campbell's amusement, like strange dogs.

As for Richard Burton, we met when we were both serving on the board of the Welsh National Theatre, a scheme that was the brainchild of my close friend the Welsh actor Clifford Evans. We also met in Spain, where I was a screenwriter for the Bronston company, which was then making such films as *El Cid, Fifty-five Days at Peking,* and *The Fall of the Roman Empire,* and where Burton was finishing up the battle scenes for *Antony and Cleopatra.*

The point is this: both men, when I encountered them, had that self-destructive air about them of which I have spoken. Thomas, though he was only in his middle thirties, had already done his best work, and the visible mark of death was already upon him. He was only thirty-nine when he died, a tragic death that made a great impact as the sort of end appropriate for a poet and a Welshman. It was the kind of death suffered by Poe, Baudelaire, Rimbaud, and other *poètes maudits,* and it made him a literary icon. When I knew him he was already sick and sodden, given to fits of gasping, racked by coughing from the perpetual cigarette. As for Burton, when I would join him and his little gang of hangers-on in the bar of the Castellana Hilton, his head was heavily swathed in bandages as the result of a drunken fight he had picked with several other drunken Welshmen on the platform at Paddington Station. He was much given, like the miners among whom he had spent his youth, to enthusiastic bouts of brawling. I recall that his director, Joe Mankiewicz, was much concerned about finding a way to place a metal helmet over the thick layer of bandages in such a way as to prevent the noble Roman from looking like an idiot.

If Thomas had written almost all his best poetry and prose at the time we met, Burton still had many movies and plays left in him. Yet he too seemed to contain within him some intimation of disaster. They seemed to take some inward and private satisfaction from this, and the faint truculence of their manner and expression appeared to be a warning, to their friends, their family, their public, that they were not to be turned aside from embracing their fate. They had the compulsion of so many gifted and intelligent Welshmen, especially South Welshmen, to court catastrophe. They knew very well what path they had chosen and resented anyone who tried to deflect them from it. It is not surprising that Burton's best roles portrayed men in the grip of a self-destructive demon: Hamlet, Othello, Coriolanus, Faustus, the espionage agent in *The Spy Who Came in from the Cold*, Henry VIII in *Anne of the Thousand Days*.

And yet . . . and yet . . . Should we really consider the Welshman's propensity to flirt with failure as one of his vices, or should we regard it, on the contrary, as one of his virtues? Who, after all, are the so-called failures? Lear, Othello, Coriolanus, Antony, Brutus? And who are the people who represent so-called success? Heads of advertising agencies, stockbrokers, franchisers of hamburgers and fried chicken? Where would a Welshman with any poetry in his soul prefer to spend a day: on the golf course with a stockbroker, or at the inn with Falstaff? And who would dare to call Dylan Thomas and Richard Burton the failures, and the bankers and stockbrokers the successes?

And there they are—the men in the Cardiff jerseys—giving an actual demonstration of it down there on the field, even as these thoughts are running through my head. The Cardiff team is doing what I have seen so many Welsh teams do over the years:

breaking away, handling and dribbling brilliantly, storming down the field right on to their opponents' line . . . then dropping the ball, fumbling, failing to score . . .

It is as if they wanted to show the other team, show us in the stands, that they *could* have scored, if they had wanted to—nothing simpler. Yet the pleasure of scoring the try, of putting points on the board, would have been nothing compared with the agonizing pleasure of failure. The triumph of crossing the line and touching the ball down is somehow not as vivid and intense as crashing down in failure at the last possible second, when the thing is within your grasp. And the feeling is particularly satisfying if you can contrive to do it on the final play of the game, when you are only a single point behind. How many times have I trudged away from Cardiff Arms Park, after Wales or Cardiff have lost by a whisker, hearing the people around me happily moaning: "We *could* have done it—we *could* have won . . . but what a marvelous way to *lose!*" This perverse gratification is quintessentially Welsh. It constitutes the major theme of the earliest Welsh literature. The Welsh are the great connoisseurs of catastrophe and debacle.

But I must not exaggerate. Not all Welshmen, even Welsh poets, possess a fatal hankering to do themselves in; witness my boyhood friend Dannie Abse, now one of Wales's leading poets and prose writers, a man of great probity and good sense, devoted all his life to his profession as a doctor. And Welsh footballers like to succeed, too. Their taste for losing is, mercifully, only sporadic, and has not hindered them from frequently carrying off the Triple Crown (victories over England, Scotland, and Ireland in a single season) and the International Championship (victories over those three countries, plus a victory over France). Moreover, in the real-life contests of which football games are the surrogate, the Welsh contingents have not always been found on the losing side. Were they on the losing side at Crécy and at Agincourt? Were the Welsh Guards, the Welsh Fusiliers, the

Welsh Regiment, the South Wales Borderers, the Monmouth-shires on the losing side in the world wars which have marked the century that Churchill called "The Terrible Twentieth"?

And yet—yes—if there is no other way, if they are fated to lose, then the Welsh go down to defeat with the kind of ecstasy which one senses was characteristic of their Celtic ancestors. In their bright war paint, uttering their ferocious cries, the Celtic warriors would drop dead defiantly at the very feet of their admiring enemies.

All the same, winning or losing, scoring or not scoring, what a lovely spectacle it is, this British football.

The Neath scrum half snatches up the ball. He darts around the pack. He sends his backs sprinting up the field. In no time at all the winger is bolting down the touchline before the Cardiff fullback can collar him and bundle him into touch with a tackle worthy of my Tommy Stone of long ago.

I like this impulsive and uncontrived character of the British game. I like its improvisational quality. It has the air of a true game, of something played for pleasure. There is some marvelous running and catching in the American game, when the quarter-back lofts the ball 40 or 50 yards into the outstretched hands of his wide receiver; yet there is a dour atmosphere about the American game that is absent from the British.

I lean back in the sunshine. The Cardiff three-quarters, in their turn, are mounting a beautiful, flowing attack, but even before Ken Reynolds can receive the ball, I hear the veteran critics behind me setting up their quavering complaint: "'*E 'on't passsss, that Ken Reynolds!*" Some people are hard to satisfy.

There is a story that the Welsh tell about Gareth Edwards, the legendary Welsh player whose statue stands in the pedestrian mall that is now Queen Street.

Gareth is captaining the Welsh Fifteen against the English

Fifteen at Cardiff Arms Park. Two supporters, whom we will call Dai and Ianto, have traveled down to Cardiff from the Valleys for the match. They have only been able to afford one ticket between them. They toss a coin outside the ground for who will use it and see the game. Dai wins. They agree that Dai, up in the grandstand, will keep Ianto, outside in the car park, abreast of what is going on.

The game starts, and Dai pops his head out of the grandstand at intervals and gives Ianto a running commentary.

"Welsh player carried off, Ianto!"

"*Diw!*" says Ianto.

"Two more Welshmen injured, Ianto!"

"*Diw, diw, diw!*" says Ianto.

And so it goes on: one Welshman after another knocked out of the game, though the Welshmen are still managing to hang on and prevent the English from putting any points on the board.

But finally Dai appears again. "Fourteen men carried off, Ianto!" he shouts dolefully. "Only one Welshman left!"

"Who is it, then?" asks Ianto. "Is it Gareth?"

"Gareth it is!" says Dai—and at that moment a tremendous roar goes up inside the ground.

Dai dashes back inside. A minute later he appears again.

"It's all right, Ianto!" he shouts. "*Gareth has scored!*"

I must say that by the time the public house heaves into sight, my feet are dragging and my tongue is hanging out. It has taken me two hours to walk across the city from the Cathedral Road to Roath Park, a long stretch on hard pavements for a middle-aged man, even with the help of Admiral Pickard. I was beginning to wish, an hour ago, that I had brought another of my collection of walking sticks: the one with the flask concealed in the handle. Moreover, yesterday's sunny weather has turned into a chilly drizzle. " 'Tis the hard grey weather that breeds hard Englishmen!" Yes—and hard Welshmen too.

Still, the long walk has been evocative. Sophia Gardens, Duke Street, the castle, Queen Street. As I have just mentioned, Queen Street, where the trams once clanged and swayed and the trolleys hissed along, has been turned into a pedestrian mall since I was here last: a nice idea. A bit disconcerting, though, to see that at the top end of the precinct, near the castle, is a towering statue of Aneirin Bevan, once a minister in the postwar Socialist cabinet. He stands on his pedestal in a typically hectoring posture, his eyes bulging and his jaw thrust out, leaning so far forward that at any moment you expect him to topple over, an appropriate attitude for a Socialist politician. His presence in the capital of Wales puzzles me; neither he nor his colleagues in the Labour party ever did much for Wales or the Welsh.

Bevan and his friends disapproved of nationalism, especially the nationalism of small countries. Like the Russian Communists, the British Socialists were one-worlders. One of the few

Labour politicians who did anything constructive for Wales was James Griffiths, tall, pale, quiet, courtly, with the meander of violet pit scars on his forehead. I wish it was the statue of honest old Jim Griffiths that stood in Queen Street, instead of that of Nye Bevan, the Bollinger Bolshevik. Churchill, usually magnanimous where his political opponents were concerned, called Bevan "that squalid nuisance." When I used to function as Our Political Correspondent, and was sent to cover Bevan's meetings at the Corey Hall and elsewhere, I recall what a tub-thumping blusterer he was. He had the *hywl*, right enough. Too often it is the biggest loudmouths who get the biggest statues.

Queen Street is barely recognizable; most of my old landmarks have been torn down or rebuilt. It does not possess the same character that it did in the days of the handsome old Edwardian shop fronts with their broad expanses of glass; modern stores are more uniform and utilitarian. But there is just as much color and bustle, and the shoppers certainly seem more prosperous, more assertive, better dressed. And, as at Llandaff, the people strike me as being younger, but that might be because of the fact that they are healthier and longer-lived, or simply because I myself happen to be growing older.

At any rate, for old times' sake I suddenly decide to swing left and cut down Park Place. On my right are the Park Hotel (scene of some notable carousing, that) and the site of the Park Hall Theatre, my favorite cinema in downtown Cardiff in the 1930s—no mere cinema, indeed, but a grand and palatial picture palace. Here, often by effecting an illicit entrance through the lawyer's office at the rear, I saw many of the most exciting films of that era: *The Invisible Man, The Thirty-nine Steps, The Lady Vanishes, King Kong, The Scarlet Pimpernel, Doctor Cyclops.* No wonder that, when I eventually turned to writing, my passion would always be for a well-conducted narrative.

A few steps away, on the other side of the street, is the New Theatre, which, with the old Empire in Queen Street and the

Prince of Wales's in St. Mary's Street, was one of the three principal homes of live entertainment at that date. But whereas the Prince of Wales's has collapsed into grime and neglect, I can see that the New Theatre, thanks no doubt to its superior size and better location, has continued to flourish. It is now the headquarters of an organization that was not even a wistful dream when I was a boy in Cardiff: the Welsh National Opera Company. A poster outside it tells me that tomorrow the company is to open its new season with a performance of Verdi's *Falstaff*.

Impulsively, I duck inside and head for the box office, taking out my wallet and feeling for the British bank notes that have simultaneously grown smaller in size and larger in value than the ones I was used to. I ask for a seat in the stalls.

The young man behind the guichet shakes his head, his smile polite but pitying. "I'm sorry, sir. The entire house is booked up for tomorrow evening."

Oh well, I will try for a later night. I extract some bank notes.

"Sorry, sir. No seats available."

A matinee, then?

"No, sir. No seats of any kind, not for three weeks, not for the entire run."

Not even standing room?

"Not even standing room, sir."

I turn away, disappointed. Of course, I should have realized it would be foolish, even with the prices of theater tickets what they are today, to hope to find a seat for an important musical event in Wales, especially for an opera, with Welsh singers.

Tucking my wallet away, I gaze slowly around the foyer, resplendent in scarlet and gold. The New Theatre always possessed a dashing style and an air of architectural distinction that the other theaters lacked, and in the hands of the Welsh Opera it has been restored to the luxurious appearance it must have had at the turn of the century. It was here that my father and mother, in the first flush days of their marriage, came to watch the great actor-managers of the day: Irving, Beerbohm Tree, Martin Harvey, George Alexander, Forbes-Robertson. In the years of the Depression and in the early 1940s, when my mother and I were inveterate theatergoers and I was Our Theatrical Correspondent, its lofty standards had to be lowered a notch or two, and instead of straight plays it was compelled to book programs of music hall or variety, which Americans call vaudeville. However, those years represented the glorious sunset of British variety, coinciding with the Golden Age of radio. If anything, variety was more popular in those desperate decades than live theater, or radio itself, and almost as popular as the cinema. And the individual acts, particularly the comic acts, were outstandingly witty and warmhearted, honed to a high finish, miracles of pace and timing, spiced with topical allusion and the sly double entendre that has always been the leading staple of British humor. It was a real folk art. Though their names may now mean little, those people who watched them perform will always remember them with gratitude and affection. Robb Wilton, Max Miller, Gillie Potter, Arthur Askey, Gert and Daisy Waters, Flanagan and Allen, Monsewer Eddie Gray, the Western Brothers, Old Mother Riley, Wilson, Keppel and Betty—their fun and high spirits did more than is generally recognized to help the country through an excruciatingly bad patch.

The National Museum with the City Hall standing beside it are as impressive, I am glad to note, as they were in my boyhood: massive affairs, erected when Cardiff was at the peak of its fortunes, embellished with writhing copper dragons and other exuberant beasts. Florid, overblown, theatrical, slightly dotty, they suit the Welsh very well as the centerpiece of their national capital.

The blooms in the flower beds around City Hall gleam brilliantly in the rain, and in front of the museum are the pretty gardens where I used to loiter for hours as a boy, lolling on the grass and eyeing the girls. In the middle of the gardens is a ring of rough-hewn sarsen stones, arranged in a circle like a miniature Stonehenge. I venerated this ring for years as a relic of the Bronze Age, only to discover that it was erected shortly before I was born in order to mark the site of a National Eisteddfod. These Eisteddfods, or cultural festivals, are held everywhere in Wales, but the "National" is an important annual event staged alternately in North and South Wales. Here respectable Nonconformist ministers, wearing horn-rimmed spectacles and with gym shoes peeping out from beneath their flowing bardic robes, pretend to be Druids, waving jeweled swords and quaffing ale from the horns of oxen.

A statue of Lloyd George stands with its back to the sarsen circle, brandishing a fist at the National Museum across the road. Sculptors liked to portray him in this bellicose attitude. At Caernarvon he stands shaking his fist at the castle, and, since the castle was a symbol of English domination, this is understandable. But what can the National Museum ever have done to make him angry? In fact, he was not so much an angry man as a man given to the Welsh capacity for permanent indignation. He was passionate rather than rancorous, a man of charm and humor, of easy and abundant emotion, a superb orator, whereas Aneirin Bevan was a mere spouter. He was prototypically Welsh in that eventually his passions, which had fueled extraordinary achievements, turned sour and betrayed him. Like many prominent Welshmen, he seems to have had a secret contempt for success, a secret hankering for failure. Or perhaps, like many Welshmen, he simply grew impatient and bored. His powers, as uncanny as Merlin's at the height of his career, deserted him. He spent his last years, after he had ruined himself and his party, in obscurity and virtual disgrace. He was one of the few men whom, not just in Wales but in any country, one would not hesitate to call a genius. And of course he was right: failure is a kind of grace. It is a poor sort of man who cannot face the fact that we are all failures in the end. Life itself, after all, is a losing battle. (And how very Welsh I show myself to be, writing that sentence.)

All the other, older statues still stand in their accustomed places. I greet them like old friends. There stands the sanctimonious, frock-coated old skinflint John Corey, the coalowner. A few yards away stands Lord Ninian Stuart, one of the Butes, a brave figure in his field officer's uniform, with his map case and binoculars. He gave his life at Loos, in 1915—the battle, incidentally, in which my old regiment the Welsh Guards first saw action, and in which Rudyard Kipling's son was killed fighting with the Irish Guards ("The Irish march to the sound of the guns/ Like salmon to the sea"). And there, a few feet beyond the railing, is my favorite statue of them all: Goscombe John's statue of Lord Tredegar, high up on his horse, with panels around the plinth depicting the Charge of the Light Brigade at Balaklava, in which the young Tredegar rode at the head of his troop. The Tredegars, like the Butes, were coal barons—but much, surely, can be forgiven a rich man willing to put aside his privileges to face fire in the service of his country. And—the *Charge of the Light Brigade!* . . .

If City Hall and museum and city center still correspond to the image preserved in my memory, what a jolt I get when I reach the lower end of Queen Street, where it becomes the Newport Road. The whole district from Churchill Way right down to the Royal Infirmary has been totally transformed.

Here has risen, or is in the process of being erected, a kind of Cardiff Manhattan: an area of skyscrapers, albeit superior to those that disfigure modern London, well spaced out and on the whole inoffensively designed. In fact the entire area around the old Taff Vale railway station was dingy and squalid when I was a boy. Development has definitely improved it. I walk through it admiringly, impressed, yet somehow perversely missing the ancient dirt and drunkenness in the vicinity of the old pub called The Sandringham. In spite of its grand name, this was a working-class pub, always a thrill to walk past in those days of spit and sawdust, its open doors exhaling the reek of beer and its customers (among them my Uncle Jack) staggering out to fight or collapse in the street.

It was here that many of Cardiff's characters used to forgather. I remember a sandwich man, resplendent in full Edwardian fig, frock coat, white spats, sponge-bag trousers, patent-leather shoes, boiled shirt, and top hat. Here was the regular pitch of a newspaper seller, a figure who filled me with dread and who would wander intermittently through my dreams for sixty years. He was Cardiff's Elephant Man. Dwarfish, he wore a greasy cap with a huge peak and a filthy muffler and yelled *"Sou' Wes' Echoooo!"* in a twangy voice. One side of his face, from the forehead down to the shoulder, concealing his left eye, his left cheek, and the left side of his mouth, was a bulging, drooping, shapeless mass of pitted gray flesh. His name was Billy Benjamin, and he was sharp-witted and popular and sold a lot of papers. I would go out of my way to goggle at him, but he was used to it and only used to grin at me, as if his disfigurement was a commercial asset. Passersby would hand him their pennies and take their papers and exchange a joke with him as if his appearance was the most natural thing in the world. They had got used to it, as people will get used to anything, and as Billy himself had got used to it.

All the same, he must have been something extraordinary for me to have remembered him so vividly; after all, the streets of Cardiff in those days were crammed with figures which nowadays would stop the traffic. As a child I regarded them as perfectly normal and did not flinch from them at all. There were the drunks, prone in the gutter or propped up against the walls of pubs like The Sandringham. There were the beggars, with cardboard placards around their necks, holding out battered tin cups. There were the one-man bands, the knife grinders, the barrel organs with their moth-eaten marmosets in crimson velveteen smoking caps and jackets. Above all, in those days of the Depression there were the miners and the ex-servicemen, limbless or doubled over as they coughed their lungs out, the miners the victims of pneumoconiosis, the soldiers of phosgene gas.

As a child, holding my father's hand and stopping on our walks to greet his friends, most of whom had served in France, or Gallipoli, or at sea, I took it for granted that the world was full of freaks and cripples, men with one eye, one arm, one leg, who coughed all the time, or were half deaf as a result of being artillerymen and loosing off those monstrous barrages that preceded the attacks on the Western Front. The streets of Britain were Swiftian places in the 1920s and 1930s. I can recall, as late as 1938, entering the Cardiff Royal Infirmary carrying two big Christmas cakes, thick with icing and marzipan, that my mother always used to send along as a Christmas gift, even though our own Christmases in those Depression days had become exceedingly lean. I was directed by Matron to take them to the Mametz Ward, where, twenty years after the end of the Great War, still moaned, wept, twitched, and hobbled the ruined remnants of the Welsh Division. *Mametz.* The names of those ghastly engagements of a ghastly war are still capable of sending a shiver through someone of my generation:

> *If you want the old battalion, I know where they are:*
> *They're hanging on the old barbed-wire.*

Oddly enough, it was only when I began to reach middle age, in my early forties, that I really started to understand how much the Great War had influenced, determined even, the whole course of my life. It was only then that I was prompted to take a closer interest in it. It had ended a mere six years before I was born, but like all young men I was too busy living my own life, in my own way, to perceive how the present is linked to the past, and flows out of it. Young people are great solipsists.

Sometimes I think we may be nothing more than the victims, prisoners, or hostages of an earlier generation, blindly acting or reenacting the tragic problems which it has bequeathed to us. And there is more to it than that: it is the configuration not merely of the generation immediately preceding our own that decides our fate but of all the generations before them. One generation squeezes the next generation in its grip, and we in our own time only have the illusion of free will. Humankind is always, as it were, a step behind. The Great War ended in 1918, and I was born in 1924, so it was fairly easy for me to comprehend, once the connection had dawned on me, how my own destiny had been hatched from it. But I was also born in a particular place, in South Wales, and I needed to appreciate, too, that my life was the product of the whole history of Glamorganshire. Difficult and almost impossible to grasp as it is, the fact is that the story of my life does not just begin with Gwilym White or Moses White but courses back through Joshua White and Rawlins White to the Wars of the Roses, the Norman Conquest, the Rule of the High Kings, and the Roman Occupation, the Iron Age, the Bronze Age, the Stone Age. Surely this must be one of the causes why I am making this September pilgrimage, in many ways so pleasurable, in other ways so painful. I must have had it in mind that the time had come to try to shimmer back through the lives of the young Guardsman, the sailor, the schoolboy, the child who stood in the doorway at the Cathedral Road, time to try to drift back through the earlier lives I led before they were ever born. Somehow, as a son of Glamorgan, I must be the comrade and coeval of Sir Henry Morgan, the bowmen of Agincourt, King Arthur, Caratacus. Why else should I have been mulling through the events of Welsh and South Welsh history? They are not just a ragbag of random facts; they are my bone, my sinew, and my marrow. They are the hints and markers that brought me from the misty purlieus of the past into the doorway of the Cathedral Road, and on again from there.

"Only connect," said E. M. Forster. Few people today, in Wales or England or Europe, are much given to connecting up their familial and other origins; they are too caught up in their daily business. They know that the bloodlines must run deep, but there is a generally accepted cutoff point at about the level of the grandparents or great-grandparents. It is the same in America. Most Americans will speak of the Old Country—though they generally have to be pressed, first because they lack a burning interest in it, and second because it is part of the American compact that newcomers should surrender themselves to the melting pot in the interests of their new nation. To become an American, as the oath to new citizens specifically spells out, it is necessary to renounce all former ties and associations. Thus an American might tell you that his family was originally Finnish or Polish or Hungarian but would be unable to tell you from what part of Finland or Poland or Hungary it came, and the odds are that he could not point out Finland or Poland or Hungary on the map.

Sometimes the ancestral obliteration is total. More often than not, when I meet a Jones, a James, a Williams, a Humphreys, an Evans, and inform him that their name is Welsh, I am met with a blank stare. What and where is Wales? As for history, the majority of Americans assume that it began in 1776. They know next to nothing of the colonial period, the struggle for supremacy by the English, Spanish, and French, and the long, sad story of the American Indian. Yet, of course, though the American is unaware of them, the scarlet threads are there, linking him with his ancestry and his past. Indian America, colonial America, his European or Asian or Latin background— none of them can be wholly reduced in the melting pot or by the pressure of modern living. A part of them is irreducible; he carries them with him in his genes, his instincts, his folk memory, the advance of the nation.

My American Jones or Williams may have no active memory of Glamorgan, or Gwynedd, or Dyfed, yet when I look at them I can often see how very Welsh their faces are, and their mannerisms, and their actions and attitudes. The blood of the dragon is in their veins. It is not easily diluted.

The Royal Infirmary, as I pass it, has exactly the appearance it had in 1938, though the poor maimed creatures in Mametz Ward have long since been standing at ease on the tranquil parade ground of the dead. It looks doubly depressing and barracklike in the drizzle. I hurry past it. My lifelong precept has been to steer clear of doctors, lawyers, bookies, and policemen, and, in spite of the fact that many of my mother's sisters were nursing sisters and matrons in South Wales hospitals, I have had mercifully little to do with hospitals and doctors' offices. Recently, however, since my wife's illness, and the obsession in America with every conceivable form of disease, it sometimes occurs to me that the world is becoming one enormous hospital ward.

I turn my head away and swing sharp left, cheering up as I enter the City Road. I suppose we all have our favorite thoroughfare in our native town; after Bute Street, I think that the cheeky, smelly City Road must be mine. But whereas Bute Street has become a ghost town, the City Road remains as busy and perky as ever.

Most of the shops I knew as a small boy, when for a time I lived in this part of town, seem to be gone: Mr. Baby the greengrocer, Mrs. Hussey the baker, Mr. Knight the butcher, Mrs. Pascal at the sweet shop, where we bought gob-stoppers, licorice sticks, and sherbet fountains. So is Mr. Fligelstone the pawnbroker; there used to be long lines outside Fliggy's on Friday nights. Long lines outside the pie shop, too, where on

Saturday nights people would bring their basins to be filled with steaming helpings of faggots and peas (faggots, I hasten to add, consist of savory ground meat cooked in a piece of the lining of a sheep's stomach, a kind of miniature haggis). Now the aroma of the pie shop seems to have been superseded by the whiffs of curry and cardamom curling out of the doorways of the score of Indian restaurants that appear to have supplanted the older Chinese restaurants everywhere in the British Isles.

I recall how grumpy I used to be when my mother asked me to go out with a basket and a shopping list, after the glory days of maids and housekeepers were behind us, in order to fetch a couple of chump chops from Mr. Knight or a cottage loaf from Mrs. Hussey. How gladly this afternoon, in the rain, would I step, basket in hand, into the small, bright, stuffy shops, if they could be magically resurrected. Strange that I should feel such a stab of nostalgia for such ordinary things as the smell of apples and cabbages, the sight of a blue-and-white-striped apron, the sound of a knife being whetted on a steel, the scent of newly baked baps and Welsh cakes, the clink of the top being screwed back on a jar of bull's-eyes, the glimpse of the garish covers of *Modern Boy, Wizard, Hotspur,* and *Rover* on the rack outside the newsagent's. Why do we assume that the background settings of our life at each successive stage are permanent and solid, when they are only painted cloths, soon to be folded up and whisked away to the prop room? I would like to see that row of poky little shops again, looking at them this time much more carefully. I would like to walk into my mother's kitchen and put that laden basket on the table.

The kitchen. In households all over the world, and particularly in Wales, the kitchen is the most important room in the house, its physical and psychic center, its engine room, its powerhouse, the place from which radiates its warmth and vitality. My mother's kitchen never quite became the center of our domestic life, but, in the years immediately after my father's death, it came very close to it. My mother was by nature a homebody and a homemaker, and while she was perhaps the most beautiful of a family of eight sisters, many of whom were striking-looking women, she lacked their ambition and assertiveness. She was gentle, sweet-natured, and retiring, and in the years of my father's affluence he delighted in cosseting and pampering her.

When the money dwindled, however, and the servants departed, she showed she was made of the same mettle as her sisters, adjusting quickly and bravely to her altered circumstances. She had always had a greater gift for cookery than her more outgoing and impatient sisters, but now she blossomed into a cook of quite exceptional skill and resource. In a sense, the kitchen became her redoubt, her stronghold, her place of retreat, the place where she felt least vulnerable. Life had dealt her a number of sudden and devastating blows, blows for which her previously sheltered and privileged position had not prepared her. In a short space of time her existence had been turned topsy-turvy and she had been made aware of the chaotic and meaningless nature of things. In her bright and shining kitchen, with her implements and ingredients ranged neatly around her, she could regain some feeling of control, some sense of order. Many women retire to their kitchens in this way at times of stress and bereavement. A kitchen, after all, is a warm, fragrant, steamy, dreamy, womblike sort of place. Nor can it be entirely accidental that the kitchen is usually the room at the rear of the house, the room remotest from the hurly-burly and random din of humanity passing by in the street outside.

Although her retreat into cooking was more marked after my father's death, my mother had already begun her apprenticeship while he was in the sanatorium and in the doleful years that followed his return home. It was as if, while the husband was slowly dying in the bedroom overhead, the wife was trying in the kitchen below to bring to house some semblance of health and well-being. The preparation and consumption of food often possess such a significance, of course, and often serve as an expression of love. My mother, though shy, was not at all undemonstrative or afraid to show her affection, in the Welsh way, by means of plentiful hugs and kisses. But cooking elaborate meals became an additional way of showing us how much she cared for us, how determined she was to keep up our morale and give us at least the appearance of good cheer.

She came to master the full range of the art of cookery. She was a dab, as the Welsh say, with the conventional dishes: baron of Welsh beef, saddle of Welsh mutton, shoulder of Welsh lamb glazed with honey, ham with parsley sauce, hot pot and leek flan and the delicious broth that the Welsh call *cawl*. She had an exceptionally nice touch with fish: salmon, trout, plaice, sole, haddock, turbot, mackerel, Fishguard herrings. But it was with puddings and with pastry that she really entered into her culinary kingdom. With the aid of a copy of Mrs. Beeton, lacking its covers, tattered, spattered with stains, more thumbed through and pored over than any Bible, she covered the whole panoply of British puddings: Guards pudding, Queen Anne's pudding, Cabinet pudding, Snowdon pudding, roly-poly pudding, spotted dick. America boasts no puddings like those; its roll call of what it calls desserts is brief and insubstantial. No wonder I often awake in the middle of the night, in Tennessee, with the scent of hot jam roll in my nostrils and the taste of it upon my tongue.

As a pastry cook, however, my mother became a nonpareil. When I remember her in her kitchen, I recall her as bending over her pastry board, surrounded by her saucepans and mixing bowls, in her frilled apron, flour up to her elbows, blowing a straying lock of black hair away from her forehead. At four o'clock the apron was taken off and folded away and a smart afternoon frock was substituted, so that she could preside over what she considered the high point of her day: the ritual of the tea table. It was at teatime that she could display the array of breads and pastries that had been taken hot from the oven only moments before: brown bread and white bread, cut wafer thin, Welsh cakes, Eccles cakes, sponge cakes, maids of honor, Bakewell tarts, lemon-curd tarts, Battenburg, and gingerbread. Since my father's illness she had parted willingly with her pearls, her diamonds, her furs, but nothing would have induced her to part with two things: her piano and her silver tea set. Flanked by a pair of cake stands, she sat behind her big silver tray with its accoutrements: the teapot, the hot-water kettle with its spirit lamp, the slop basin, milk jug, and sugar basin. The tea was poured into Worcester cups and the bread and butter and cakes handed around on Worcester plates. On special occasions she brought out her mother's precious Nantgarw and Swansea. A tray stood ready so that the first cup of tea could be carried upstairs to my father.

My mother made such remarkable progress as a pastry cook that within eighteen months the news of her expertise had spread beyond her own kitchen. Commissions flooded in. Her kitchen table began to be laden with Christmas cakes and anniversary cakes, and with wedding cakes that were towering masterpieces of icing and marzipan. It became crowded with the aunts and nieces and outside assistants who were pressed into service. As I scraped a small, grimy finger around the empty bowls, I would be hemmed in by the hips and bosoms and quivering flesh of warm and white-aproned women, all of them, in those days before mechanical gadgets, whisking, sifting, beating, grating, stirring, rapping and tapping with wooden spoons. The sums that my mother earned from these efforts helped to keep the household afloat. She would have earned a great deal more if she had not been so diffident about pressing for prompt payment, had not given so much of her handiwork away for nothing, and had not been so scrupulous about using only the most expensive ingredients (though what great artist can bear to scamp on his materials?). She was a meticulous cook but an inexperienced businesswoman, so it was ironic that in the room directly above her head she happened to have, if only he had been in a condition to function, a man who had once been one of the most successful Welsh businessmen of his generation. All this activity ceased, of course, with the onset of the war, with the advent of scarcity and the introduction of ration books.

A word about my mother's seven sisters, the aggregation of aunts, as it were, by whom I was brought up "by hand," like young Pip in *Great Expectations*. I remember them functioning throughout my childhood as a kind of laughing, chattering, galvanic, restless Greek chorus. They were indisputably a remarkable group of women, for the most part highly independent and strong willed. They were also, in the way of Welsh women, very female females, a comely and sweet-smelling crew. Throughout their lives they stuck by one another and gave each other close support, and there were certainly times when I felt sorry for their husbands, who were deputed to play decided second fiddle to that phalanx of women with their passionate sense of solidarity. While my maternal aunts were a constant presence in my young life, their spouses, unlike my paternal uncles, with two exceptions, were not. The exceptions were my Uncle Arthur, Claire's husband, a fine, soldierly man, who took special care of me after the death of my father, whom he had revered, and my Uncle Mac, Paddy's husband. I had a special liking for Mac because he was a seaman, the master of a succession of oil tankers. We therefore had much in common.

The oldest of the sisters was Agnes, known as Ness. Ness was the most worldly-wise of the eight, and the one with whom over the years I had some of the most serious talks. She had been an exceptionally handsome and physically appetizing woman, but she had never married, perhaps because, though she liked men, she had a low opinion of their character. However, there had been an engagement, I gathered in a roundabout way, to an infantry officer who had died as a result of wounds sustained on the Somme, and after World War I there was a long and mysterious liaison with a prominent surgeon in Bath. She became a hospital matron, and in later life was much sought after as a guest at medical functions because she had been among the first dozen women to be enrolled as state registered nurses. She had started her nursing career when Florence Nightingale was still alive and was the embodiment of the Nightingale tradition. As I mentioned earlier, she became an obsessive and disastrous devotee of the art of knitting, though she might have done better at it if she had not been such a compulsive reader at the same time. Her favorite authors included Hardy, Bennett, Galsworthy, and Maugham, and she had a standing order at Boots circulating library for the latest novels by Walpole, Deeping, Hutchinson, Raymond, Cronin, Mackenzie, and the other popular novelists of the time. A useful aunt for a future writer to have.

I wonder how many writers are able to recall the exact moment when fate decided they would take to authorship? I believe I can. It happened one evening after tea in the house of my Aunt Claire and Uncle Arthur in Whitchurch, a suburb of Cardiff, in the summer of 1931. I was seven years old, and my Aunt Margaret, who was a schoolmistress, took me on her lap and recited two poems to me: one was Alfred Noyes's ballad "The Highwayman," and the other was Walter De la Mare's "The Traveler." After sixty years I can still remember that she read them in that order, and hear the pitch and timbre of her voice, and feel the clutch of her arms around me. From that moment the die was cast.

Both my Aunt Claire, to whom I have always remained very close, and my Aunts Mollie and Phyllis were nurses, and really only my mother and my Aunt Lal were stay-at-homes. Lal possessed a temperament more unworldly and angelic than my mother's, if such a thing was possible. I lived with her in Cadoxton, near Barry, for almost a year after my father first fell ill and it was necessary to remove me because of the risk of contagion. She died in childbirth only a short time later, though at that time I would not have known what childbirth was. Peace be to her gentle shade.

Would you believe it, after half a century the same old car dealerships are still here, in the City Road, some of them under the same names? Amusing to learn that the wicked still flourish. There are no large open-air lots, only cramped shop fronts with two or three cars on display behind them. It was always a mystery to me how they managed to slide them in; I guessed they did so in the same way that my Uncle Evan used to slide his model ships into bottles. But the cars!—BMW, Mercedes, Saab, Volvo, Lancia, Alfa Romeo—none of your cheap and flimsy Morris Cowleys and Austin Sevens of yesteryear. Another sign of better times.

Good God—what is that that I can see—across the other side of the street? Surely!—it can't be!—yes!—the old Gaiety Cinema. I would have given long odds that the Gaiety would have fallen victim to the wrecker's ball years and years ago. But there she is—shabby and chopfallen like the Prince of Wales's, with placards revealing that she has sunk to the level of a bingo parlor—but still the same Gaiety. Insulting to call her a cinema; like the Park Hall, she was a pleasure dome. It seems natural, somehow, doesn't it, to describe cinemas, which offer us the darkness and shelter and dream retreat of the womb, as female, like ships? And the Gaiety is truly female, in that on either side of the entrance, gleaming in the wet, there rise two sumptuous copper-sheathed cupolas, like the stupendous breasts of Kay Francis or Joan Blondell or some other goddess of the early talkies. It was on that low wall over there that I can remember sitting and weeping for the death of Leslie Howard, the doomed poet in *The Petrified Forest*, who had arranged to have himself shot by the gangster Duke Mantee in order to liberate the local Madame Bovary with his insurance money. But then, as I said before, I tended to weep rather easily. A little later I would weep for the deaths of Julien Sorel and Lucien de Rubempré—and I am not quite sure that I ever really got over them.

I also associate the Gaiety with a real death. My father and mother had taken me to see *The Jazz Singer*, though it was not the fact that it was the first talking picture that would make an impression on me. What I remember is my father buying a newspaper outside the cinema, scanning the headline, and saying, "Good God! Seagrave is dead!" Even as a child, Sir Henry Seagrave was a bigger hero to me than Tommy Stone. He was my *beau idéal*. Somewhere I still have my model of his Golden Arrow, the beautiful machine in which he set the world's land speed record in 1929. Boys followed the world land and water speed records avidly in those days, as well as Professor Picard's attempts on the stratosphere record and Charles Beebe's exploits in his bathysphere. Seagrave, George Eyston, John Cobb, and Sir Malcolm Campbell were household names. Campbell was the first man to achieve 300 miles an hour, in his magnificent Bluebird, and Eyston in his Thunderbolt and Cobb in his Railton got up close to 400. Nowadays, when no one cares (the last activity of this type to engage the public interest was the breaking of the sound barrier) the official land speed record stands at well over 600 mph. Those were very daring men, and their deaths in their blazing cars and disintegrating speedboats were Wagnerian. Seagrave died, Eyston died, Cobb died, and Campbell's son died in a later version of Bluebird. No other single sport has been as punishing as that concerned with the pursuit of speed. Of the twenty winners of the World Racing Championship since 1950, nearly half were killed and several more severely injured.

I could not have suspected, then, standing with my parents outside the Gaiety, that in time I would spend fifteen years writing or patching up movies, as a way to sustain less lucrative literary activities, and that my first novel and first movie would in fact be about motor racing.

A quick turn to the right. A short stroll down the Albany Road (the Butes filled Cardiff with these pretentious Scottish street names). The rain is coming down harder, if anything. But no matter, I can finally see my ultimate destination in front of me.

The Claude Hotel is an imposing, freestanding Edwardian structure, three stories high and built of a light granitic stone, situated at the foot of a steepish little hill and dominating its own little circle of shops and churches. Its name sounds very grand, though it is probably only a corruption or Anglicization of some Welsh word like *Clwyd,* which means "a gate." Probably, not too long ago, a farm stood here, perhaps even one of those farms in the area that are known to have been owned by old Rawlins White.

The sight of it makes my heart flutter. I had been in two minds whether I had really traveled 4,000 miles to visit Llandaff Cathedral. But I know for a fact that I had had it firmly in mind from the moment I left Tennessee that I was going to spend at least an hour in the Claude Hotel.

I have close links with this part of Cardiff. I used to attend that Ruabon-brick infant school a couple of streets away. I remember little about it, except that once I toddled into the middle of the classroom on St. David's Day, wearing a coat of chain mail made from a silver-painted potato sack, carrying a cardboard shield with a dragon on it, and brandishing a wooden sword, and recited a speech in Welsh, followed by a solo rendering of "God Bless the Prince of Wales." Those are not the kinds of moments a man easily forgets. My real star turn as a child, by the way, was to dance the sailor's hornpipe, got up in a little sailor suit and wearing a little sailor hat. It had been taught to me in an evil hour by my Uncle Alf, who had served in the Navy as an engine room artificer. I have been known to perform it in later years, though circumspectly, and only on bibulous occasions.

Six o'clock. The double doors to the public bar and to the private bar of the Claude Hotel stand open. I head for the public bar and march in, and after a few moments, with the briefest of glances around, I march right back out again.

In the days when I used to frequent British pubs, the public bar seldom resembled Buckingham Palace. But it was a place with genuine character: gleaming mahogany, shining brass, stained glass, a sense of the solemnity that ought to accompany the ceremonious drawing and downing of a good pint of beer. Now I find that the public bar at the Claude, like the public bars I encountered recently in London, has been turned into a hideous "games room." The brass and mahogany and stained glass have been sent to the scrap heap, or dispatched overseas to decorate American restaurants. The sturdy old chairs and the tables of intricate ironwork have been replaced by plastic. And what of the canned music? How can a man do any serious thinking and drinking with that racket going on? Canned music is one of the nuisances of modern civilization. When my plane is demolished by engine failure or a terrorist bomb, will I really have to die to the strains of Lawrence Welk? There is no point in making an inordinate fuss about these things; nonetheless, I found it disconcerting, when I was in London, to go into a familiar old hostelry like, say, the Salisbury in St. Martin's Lane, and find it awash with jukeboxes and one-armed bandits.

Pleasant, then, to walk around to the entrance to the private bar, take a deep breath, and encounter an altogether different atmosphere—an atmosphere of calm and a comparative silence, except for a minor seepage of noise from the ghastly games room. Better than that: as I stand in the doorway, taking off my raincoat and shaking the moisture from it, I realize that in forty-five years the room has scarcely changed. Even the air has the same stale, sweetish tinge. It still has the same spacious, high-ceilinged, seedily handsome appearance, with its wide leaded windows and the broad tiled fireplace at the lower end of the room. Amazing. After forty-five years, after all the singing and shouting, the whispers and whimpers, the squeals and the giggles, the sobs and the sighs, the private lounge at the Claude Hotel is still the same. Carrying my pint of mild-and-bitter to a table, I feel very queer and mortal. "What is life? Two weeks beside the sea," murmured Cecil Rhodes on his deathbed. And what has my life been? A couple of drinks in the Claude Hotel. Once more I feel as if my life has somehow got squeezed up, as if instead of the stranger from Tennessee who has wandered in out of the rain it is the young sailor, the young soldier, Our Theatrical Correspondent from the *Western Mail*. At any moment the sirens will start to wail and the antiaircraft guns near the church up the road will begin to snarl and thump.

At this time on a Monday night there are only a couple of patrons in the lounge. It will fill up later. One of the things in Britain that is never going to alter, however much they muck about with the decor of the pubs, is the popularity and importance of pub life. It is part of the country's enduring fabric. In the early 1950s, when television began to take hold, it was commonly supposed that the public house was doomed. Television was also expected to impose a uniform culture on Britain, wiping out regional customs and ironing out regional accents. Nothing of the sort happened. Not television, or computers, or the Common Market can do much to alter the local loyalties of the British. The sense of national character and individual identity, which the Socialists used to consider so obnoxious, are altogether too tough and impermeable—which is good news for Wales, and for small countries everywhere.

I lay Admiral Pickard on a chair. I take a sip of my beer. I close my eyes. The subdued clink of bottles, the snatches of conversation, the muddled music from the public bar begin to make me sleepy. . . .

The big room was different, on that evening long ago. That night it was chock-a-block with humanity. The street outside was a seething mass of men and women, young and old, swaying and jostling, slapping each other's shoulders, bawling and breathing fumes into each other's faces. More than half of them were in uniform: light blue, dark blue, khaki. Most of them were British—Welsh, English, Scottish, and Irish—though there was also a generous sprinkling of Australians, Canadians, New Zealanders, South Africans, Rhodesians, Americans.

V-E Day. May 8, 1945. I had already fought my way to the bar half a dozen times. I was growing deliberately and uproariously drunk. I was twenty. The war which had lasted nearly six years and punched a sizable hole in my young life was over. These were the days when decent liquor was in short supply. When you ran across it, you put down as much of it as you could as quickly as you could.

I had something to celebrate: the fact that I had survived. I had not expected to. As a rule young servicemen seldom trouble about such things; they fancy themselves invulnerable. The ones who worry are the men who are middle aged, who want to get back to their homes, their wives, their children, their steady jobs. But in my case there had been a kind of shadow over me, something a superstitious Welshman could not ignore. The shadow was the knowledge that the three men who had been head of my house at school immediately before me had all been killed in action. I call them men; really they were scarcely more than boys. The eldest of them, Michael Gisby, who had left Emmanuel College at Cambridge to be shot down over the Ruhr as the pilot of a Lancaster, was only twenty-three. Alec Biggs had perished in the freezing waters of the North Cape on a convoy to Murmansk. John Kuypers had died in the Western Desert, when Auchinleck was trying to steady the line in front of the Suez Canal. I was the fourth man up. It seemed to me the odds were against me.

Well—now it was V-E Day. My number had not come up. I had managed to scramble through. Surely that was worth a drink?—or two?—or three? Actually, the fact that I had come through, that here on V-E Day I found myself standing on my feet, among the seething mob in the Claude Hotel, with a glass of rum in my hand, was to have an effect on me that would last long beyond that night. I was to live afterward with a heightened sense of existence. I was to feel that my life had been made over to me as a miraculous free gift. I daresay innumerable ex-servicemen have felt the same. In me, it was to produce a curious kind of double vision. Out of one eye (the English eye) I would view existence responsibly, rationally, feeling obligated to do something positive with my life, to shape it and give it meaning. I owed that to my dead friends, who had been robbed of the chance to do the same. Out of the other eye (the Welsh one) I would view life impulsively, hedonistically, as something to be exulted in and enjoyed, luscious as the taste of fruit. Thus my life would turn out to be an odd blend of the longsighted and the shortsighted, of sobriety and insobriety, depending on which eye I happened to be looking through at the time, leading of course to some very peculiar results whenever I tried to look out of both eyes at the same time.

That evening, at least at the start of it, I was looking through the Welsh eye. It was one of those turning points when we all knew that, for each one of us as an individual and for the country as a whole, one era had ended and another had begun. Soon I would be shedding the uniform I was wearing and would be plunging into what everyone in that hot, sweaty room felt was going to be a brave new world.

It was a piece of fantastic luck that I happened to be on a week's leave at this particular time; I still had three glorious days left before I had to report back to Windsor Barracks. I had brought along with me to share in the merrymaking a handsome, lively young nurse whom I had taken out a couple of times earlier. Nest Lewis was one of those fine, high-spirited Welsh girls who add color and laughter to life. (Nest is the Welsh equivalent of Agnes, and was, incidentally, the name of Gerald the Welshman's mother.)

Nest was also wearing uniform. She had just come off duty and had had no time to change. I had my arm around her waist, and she had hers around mine, and we were rocking from side to side and slopping our drinks and singing our heads off with the others. We were both tall and could see over the heads of the people around us. And as we were swaying and singing I caught sight of another girl, a small, dark-haired girl, also in nurse's uniform with a red cross on its breast, smiling and joking with the circle of servicemen around her.

"Genuine passions," says Balzac in *La Cousine Bette* (and who knew more about the passions than Balzac?), "have no instinct of their own, and natural instincts are infallible. Nature's action in such cases is called 'love at first sight': But 'love at first sight' is really, quite simply, 'love at *second* sight.' "

So, as the dark-haired girl in the corner and I looked at one another, first sight and second sight fused into the celebrated *regard rouge*. Cynics would say that what we were recognizing was only ourselves, a flattering mirror image of what we imagined or would like ourselves to have been, not really another distinct and individual creature at all. Even if there is some truth in that, I think I could put it more charitably: we were seeing something that we sensed would complete the other half of our nature, that supplied another side to us that we had always sensed was lacking.

And as I sit here on this chilly Monday evening, with Admiral Pickard and my wet raincoat on the chair beside me, I can still see the May sunshine as it slanted in through these same leaded windows opposite me, bathing the heads of the happy mob and illuminating the figure of the girl in the corner.

The girls of Cardiff are known for their beauty. This one struck me as beautiful enough to take her place beside the "gentle gold-torqued women" who throng the pages of the *Mabinogion*. Except that this girl was dark, I felt like the messengers of King Arthur when they made inquiries about the girl who came to the shepherd's hut every Saturday to wash her hair, leaving her gold rings in the bowl as payment:

> She was dressed in flame-red silk, with a torque of red gold around her neck studded with precious pearls and rubies. Her hair was yellower than broom, her skin whiter than sea-foam, her palms and fingers whiter than shoots of marsh trefoil against the sand of a welling spring. Neither the eye of a mewed hawk nor the eye of a thrice-mewed falcon were fairer than hers. Her breasts were whiter than the breasts of the white swan, her cheeks were redder than the reddest foxgloves, and anyone who saw her would fall deeply in love. Wherever she went, four white trefoils appeared behind her, and for that reason she was called the Girl of the White Track.

That was how she affected me. That is the reason for my grief when eventually I would see her lying helpless and motionless, unable for months to move even an eyelid or a finger. It was the explanation for my intemperate reflections in Llandaff Cathedral. The normal processes of aging, of everyday wear and tear, I could have accepted. But *that*? . . . It only seemed an additional cruelty, that the damage to her brain had the effect of making her shed the actual number of her years, smoothing away the lines of her face so that her expression had once again become that of the young woman I saw that evening standing in the corner among her khaki-clad admirers.

I shift in my chair. I am growing stiff. It feels damp in here. No slanting May sunshine—just the regulation Welsh downpour. It is coming down faster, more heavily now. I can hear it hammering on the roof.

I wonder why I felt such a compulsion to come back to this featureless spot? Of course, Valerie and I had always promised ourselves that one day we would revisit the places where we had lived: Audley End in Essex, Grange Road in Cambridge, Hamilton Terrace in London, Minsterworth Court in Gloucestershire. You always imagine there will be plenty of time for such things; then, all at once, you wake up and find that time has run out. As John Owen, the Welsh epigrammatist, wrote:

*Thou ask'st what years thou hast? I answer None:*
*For what thou hads't, thou hast not: they be gone.*

Perhaps I walked across Cardiff tonight because I felt, in my foolish Celtic way, that it might help to heal her if I somehow went back to the beginning. At Llandaff I failed to find a clue to healing among the priests; perhaps I could find it among the publicans.

We were so strong and alive on that May night. Our lives were full of energy and promise. Ironic that one can draw no sort of virtue from that, that there is no way to tap it, that the vital qualities of our youth can do nothing to redeem and fortify our age.

"*However amusing the beginning of the comedy, the last act is always bloody.*" As usual, Pascal was right. The curtain rose on a carefree crowd in the lounge of the Claude Hotel. It is falling on a solitary sickroom 4,000 miles away.

And yet—forty years ago—the gods granted us a *dies faustus*, a splendid, gaudy day. I helped to trundle the piano out of the bar, through those double doors over there, out into the middle of the street. We set it down opposite the Baptist chapel across the way. There must have been a couple of hundred of us. Above us, from the upper floors of the Claude, banners were hanging, banners with the red dragon of Wales. Someone sat down on a crate in front of the piano and began to play: "White Cliffs of Dover," "Roll Out the Barrel," "Underneath the Arches," "Run, Rabbit, Run," "Umbrella Man," "We'll Hang Out Our Washing on the Siegfried Line."

We danced around the piano. We danced *on* the piano. We danced up and down the street. We danced in ragged lines, in ragged circles, in ragged squares. The whole world was laughing, crying, kissing, hugging, slapping backs, arms around each other's necks, each other's waists, each other's shoulders. The whole of Wales was singing.

The spring dusk fell. The lights in the pub came on. The music grew slower and slower, dreamier and dreamier.

Valerie and I were holding each other. We were dancing together in the street. We were dancing together for the first time.

Standing in the little town square, as the country bus zigzags away along the curving road to Brecon, I am glad to see that in the past forty years the Bear Hotel has changed, outwardly at least, to an even smaller degree than the Claude. I linger for a moment, letting my glance stray over it, while the image of it I have been carrying for so long in my mind settles upon it with the accuracy of a piece of tracing paper laid over a drawing. I feel a deep sense of satisfaction. If anything, the facade of what had originally been an eighteenth-century town house, converted in the nineteenth century into a hostelry, is even more handsome than I remembered it.

Since I left Cardiff a couple of hours earlier, the weather has slightly relented. We are now enjoying what British broadcasters refer to as "occasional intervals of sunshine." The sun is penetrating the rents in the murk, as if a gray material has been slashed and stuffed with yellow rags. The bright rays slap with a sharp brilliance on the white plaster of the walls, the intense black of the stringcourses, the moldings of the windows. In case the traveler is in any doubt, the words *Bear Hotel* are repeated three times, once between the top-floor windows, once on the antique lantern hanging above the portico, and once on the portico itself. For good measure, beside the portico hangs an inn sign with a bear prancing merrily against a background of the surrounding Black Mountains. Even if you were illiterate, or drunk, you would know where you were by the picture of the bear on the painted sign, which I suppose was the original purpose of such inn signs. No doubt there were real bears in these mountains, at least until the time of Owain Glyndŵr or thereabouts; that, or else the sign betokened that this little town of Crickhowell (*Crug Hywel,* "Howell's Crag," in Welsh) was once a fiefdom of the Earls of Warwick, the great Marcher family whose coat of arms consisted of a bear with a ragged staff in its claws.

There is a pampered look about the building which it definitely lacked on the rainy day when Valerie and I arrived here on our wedding day, forty years ago. Britain was just emerging from World War II, during which nothing was painted and the ornamental railings that graced buildings like the Bear were torn down and carted away to provide scrap for munitions (a silly policy, since almost all of it was found to be completely useless). Everything was patched and peeling. Now the front of the hotel is a festival of geraniums and snapdragons, the window boxes on fire with petunias and impatiens, the lamps and lampposts draped with hanging baskets. Cotoneasters are trained around the archway, still bearing the words *Post Horses,* that leads into the big cobbled yard beyond.

As I hold the single bag that contains all the belongings I have brought with me from America, it occurs to me than I shall not be carrying into the Bear many more worldly goods than I carried into it almost half a century ago. The thought pleases me. It is as if I am duplicating that earlier and happier day. I have already taken pleasure in the way in which the journey up from Cardiff has been a virtually identical repetition of the journeys I used to make here in my teens and my twenties. It gives a sense of continuity to what in many respects has proved to be something of a disjointed and at times distracted life.

Then, as now, it should have been a simple journey. Crickhowell is no more than 25 miles due north of Cardiff. But, like everything in this endearingly cockeyed little country, it can only be reached in a devious and roundabout fashion. In Wales you can never approach anything directly; you have to do it obliquely, often by starting out in precisely the opposite direction. If you look at the map, the shortest and most obvious way to reach Crickhowell is to take one of the roads that lead straight up the Valleys, as Glamorgan folk call North Glamorgan. But those roads, through the coal-mining villages of Bargoed, Ebbw Vale, Blaina, and Brynmawr, are as serpentine as the black shafts and trackways below them. And since I am heading for the delectable ranges of the Black Mountains, I have no desire to take the edge off my first sight of them for several years by coming at them through the sooty tangles of the Welsh Rust Belt.

Accordingly, after arranging to keep on my room at the Lincoln Hotel, I took the train at Cardiff Central and set out not due north but due east. The little local train with its couple of coaches would bring me cranking around to Crickhowell through a softer and a greener landscape, and although today's ride was swifter and smoother, like my ride down to Wales from Paddington, it was still recognizably the same one I had made many times before, arousing many of the same sensations. Except for the posters, the station at Abergavenny, which is as far as the train would take me, looks exactly as it did in the 1930s, and the long descent of the steep hill to the bus station has altered not a jot. The Atomic Age has made little outward impression on those stolid villas with the big bay windows beyond the privet hedges.

Already, in Abergavenny, where I have to kill an hour before boarding the bus that will take me the final 6 or 7 miles westward to Crickhowell, I can feel the special atmosphere of rural Wales. Maybe I am doing little more than recapturing the impressions that this corner of Wales produced on me in childhood and youth. Yet I do really seem to sense a distinctive and individual quality in the very air I breathe, as I carry my bag along the twisty and congested high street of the modest market town toward the Welsh Guardsman, where I mean to down a sentimental pint. "That cordial air," Gerard Manley Hopkins calls it, in one of his sonnets, and indeed there is something invigorating and enfolding about it. It seems to stroke you. The feeling of being embraced is enhanced by the way the dark folds of the mountains press down into the valley as it winds away from the English lowlands into the heart of Wales. To the north are the peaks of the Sugarloaf, Table Mountain, Pen Cerrig Calch, Pen Allt-Mawr; to the south are Blorenge, Garn Caws, Mynydd Llangeynidr. Beyond the valley with its farms is dense and matted country. The mountains slink along beside the road and river. There is nothing grand and remote about them, like the mountains of Snowdonia; they crowd you and elbow you. The effect they make on you can be like the effect the Welsh people themselves often make on strangers: intimidating. I always feel nervously alive when I am in the Black Mountains, as if my nerve ends are exposed.

As the bus pulls out of the station and drives along the narrow country roads, the passengers settle down to a typical Welsh discussion of the personal habits and peccadilloes of their family and friends. What else are bus rides for? This is the kind of good old gossip which you used to hear on the train from Paddington and which I missed on my way down from London. Now the people around me are going at it hammer and tongs: all the local scandal—divorces, adulteries, social diseases, bankruptcies. All good knockabout stuff.

The woman sitting beside me is one of the most vocal of the lot. She is small, shapeless, spherical, in her late fifties, with her short, wiry, black hair starting out all over her head. She wears a knitted purple skirt and a purple silk blouse and hugs a string bag overflowing with vegetables. The seat rocks under me as she twists around and bounces about, hissing and whispering and spraying out indiscriminate slander. She keeps appealing to me, of all people, a total stranger, to confirm the scabrous snippets she is flinging around.

"Isn't that so?" She gives me a bump with the string bag. The carrots are sharp and painful. "Isn't that the truth, now?"

Another bump. "Isn't that what she said?" Fortunately the questions are rhetorical and need no answers. Nonetheless, I find myself slowly slumping lower and lower in my seat.

Fragments of accusation and invective fill the air like flying shrapnel. Most of the exchanges are good-natured, music-hall humor, meant to elicit laughs, but some have a hint of the malice and sarcasm that Gerald the Welshman noted about Welsh conversation all those centuries ago. He would still feel completely at home among these people, and I wouldn't be at all surprised if he joined in. He was very fond of the tart phrase, himself. When the bus sets me down, slightly breathless and light-headed, in the little square at Crickhowell, opposite the Bear, I can see through the rear window as it bumps off again toward Brecon that the passengers are still laughing and gesticulating and clecking away with the same animation.

If the outside of the Bear had struck me as being more spick-and-span than it was forty years ago, so does the inside. As I step through the front door with my bag, I see that its appearance and arrangement are recognizably the same. What has changed is the general atmosphere in the lounge and the bar, which in the aftermath of the Depression and the war years was notably drab and gloomy. In the winter of 1946, when Valerie and I first came here, Britain was suffering from a more serious state of deprivation than it was during the war, and the calorific intake of Britons had been officially set at 1,200 calories a day.

No sense of restriction now. The ale and the spirits are flowing, and the bar is alive with the banter and backslapping of a crowd of men and women who, when I have joined them, I learn have come to the Black Mountains for a conference on mountain rescue. The noise and laughter are further enlivened by what I gradually identify, to my astonishment, as the music of Mozart's oboe quartet, piped in over the loudspeakers. I have known this work from boyhood, in the old recording by the Griller Quartet and the inimitable Léon Goossens, but I had never expected to encounter it in an out-of-the-way place like this. Mozart! Alas, in the days ahead I am destined to learn that one can have too much even of Mozart. Apparently the oboe quartet is the one piece of music that the Bear Hotel possesses, and whenever it comes to an end it promptly starts up from the beginning again. Even Mozart can grow tiresome after the twentieth repetition.

Fortunately I am ignorant of this by the time I have had a snack at the bar, swapped some stories with the mountaineers, and been shown upstairs to my room. I had briefly scouted the rooms while booking in and had been absolutely bowled over to discover that the identical room where I had spent my honeymoon had just that moment fallen vacant. Some Welsh instinct had told me that it might be.

I drop my bag on a chair and go across to open the window. The busy and sunlit little square below me looks exactly the same today as it did then. Only I have changed. I would give everything I possess if Valerie could stand here beside me, leaning on the sill, breathing in the autumn air, enjoying the brilliance of the late-flowering geraniums, petunias, and snapdragons.

That night, in a dream, I get up from the bed and cross again to the window, open it, and lean out.

The view has completely altered. The square is utterly silent and deserted, the shops and houses are blank and shuttered. It is lit with a strange dull-bright radiance, a pewterlike glimmer, and I think it must be dusk or dawn before I realize that it is snowing.

The floor of the square is laid with large black-and-white squares, like flagstones, and here and there on the flagstones are squat, irregular patches of what look like dark purplish rocks. Looking up toward the sky from which thick flakes are falling, I can make out a series of shapes, some black, some yellowish white, gently bobbing and swaying about, as if blown by the wind. Then I see that they are large chessmen, and that they are suspended from the sky on strings or wires.

Is it the sky, or is it some sort of ceiling of soft, white cotton? Then I realize that it is neither, and that I am looking up toward a milky film that is the surface of the sea, and that it is from this that the big chessmen—kings, queens, knights, bishops, rooks—are hanging.

The town square is under the sea. It is snowing into the ocean: large, lazy flakes, like frozen tears. And now above the roofs of the shops and houses I can discern a subtle shifting motion, as if behind the square is suspended a background of cloths or tapestries of shot silk, moving gently and constantly with the action of the breeze and the tide. There is something immeasurably soothing about the rippling and weaving of those richly colored silks.

Then, as I lean on the windowsill, watching the lovely and unearthly spectacle, there comes into my mind the memory of the peep shows we used to construct in our lockers in the dayroom of my school in England. They were very elaborate and could take days to build. We competed with each other as to who could manufacture the most spectacular and imaginative. We used any glittering materials we could hoard or scrounge: silver paper, colored cellophane, scraps of tinsel and tissue paper. The lockers were narrow and deep, and we turned them into miniature Aladdin's caves, artfully lit by flashlights and Christmas bulbs. There were ships, automobiles, aircraft, fantastic figures that could be made to move by manipulating hidden strings.

It now comes to me that what I am gazing at from the window of the Bear Hotel is a peep show, like those peep shows at school. The square is a stage set, an illuminated box, and outside it, beyond the shifting and shimmering cloths of the backdrop, there is nothing. Beyond them is only blackness, infinity, a universal void.

And then, as I watch, the black-and-white squares on the floor of the square tremble and curl at the edges, gently detaching themselves, beginning to float upward through the wintry, watery light. And when they reach the level of my window, they change slowly into a flock of black and white birds, all flying upward and away out of sight.

I follow their flight with a sense of sorrow and joy, a feeling of mingled heartsease and desolation.

Once I knew these Black Mountains of Glamorgan, Brecon, and Monmouthshire very well. Waking next morning to a day of alternate showers and sunshine, I am tempted to head for at least a dozen different places.

There is Caerleon, the Roman Isca, headquarters for four centuries of the Second Legion. I could stroll about on the broad expanse of its grassy forum. Or there is Tintern, no more than 20 miles away, where I once used to fish for salmon with Jock Shelley. It was always enjoyable to picnic at Tintern, one of the best preserved of the great Cistercian foundations that were sacked by Henry VIII and his gang of Tudor real-estate developers. Or there are the Three Castles—Grosmont, Skenfrith, White Castle—a triangle of well-preserved fortresses built by the Marcher barons to guard the entrance into Wales afforded by the tongue of lowland thrusting between the Black Mountains and the Forest of Tintern.

Another favorite outing we used to take in the old days was to Llanthony, a Cistercian priory even more remote than Tintern, tucked into the valley of the Honddu only 6 or 7 miles across the mountains to the northeast of Crickhowell. Close to the broken pillars and fallen buttresses of the priory is a venerable public house, where (Welsh weather permitting) you can sit on a bench beside the front door and eat bread and cheese and drink excellent ale. Llanthony was once the private property of Walter Savage Landor, whose friends the Lakeland Poets took their ease on that same bench. And if you have a taste for these literary outings, then no spot is more evocative than Capel-y-ffin, 3 miles farther up the Honddu, even more unknown to the tourist and casual visitor than unfrequented Llanthony.

I stumbled on Capel-y-ffin more than forty years ago, when it was at the lowest point in its fortunes and was practically derelict. Here an eccentric Anglo-Catholic who called himelf Father Ignatius built his own monastery at the end of the nine-teenth century. As as young clergyman in London's Dockland, he had been a fiery social activist, which had landed him in trouble with his bishop. There were also hints of graver offenses, in the shape of trouble with choirboys and altar boys, which his superiors, in accordance with the usual practice, had hushed up. He thereupon went off to Wales and founded what was virtually his own religion. There in the Black Mountains he established his own version of the Abbey of Theleme, complete with an impos-ing abbey church around which were grouped commodious living quarters. In it he celebrated masses adapted to his own taste, in gorgeous vestments of his own designing, no doubt assisted by a choice flock of choir- and altar boys. When he died he was buried, like an abbot of old, in front of the altar of his own church, though soon after his death the entire edifice suddenly collapsed and fell in ruins about him.

Father Ignatius's monastic experiment failed to survive him, and the buildings lay empty until, in the 1920s, the artist Eric Gill, another free spirit, established there a quasi-religious com-munity of his own. Gill was a sculptor—his Stations of the Cross are in Westminster Cathedral—but is better known today as a magnificent wood engraver and a designer of typefaces. Much influenced by the ideas of Chesterton and Belloc, he founded a guild or commune of Catholic artists and artisans (among whom was included the Welsh poet and painter David Jones) at Ditchling in Sussex, and subsequently transferred it to Capel-y-ffin. I was very fond of visiting the place where those earnest souls had once lived and worked. Above the neat cloister was a small upper room where they attended Mass. It was perfectly plain, white-washed, with the atmosphere of seemliness and simplicity redolent of another small chapel, Matisse's chapel at Vence. Though not a believer, I used to like to sit there, in the stillness. It had the feeling of the small upper room at Galilee described in the Gospels. In the tiny churchyard at Capel-y-ffin you can see the small square tombstones fashioned by Gill for his friends and associates, and for local farmers and their wives. Fortunate bones, to rest for eternity under a stone with an inscription cut by the hand of Eric Gill.

I am not, though I have my share of Welsh melancholy and morbidity, a frequenter of graveyards, as many of my friends are. They like nothing better than a Sunday-afternoon stroll around Kensal Green or Père-Lachaise. And yet there is one grave in the Black Mountains, a mile or two from Crickhowell, that I have visited more than once. This is the grave of Henry Vaughan, one of the greatest of our Anglo-Welsh poets, who died in 1695 and is buried in the graveyard, close to the wall of the church, at Tretower. He was a country doctor, like Sir Thomas Browne, educated as so many Welsh professional men were from Tudor times onward at Oxford, whence he returned to Wales as a young man to live out the remainder of his life. On the title page of his works he added the word *Silurist* after his name, to denote that he was a descendant of the Silures, the Celtic tribe which inhabited those parts. Because of the musical quality of his verse, he became known as the "Sweet Swan of Usk," and it is with a wide view of the river Usk in front of him that he now lies, beneath a slab on which are inscribed his name, the dates of his birth and death, and the word *Peccator*, "A Sinner." Once, when I went there to pay my respects, I found that the last name written in the visitors' book in the little church was that of Edmund Blunden, a quiet and contemplative twentieth-century poet, also an Oxfordian, who had much in common with Henry Vaughan. I was pleased to be able to write my own name beneath Blunden's tiny signature.

But it is not to Tretower, Llanthony, or Capel-y-ffin that I decide to go today, neither to Tintern, Caerleon, or Three Castles. Today I shall not be mooning around any graveyards, although the ashes of the man to whom I intend to dedicate the next few hours were scattered twenty years ago on the mountains that rise behind the Bear and are blown around them by the pendent winds.

There is a steep lane directly behind the hotel, and after one of those big British breakfasts that I have grown unaccustomed to during my years in America, I seize Admiral Pickard and turn up into it.

A quarter of a mile of sharp climbing brings me out into a narrow country lane that goes curving up into the hills. Autumn is very much in the air. There is a sharpish edge to the wind. The sunshine is fitful, with low cloud going over and shadows racing up the mountainside. In ten minutes I am completely clear of the last house, walking briskly into an upland landscape that has scarcely altered in half a century, pausing wherever there is a gap in the high hedge in order to look down into the valley.

Crickhowell retains the compact and well-defined outline it had in the 1940s. Henry Vaughan, who rode these hills with his medical saddlebags three centuries ago, would have no difficulty in recognizing it now. The only difference is a small rash of modern houses and bungalows at one or two points on the outskirts. They are something of an eyesore, I suppose, but produce in me only a mildly jarring sensation. For there is something extraordinarily reassuring, as I gaze down into the pastures with their grazing cattle, about the spectacle of this little British country town. All the time I was roaming around Europe, Africa, Mexico, South America, Texas, Tennessee, its people were placidly pursuing their age-old avocations. Wars and revolutions have passed over it, where it lies cradled in the arm of the river and in the shelter of the hills. For a thousand years it has retained its essential shape. When we are young, we have the arrogant conviction that during the course of our lifetime the whole world must inevitably change and be utterly transformed, simply as the result of our having lived in it. When we are old, it is comforting, if chastening, to realize that in spite of all our impatience and sense of personal importance, most of the world has hardly changed at all, and never intended to.

Clusters of blackberries still hang thickly in the hedges. I pick and eat them as I walk. They are sweet, overripe, deliciously cool and moist. Will I find the village of Llanbedr as little changed by the years as Crickhowell? One part of me hopes so, yet I recognize that, in spite of what I have just said about the comfort of permanence, another part of me hopes sneakily that there might be at least a minimal amount of alteration. To revisit the scenes of one's youth is in itself a painful reminder of the passing of the years. The blow is only softened if the scenes and surroundings have been at least minimally changed. If they stand there, looking precisely the same, they reproach us, and in some obscure fashion we resent them. Better and kinder if their outlines have softened or shifted, if only by a fraction.

Llanbedr has always been important to me, a special place, very private, very personal. It has been necessary to share most of the other locations of my life with hundreds or thousands of other people. Llanbedr has remained mine alone, a retreat, unknown to the outside world, inviolable. Its image is a touch-stone, a talisman. For fifty years I have carried its image with me, an image of a secret garden, a Cythera. Once it existed in actual time, but over the decades it has been magically transferred, little by little, into the realm of memory, of the imagination. It has become timeless, preserved in a shining, amberlike manner in some distant corner of my brain. Llanbedr, with its church, its public house, its bridge, its river, is my quintessential Wales, my quintessential youth.

Llanbedr, above all, is the place where Boris de Chroustchoff and his wife Ida lived in a cottage at the end of a winding, woody Roman trackway that meandered toward the inner reaches of the mountains. As I step out along the upland road, quickening my pace in my eagerness to reach my destination, I am conscious that my heart is beating painfully. Will it be more bearable to find Boris and Ida's cottage intact, untouched by time, or would I feel perversely glad to find it neglected and laid waste?

It was, by any reckoning, a remarkable cottage to find in a Welsh *cwm* at any time, but particularly in the 1930s and 1940s. How could you expect to encounter, in such an unlikely corner of the world, in a province of subsistence farmers and sheep herders, a dwelling whose four or five small rooms would turn out to be an Aladdin's cave crammed with African jujus, Oriental masks, Persian paintings, Turkish silver, dinner services from the Russian imperial porcelain factory, incunabula, pictures by Kandinsky and Larionov? And how had all these treasures been transported up that cobbled Roman trackway, too narrow to admit the passage of a furniture van or even one of the small Morris Cowley cars of the period? The answer was that Boris himself had carried them there, on his back, across the bridge, along the bumpy path to the cottage.

There was a great deal of Tolstoy about Boris. He resembled Levin in *Anna Karenina*. He was by birth an aristocrat, born into a family of great fortune and estates, but he liked to effect the Tolstoyan high-necked blouse, baggy pants, and broad leather belt. His features were a blend of the aristocrat and the peasant: a high forehead combined with small, twinkling blue eyes and knobby, scarlet cheeks. There was a Mongolian slant to the eyelids and a pronounced Slavic cast to the whole face. He was short, but wide shouldered and immensely strong, as his feats as a lifter and bearer of heavy loads testified. He carried himself in the peasant way, hunched forward, and when he walked he took very short, rapid steps, shooting along at such a speed that, though I was thirty years younger than he was, I had difficulty in keeping up with him during our daylong rambles in the mountains.

This unusual inhabitant of South Wales had been born in Russia in the 1890s. Although I knew him for four decades, I never knew the exact place and date of his birth; in fact, I never gathered more than a vague hint or two about the details of his earlier life, since he was inordinately and unnecessarily secretive in the typical Russian fashion. His father or grandfather had been the imperial ambassador in Rome and Madrid, hence the sumptuous dinner services. From his general demeanor and the few hints he dropped over the years, I gleaned the impression that he had enjoyed one of those idyllic, ecstatic childhoods described by Vladimir Nabokov, his exact contemporary, in *Speak, Memory:* "In regard to the power of hoarding up impressions, Russian children of my generation passed through a period of genius, as if destiny was loyally trying to do what it could for them by giving them more than their share, in view of the cataclysm that was to remove completely the world they had known." It is more than probable that Boris and Nabokov knew of one another, though Boris was at Oxford when the Russian Revolution broke out and Nabokov was at Cambridge; but whether, with their spiky, quirky Russian temperaments they would have become friends is another matter. Boris intensely admired Nabokov as a writer, particularly his witty and erudite footnotes to his edition of *Eugene Onegin,* and shared with him an appetite for botany and arcane intellectual pursuits. With Nabokov it was butterflies, while Boris became an accepted authority on edible mushrooms, on certain categories of rare books, and on the coinage of the Moorish kingdoms of Spain.

After the outbreak of the October Revolution, Boris was never able to return to Russia. He never spoke of his family or its fate. Probably his parents and relations perished in the continuing horror that has been Russian history since 1917. Evidently he had a certain amount of money, at least at that time, for in the 1920s he set himself up as an antiquarian bookseller in Museum Street in Bloomsbury. From other sources, I gathered later that his methods as a tradesman seem to have been highly individual. He was anxious that his precious books should not fall into the wrong hands, so he would lurk behind the bookstacks, sizing up the customers who were browsing among the shelves. If one or other of them had an appearance that struck him as unsatisfactory, he would scuttle forward, snatch the book out of the customer's hands, and with a cry of "Not for sale! Not for sale!" return it to the shelves.

Not surprisingly, his business failed to thrive, and he was left with a large stock of valuable books on his hands, which eventually ended up filling most of the space in one of the two bedrooms at the Milaid Isaf, as his Welsh cottage was called. A fair amount of his capital was also lavished on his first wife, a beautiful and extravagant creature called Phyllis, who left him to live with Philip Heseltine, the composer. Heseltine, who used the pseudonym Peter Warlock, one of the greatest of British songwriters, killed himself at the age of thirty-six. These meager details only came to me by a sporadic and indirect route, largely through an Oxford friend of his called Lionel Jellinek, who eventually became a high-court judge. By the time I met Boris, in the summer of 1939, his circumstances had been greatly reduced—though no man ever contrived to live so well on so little. His Tolstoyan proclivities served him well, and he obeyed Voltaire's injunction to cultivate his own garden. He grew his own tobacco—probably the first tobacco to be grown in Wales—

and raised a wide and unusual range of vegetables. He was a close reader of seedsmen's catalogs. He made his own wines and liqueurs from his vegetables and fruits, and gave me my first taste of yogurt, of which he kept an ongoing supply from a basic culture. In the 1930s yogurt was a very exotic comestible indeed, virtually unknown, retailing in London for a guinea a pot, and eaten not as a dessert but as part of a regime ordered by Harley Street doctors for invalids and for sufferers from consumption. The simple, peasantlike existence Boris had chosen to live in one of the more inaccessible parts of Wales, after his affluent years in Bloomsbury, was largely self-contained, though for many of his supplies he was dependent on the local farmers, with whom he got on extremely well and who were vastly intrigued by this strange bird who had unaccountably landed in their midst.

It was lucky for him, when World War II broke out, that he was in fact living in such an isolated spot. He was not a British citizen, and the only official papers he possessed were those issued by the Nansen Society, a philanthropic organization founded by the polar explorer Fridtjof Nansen to provide the flood of postwar refugees with at least a temporary means of identification. Had he lived close to any important urban center, he would have been promptly picked up as soon as hostilities were declared and packed off to internment on the Isle of Man. As it was, he was spared, and only had to walk down to Crickhowell now and again to report to the local police sergeant.

He and Ida contrived to sit out the war in their Breconshire retreat quite cozily, and although wartime rationing and short-ages were a very real thing they were helped through, as I have said, by their farmer-friends, who like the peasants he had known in Russia were adept at concealing at least a few good things from the official gaze. I have no idea, again, how long he had been married to Ida. She was Jewish, a small, delicate, pretty, violet-eyed woman whose existence was absolutely and totally centered on Boris. She was expensively educated and had been used to a life of luxury, and her first years in the Black Mountains must have been difficult for her. But all she wanted, all she had apparently ever wanted, was to be with Boris, and no woman could have had a man more to herself than at the Milaid Isaf, and in wartime. She had even managed to make herself look like him, and when I first met her I assumed, from her dress and manner, that she was Russian and not the daughter of a Hampstead businessman. Her father disapproved of the marriage and had cut himself off from her during his lifetime, though after his death she inherited her share of his estate. Thereafter she and Boris lived in unaccustomed prosperity in a wooden house on Boar's Hill, on the outskirts of Oxford, which they turned into the equivalent of a Russian dacha. In the meanwhile, whenever things got tight, Boris could always sell a first edition of *Queen Mab* or *Confessions of an English Opium Eater,* or one of his Kandinskys, though such things commanded in those days only a fraction of what they would command today.

My introduction to the Chroustchoffs had come about through the good offices of an English master at my school: a short-lived, academically disastrous, but to me wholly inspiring appointment. In appearance Brian Lunn, alcoholic and epileptic, resembled Waugh's Captain Grimes or Isherwood's Mr. Norris, but he was the author of several accomplished books—the first real author I ever met—and was well connected in the literary world because of his brother, the critic and biographer Hugh Kingsmill. Brian introduced me in due course to Kingsmill, but it was to Boris, who lived in Wales and whom I could visit regularly in my school holidays, that I became closest. Looking back, I suppose that this strange Russian, already middle-aged when we met, became not just my mentor but something of a second father, since my own father had died only a couple of years before. God knows what effect this had on my character. How could a youngster, already sensing he wanted to become a writer and deeply curious about the world, not be drawn to and

influenced by such a pungently original character? The first meal
he cooked for me at the Milaid, after I had negotiated that
tortuous trackway for the first time, was a steak garnished with
*morilles* that he had gathered himself from one of his secret places
in the woods, and with it I drank my first glass of wine. Among
his other accomplishments, he was a very capable chef. During
my years in the Navy, he kept me provided from his mysterious
horde of stores with quantities of paprika, elsewhere unobtain-
able in wartime, which he instructed me to sprinkle on my Navy
food to make it edible: the most useful culinary tip I ever received
(though he did also tell me to add half a drop of Pernod to a
martini). His sense of taste was extraordinarily keen. When we
would forage in the hills for *morilles* or beefsteak mushrooms, he
would take me from one mountain spring to another. Where each
spring rose from the earth, he had fastened a pewter mug on a
chain. We would sample the water, and he would discourse on
the way the taste of one spring differed from that of another. He
not only gave me my first taste of wine, he gave me my first real
drink of water.

I think this may have been the single most important lesson
that Boris taught me. Like Lafcadio's uncle, in Gide's novel, he
impressed upon me never to value something overmuch because
you have paid a lot of money for it, and never to undervalue it
because it has cost you nothing. (My Uncle Evan Evans, he of
the many lawsuits, also once gave me an interesting piece of
advice. "My boy," he told me, when we were fishing together on
the Cardiff pilot boat, "whatever you do, don't open any envelopes that are brown, or any envelopes that have got little
windows in them." Alas, I never had the nerve to try it.) That
first sip of wine that Boris gave me was delicious—and so was
that gulp of water from a pewter mug. In later years, when I
became a persistent traveler, I was under orders to send him
menus from the restaurants I visited, and he was delighted to
hear that I had been sampling *la dinde des artistes* at Maxim's,

*ballotines de volaille Duc de Chartres* at the Grand Véfour, *étuvée de boeuf mâconnaise* at Lapérouse, *noisette de Marcassin St. Hubert* at Lucas Carton, or *pudding léger Montmorency* at Larue. Yet when we ate together at the Escargot Bienvenu in Soho, it was usually on a simple roasted fowl and a bottle of Quincy. Similarly, when he asked me to bring him back something from abroad, although I would sometimes treat him to a Parma ham or a *jamón serrano,* he would be equally contented with something unpretentious, like a box of Toscanas or a bottle of Fundador.

With any luck, most young men and women find some knowledgeable and kindly older person, amused and touched by youth and remembering their own, to help them through the earlier phases of their lives. Boris, a dedicated but discerning hedonist, was mine, to be followed a little later by Tom Henn, by Lance Sieveking, and by Stephen Glanville. I did not realize, at the time, how dearly bought his experience and his relish for simple things must have been. That trick with the paprika, that appreciation of a mouthful of fresh water—might they not have come from the experience of his Russian relatives in the czars' Siberia or in the Bolshevik gulags? In my memory, I always see the small blue eyes twinkling above the high red cheekbones, like a Slavic Father Christmas; he never let me see, and I really never suspected, the constant pain he must have felt in his condition of permanent exile. He had always loved England, and he had come to love Wales, but Russia was his country and he could never, ever, go back to it. The cheerful and stoic face that he, like me, had learned to put on at his English public school and university should not have deceived me about the extent of his loss. He had carved out, with Ida, his own little Garden of Eden in a nook in the Welsh hills: but, as Pasternak observed, "Life isn't simply a stroll across a field." It certainly hadn't been that for Boris, or for any other twentieth-century Russian. I doubt whether he was ever seriously tempted to apply for reentry to Russia, like his old

Bloomsbury friend Prince Mirsky, the chronicler of Russian literature, who went back and was swallowed up in the purges. What would have been the sense of that? The regime used constantly to urge Stravinsky to visit the Soviet Union: "Please come back," they would plead, "and we'll treat you like one of our own." "I know," Stravinsky used to reply. "That's what I'm afraid of." We are aware now of the perpetual state of fear and humiliation in which Prokofiev, Shostakovich, and every other person of intellect who was not a cynical hack were compelled to live out their days under the Soviet system. In America, I am sometimes given to describing myself to my friends as "an exile." But I am not an exile; I am a privileged sojourner in a great and hospitable country, and, although I have lived here for twenty years, I can buy an airline ticket and be back in Europe within twenty-four hours at any time I choose. For Boris, the door was barred.

There was something fine about Boris's attitude to exile. He never wrung his hands or indulged in self-pity. In spite of the fact that his whole life had been brutally dislocated by Lenin's revolution, he tried to dwell on whatever small positive aspects of life in Russia he could cull from the newspapers, of which he was an avid reader. For example, I recall how pleased he was to learn, soon after the German invasion, that the famous czarist regiment, the Preobrazhenski Guards, had been brought back into existence by Stalin, anxious to use any device, however unscrupulous, to save the country he had almost fatally weakened from being overrun. Boris exulted in the heroism of the ordinary Russian people, determined to defend themselves in spite of the bungling of Stalin and his clique. In this Boris's attitude was quite different, of course, from that of the British Socialists and Communists, whose pro-Russian stance was chiefly motivated by their admiration for Stalin and their desire to foster and spread the Marxist system. Socialism and Communism were nowhere so deep-rooted in Britain than in South Wales, and they remain so today. There have been no delegations of British parliamentarians or trades unionists who carried fraternal greetings to the Soviet Union, East Germany, or Romania in the last forty years that lacked their quota from the South Wales valleys. I wonder what Boris made of the fact, for instance, that 20 miles away from his retreat in the mountains was a Welsh mining village whose Communist sympathies were so rabid that it was commonly called Little Moscow?

As I have argued earlier, Welsh radical politics derived from Welsh radical religion. The meliorism of the Baptists and Methodists was the forerunner of the meliorism of the Socialists and Communists. The rhetoric was the same. If the Welsh miner succumbed to Communism, there was after all some excuse for it, given the grim character of his trade. But what are we to make of the British intelligentsia of the era, who embraced Stalin and all his works with such glee? For them there is no excuse; they knew very well what Stalin and his gang were up to, with the show trials, the purges, the forced removals, the collectivizations. It has always struck me as odd that the same people who were denouncing other people as Fascists or crypto-Fascists were never called to account for their overt espousal of a cause that was equally loathsome. Indeed, many of them boasted of their former membership in the Communist party as positively praiseworthy, a badge of honor, a testimony to their moral and political seriousness and commitment. They used it to further their careers, and it never affected them deleteriously in any way. Some of them even had the nerve to accept democratic and monarchical distinctions, becoming knights and barons and occupying seats in the House of Lords. The British establishment can be as cynical as the Russian in the way it adopts pliable people into its *nomenklatura*.

It may have been some connection of the Chroustchoffs with the Preobrazhenski Guards that made Boris so proud when he heard I had joined the Guards in Britain. He had always been generous with his gifts, which were seldom conventional, and I remember that he marked the occasion by sending me a magnificent eighteenth-century Japanese pillow book. During my years in the Navy and the Guards he also wrote to me regularly twice a month, budgets of gossip and good cheer in his own inimitable handwriting. Anyone who has been on active service will know what those letters meant.

Boris and Ida were grievously upset when, twenty years after the war, I decided to leave Britain for Texas. My original intention was to remain for no longer than a year or two, but I think they had a premonition that I would not return and that we would not often see each other again. In a way Boris had been responsible for my going, since he had early encouraged in me that restlessness and desire to rove which in any case was a part of my birthright. But by that time he and Ida had become very attached to my wife and our daughters. I was glad that, just before he died, he saw the dedication to him of one of my better books, appropriately enough a book of travels in Africa.

I had a premonition of my own, about his death. I have sometimes been subject, as many people have, to things of that kind. One hot summer afternoon, when I was living in London, I had a sudden overwhelming impulse to go and visit my old friend Jack Moeran, the composer, whom I had not seen for some weeks. I had no reason to suppose that he was in danger or ill health. I walked all the way from St. John's Wood to Hampstead, and can still picture the peremptory way I rapped on his front door. There was no one at home, and I turned away with a deep feeling of unease. That was the afternoon when he was accidentally drowned, in Ireland. Similarly, years later, when my wife and I were spending a summer in Mexico and were staying at Guadalajara, I had such a powerful sensation that something was wrong back home in Texas that, without stopping to phone, we jumped in the car and drove day and night until we reached El Paso. There I was told that the news had come in an hour before that my mother had suffered in Cardiff what was to prove a fatal stroke, and within another hour I was in the air on my way to Wales.

In the early 1970s I was in New Mexico, among the Navajo. I was climbing Shiprock, which in another place I have described as "a free-standing mesa of immense grandeur, breasting from the plain like a great thrusting galleon. To the Navajo, it is not a ship but the body of a sleeping god, in the form of an eagle. Always there are dust devils, cavorting puffs of loose brown soil, twisting and twirling about its base. They are like little acolytes. There are always five or six of them—more than you are likely to see at other times in the course of an entire day. They are at home at Shiprock: they are the grace notes of a living, singing landscape."

This was surely an appropriate place for Boris to bid me farewell. I had wandered a little from my Indian companions, and was gazing down the flank of the mesa. It was then that I saw Boris bustling down the trackway below me, trotting along with his quick, impatient steps, shoulders thrust forward, the way I had seen him a hundred times plunging down a hillside in the Black Mountains. As always, he was in a hurry, yet I had the impression, from the way he glanced up at me, that he was still annoyed with me for leaving Europe. He was wearing his peasant blouse and baggy pants, and loose stones sprayed out from under his sandals. He carried his small rucksack, in which to tuck away any choice and unusual objects he might encounter on the way to wherever it was that he was going. As he went slipping and sliding along, he kept his eyes fixed directly on me, the weather-beaten cheeks on the high cheekbones crinkling as he gave me a final smile. Then he flung up a hand, sketched an abrupt salute, called out a rapid and high-pitched "Good-bye, good-bye!" and hastened off into eternity.

*       *       *

There is no one at all in the village as I pass through. I would guess that even now Llanbedr possesses no more than a hundred souls, but it is eerie to see no one except a small child with a ball and a dog engaged on its desultory patrol. There is no traffic, no sound of a radio or a television. I pass the church. I pass the Red Lion, where in my Welsh Guards uniform I was treated to many a pint of cider and perry. There is a slight spat of rain as I head for the bridge that will take me to the track to the Milaid.

To reach the bridge, which is at the bottom of a small gorge over a stream called the Grwyne Fawr, you have to descend to a track just beyond the last house. For once on this trip my memory has failed me: I had forgotten that the track was so steep—as steep as the trackway down the side of Shiprock. The lapse troubles me, as if it was a small betrayal of the past, of Boris. Even while we are still living, time is busy obliterating the small details that together make up the sum of our existence.

I slither down the track, spattering loose gravel, marveling again at the pertinacity with which Boris transported his worldly goods in this forbidding place. The little crooked bridge, originally a Roman bridge but rebuilt centuries ago, looks in good repair, but again I had forgotten how closely the trees crowded together overhead, almost shutting out the sun. The narrow stream bounds over the boulders with its old force, but it seems to me that it is more littered than it used to be with dead and fallen trees. It must be, since it was here that I first taught myself to fly-fish, using my father's rods and with the help of manuals borrowed from the Cardiff Public Library, and the thickness of the undergrowth would make it quite impossible to back-cast now. And the deep pool upstream where I first saw a girl naked is so choked with leaves and debris that it is scarcely visible. I was crossing the bridge one day, on my way to the Milaid, when I spotted a girl bathing, very like the way in which Sir Peredur or Sir Lawnslot encountered beautiful girls in the *Mabinogion*. And she *was* beautiful, a Celtic naiad or dryad, though she disappeared too soon in a scramble of wet limbs and a tangle of wet hair.

I had expected that placing my foot on the path at the end of the bridge which could take me in another half hour to Boris and Ida's cottage would be a happy moment. To my dismay, I see that the entrance to the path is almost as neglected and overgrown as the stream that runs beside it. I remember it as open and speckled with sunlight; now it resembles a dark funnel, strewn with weeds and brambles. I walk forward a few yards into it, then stop. For the first time since my return to Wales, I am encountering something genuinely savage and sinister about one of the places which I frequented when I was young. Sometimes, as in the Cardiff Dockland, I had felt glum and mournful, but never that I was being threatened, or warned away. I recall that there was a grim old story, related in Gerald the Welshman's *Itinerary*, about this particular trackway. A young Welsh prince, accompanied by his retinue, together with his harpist and his falconer, was warned not to take the shortcut along the Grwyne Fawr. He ignored the warning and set out lightheartedly into that funnel ahead of me. And he and his companions, somewhere not far from where I am now standing, were ambushed and murdered. I used to find the story thrilling and romantic; now I find it frightening. Nevertheless, I square my shoulders, take a tight grip on Admiral Pickard, and go on. But after a few more yards I stop again. It is as though the path ahead was barred to me, as if I am being blocked out and turned away from my own past. It is disconcerting to have the impossibility of returning to the past demonstrated to me so bluntly and with such finality. Usually you are permitted a sentimental and consoling stroll through the places you once knew; you are at least allowed to cherish the illusion that you have not completely departed, that you retain some slight connection with them. Now I am being totally rejected, sternly cast out from this little Paradise of my boyhood and adolescence. I am being reminded that the past has got teeth in it.

I stand and stare into the inhospitable thicket of roots and branches ahead. I slowly retreat the way I came. By the bridge I turn and look back. I gaze for a long time into the stream. I realize that I shall not be coming this way again.

It is obvious that Boris and Ida's cottage, always so out of the way and of little use as a practical farmhouse, must be ruined and abandoned. In spite of what I was telling myself on the road from Crickhowell, about it being more bearable to find the place obliterated than to see it changed and in the hands of strangers, I feel a terrible and constricting sadness.

I walk back across the bridge. I begin to climb the slope. I am glad I refused to continue up the trackway, where I could have been ambushed by time and had all my memories murdered. As it is, it is possible—just—to pretend that the Milaid still stands there, lighted up and waiting for me, with the Persian paintings, the Indian tapestries, the books, the silver, the imperial porcelain, the Kandinskys, the Larionovs, the African masks.

I am surprised to find the church door unlocked. These are days when, as in medieval times, thieves roam around stealing chalices, patens, sacred vessels. They are also days when the Anglican church lacks priests and congregations, and when two out of three of the houses of God stand idle for weeks or months at a stretch. One priest has to serve several parishes.

However, the little church of Llanbedr (the Parish of Pedr or Peter) appears as neat and seemly as when I last saw it many years ago. Indeed, like the village itself, it seems somewhat better cared for than in the dreary days of the 1940s. There is a new little lady chapel, and its stubby tower is swathed in a bright orange tarpaulin to protect the work being carried out on it.

There are no workmen on the tower. There is no one inside

the church. Why is the village so silent? My guess is that all the men and most of the women go off for the day to work in the small factories in the industrial parks around Brecon, Crickhowell, and Abergavenny, while the children are probably bused off to school or nursery school. Once the men of Llanbedr were fighting the Japanese; now they are working for them.

I take a seat in one of the pews in the middle of the church. There are only a dozen or so pews, all told. I prop Admiral Pickard on the seat beside me. There is nothing grand or imposing here, as at Llandaff Cathedral with its vaulted roof and its great organ and its Christ in Majesty.

I had no deliberate intention of visiting the church when I left Crickhowell. Now I am grateful to have somewhere to sit and rest for a moment before the walk back, somewhere to settle my thoughts after the episode at the bridge. It has possibly affected me more deeply than I realize. . . . Boris . . . fishing . . . the naked girl . . . I can remember how once, fishing there, I had a kind of vision, a few unearthly seconds when I seemed to see directly into the heart of things. I was standing in the stream late on a spring afternoon, rod in hand, when the world seemed to take on a special radiance, a rapture. Everything around me, the trees, the rocks, the water itself, burned with an inner fire. It was the kind of moment that Vaughan describes in "The World":

> I saw Eternity the other night
> Like a great Ring of pure and endless light,
> All calm as it was bright.

I suppose most people, at least once in their lives, usually in childhood, have been visited by such a transcendent moment. For a second or two, I seemed to comprehend the delicate filaments that bind our existence to some invisible order of things. I understood what Trismegistos had meant when he said, "As above, so below." It was as if the river, the bridge, the water, the rocks and trees were only a reflection of something that existed elsewhere, in another dimension, in another and ideal state. I stood still at the center of a molten universe while the water flowed like flame around me. And then, at the moment when it reached its greatest intensity, the vision began to fade, and the bridge and the natural objects around me began to settle back into their familiar state: beautiful, but not with the luster and transfigured beauty they had possessed a few seconds before.

I have experienced several similar moments, though not often in middle age, when I suppose the muscle of the inner eye has grown flaccid. None of them, I think, was as vivid as the one that afternoon below the bridge, a few hundred yards from the church where I am sitting now. It is no wonder that I have been slightly shaken, and that I am glad of an excuse to relax a little before I must stir myself and say farewell to a corner of the world that is folded so intimately into the fabric of my existence.

Of course, I realize that I could have been moved to enter the church by the same impulse that moved me to attend the service at Llandaff. My ostensible aim is to snatch a breather before the tramp back to the Bear, but I could have done that just as easily by sitting under a hedge, with my back against a gate. No, I fancy that once more I may have been seized with that obscure intention to present a silent petition, to bring my most pressing problem to the attention of a deity in whom I am not really able to believe. Yet perhaps, I tell myself, seated in the kind of little Welsh church in which Henry Vaughan undoubtedly considered that he carried on a close and personal discourse with the Almighty, perhaps here there is a greater chance than there was at Llandaff that God, if he exists, might possibly notice me. In a cathedral he could be distracted by the singing, the ceremonial, the prayers, the booming of the organ. Perhaps here, alone in this little country church, on a weekday afternoon, I will stand out a little more, instead of being lost in the crowd. If it is also a slack weekday afternoon in Heaven, then perhaps the Big Welsh-

man in the Sky may also be glancing idly about. His gaze may be
attracted by the orange tarpaulin on the roof of the parish church
of Llanbedr. Who knows?

I sit as I sat at Llandaff, quietly and respectfully, as I was
taught to sit in the chapel of my school in England. At first my
thoughts are on the bridge, and the water under the bridge . . . a
man cannot step into the same river twice . . . everything is *panta
rhei* . . . "all things are a flowing" . . . The walls of this tiny
church must often have echoed the words of the hymn we used
to sing at school:

> *Time, like an ever-rolling stream,*
> *Bears all its sons away;*
> *They fly, forgotten, as a dream*
> *Dies at the opening day . . .*

From dream into dream . . . "Still glides the stream and will
forever glide" . . . The warmth of the autumn afternoon is
making me sleepy . . . "Before God can come in, things must go
out" . . . "The sacrifices of the Lord is a broken spirit." . . .

I force my eyes open and sit up straighter. "A broken
spirit." Why? Can one respect a deity who demands a broken
spirit? What use can we be to ourselves, to anyone, if we allow
our spirits to be broken? Does God really enjoy the spectacle of
broken-spirited people? There was nothing of a broken spirit
about old Rawlins White, my Patriot to Heaven, as he stood
upright amid the flame and smoke.

I rise. The lectern is a bronze eagle with outspread wings.
On it is an enormous Bible.

I go to the lectern. Since God will not vouchsafe me a direct
sign, I shall try the method of the ancients. I shall try a version
of the *sortes Virgilianae.*

I screw my eyes tight shut, as I used to do when I said my
prayers as a child in Welsh. I turn the parchmented pages,

hesitating between one page and another like someone told by a fortune-teller to select a card.

I let out my breath with a long sigh and open my eyes.

In the dim light I focus on the yellowed page with its red-ruled margin.

The verse on which my finger is resting does seem to contain a message, a genuine message, even though it is couched in the sibylline language appropriate to oracles.

I read the words aloud. My voice bounces off the white-washed walls. "Then cried the whole multitude, and said with a loud voice: Like as thou hast spoken, so will we do."

These, surely, are words of hope?

"As thou"—I?—"have spoken, so will we"—God?—"do"? . . .

Is there really some chance of recovery, however slight, for my wife's maimed left side, left arm, left leg, left foot?

I feel an uprush of gratitude.

Then my eye falls on the Gothic heading at the top of the page: Esdras I, IX, 10.

*Esdras?*

I leaf through the stiff pages.

Esdras is a book in the Apocrypha.

My message has been apocryphal.

Who says God does not possess a sense of humor?

As I walk back to the pew to collect Admiral Pickard, I remember the admonition of St. Paul: "We must not put the Lord to the test." Perhaps I have only got what I deserved.

I am quite certain that Valerie did not get what *she* deserved.

I shall walk back along the valley, under a gray Welsh sky, plucking the cool damp berries from the hedges.

"How foolish," Stendhal says, "to tease oneself with these great problems."

Absolutely.

Where better could I find, to say my farewell to Wales on the eve of my return to Tennessee, than Cardiff Castle on a warm, still, sunny autumnal afternoon? The castle, after all, is the center of the city which during my formative years was the center of my life.

I am viewing the city from a high point of the castle, where the whole of central Cardiff and its immediate suburbs are spread out in the mellow sunlight around and below me, like a map of my past.

I stand on the walkway on top of the wall that runs between one of the turrets and the gateway. Visitors pass by me from time to time to enter the interior of the castle in order to view the inner apartments, decorated by long-departed Marquesses of Bute in all manner of exotic and fanciful styles—a Moorish court, an Arab harem, a room dedicated to Chaucer's *Canterbury Tales*, an Art Nouveau nursery, a Gothic banqueting hall. I am familiar with these charming whimsies, a little unnerving in dark and provincial Wales, and no one seems to mind or pay attention to the lone figure with the silver-headed cane doing solitary sentry duty on top of the battlements.

The walkway is covered, but on the south side there is a clear prospect of the city through the tall arrow slits, and on the north side there is an unobstructed panorama of the plain of Glamorgan and the hills beyond.

Moving in close to the embrasure of one of the arrow slits, I can look down on the wide, grassy moat between the foot of the wall and busy Duke Street, with its cars and buses. Immediately below is the raised causeway leading to the gate surmounted by the sharpened black barbs of the portcullis. It was through that gate, or down the rough stones of the wall, that Duke Robert of Normandy, with the aid of some kind of makeshift rope, made his bid for freedom, possibly accompanied by his Manciple, and got bogged down in the mire. Off to the right are Sophia Gardens and the Cathedral Road, where my bag is packed and waiting for me in the hall of the Lincoln Hotel. Off to the left are the city hall, the law courts, the museum, the university, the main arteries of Queen Street and St. Mary's Street, and somewhere out beyond them the district of Roath and the Claude Hotel.

Turning around on the curtain wall with its Roman foundation, I can see the blunt masonry of the Norman keep on its towering earthen motte. Around its base, disdainfully strutting and preening, are the slowly moving dots of the white peacocks, the traditional inhabitants of the castle grounds. Behind the Norman bailey and motte are the ancient trees lining the banks of the Taff, its coal black waters coiling down from the Valleys past the Arms Park and out under Canton Bridge into the Bristol Channel. The trees are beginning to shed their foliage, and the tindery, burned-out, coppery leaves are spiraling and shimmering down.

I must leave soon. When will I be back? Will I ever be back? Gazing down from my vantage point high above the rooftops, watching the soft sunlight winking on the tops of the cars and buses and on the thick skeins of the pedestrians undulating among them, I find it curious to think that all those busy people are totally ignorant of the Whites, the Manchips, the Morgans, who were once such prominent people in the city and such an integral part of it. For something like a thousand years my relations and my wife's relations formed part of that throng down there, going intently about its business. They helped to build the city, they served the city, they bore it an obstinate love and a passionate loyalty. *"And now they have departed, and their place shall know them no more."* They have slid into oblivion with the FitzHamons, the Beauclercs, the Despensers, the Monthermers, the Clares, the Herberts, the Windsors, even the lofty and mighty Butes themselves, who refurbished this great edifice where I am now standing as a token of their wealth and grandeur, and who have dwindled in their turn, and in their turn have stolen away. In the final count, I reflect, hearing the boom and belch of the traffic and the constant low hum of the crowds, no one is indispensable, no one will be missed. The Whites saw themselves as forming part of the blood and bone of this place forever, and now the last of them is looking down at it from the castle wall and preparing to bid it good-bye.

There was a time, of course, when I felt I was altogether too much a part of it, when I felt trapped in it, when I longed to tear myself away. Most young men and women who are by nature wanderers and not stay-at-homes feel like that about their native place. I can remember the intensity of my longing to escape and the fierceness of my satisfaction when I did so. There was the usual phase when I even told myself that I hated it, that it was stifling me and threatening to choke me to death. I suppose these are feelings which many young people feel compelled to project upon their innocent native ground. Well—if I did, I recognize today that it was no more than a phase, a conventional period of revolt, and that Cardiff has been a constant background to my life, a place in which I am proud to be have been born and bred, a handsome, fine city, a city of character, mother to exceptional and individual people. It is pleasant to survey it through my arrow slit and know that I have shed all those fancied grudges, all that adolescent resentment, and that now, on the verge of saying farewell, I can allow all my affection and admiration for it to well up and take possession of me.

I have spent a busy couple of weeks since my visit to Crickhowell and Llanbedr. From Crickhowell I struck out west, then north, in order to make a round of personal visits. I strayed far beyond the boundaries of my home county to pay homage to Gwyn Jones, the doyen of Welsh literature and learning, at his home on the high terraces of Aberystwyth. There I was permitted to handle the Gregynog Press edition of his translation of the *Mabinogion,* one of the most beautiful books ever printed, and also to hold the enameled cross of the Order of the White Falcon bestowed on him by the Icelandic government in recognition of his work on the Norse sagas. Gwyn Jones's early novels, *Richard Savage* and *Garland of Bays,* made a deep impression on me as a boy in Cardiff in the 1930s, when I used to spend my rare sixpences on borrowing books from the circulating library in the Albany Road. They were among the novels that were instrumental, I think, in helping to steer me, in due time, toward the writing of fiction.

Thence I traveled to Criccieth, with its grim old castle dominating the shore, to stay with the distinguished scientist Mansel Davies. With him I visited Lloyd George's home, and his grave, and as a memento of my visit Mansel presented me with a splendid Welsh walking stick to add to my collection, its handle carved in the shape of a leaping trout, its eyes inset with garnets. And from there it was on to Anglesey, to spend some nights with Emyr and Elinor Humphreys. With Emyr, Wales's leading novelist and, I feel, a possible contender for its first Nobel Prize for literature, I toured the Bronze and Iron Age remains of that evocative island and stared sapiently at its sheep and its standing stones, neither of them in short supply. My other writing friends in North Wales, John Cowper Powys and James Hanley, are now gone, alas, from Wales, and from life, although their presence still lingers powerfully for me among the hills.

Powys, craggy and immensely forceful even at eighty, ended his days, writing fluently and vigorously to the last, in a tiny, whitewashed slate miner's cottage outside Machynlleth, the small town in North Wales where Owain Glyndŵr had established his parliament. One of Powys's last works was a long novel about Glyndŵr (all his novels were enormous boa constrictors). The front window of his little cottage looked out on the stark black slopes of Moel Hebog, the Hill of the Hawk, one of Snowdonia's fiercest peaks. He himself resembled an aged hawk. He lived austerely, subsisting on a Civil List pension, an instrument of the queen's private bounty. Together with his brothers, Theodore and Llewelyn, he was one of a writing family whose members employed utterly different but equally striking styles. Theodore, who lived to be nearly eighty, wrote in a manner that was genial, courtly, reminiscent of the eighteenth century, while Llewelyn, who died of tuberculosis in his fifties, typified Welsh gloom and pessimism at its most mordant and implacable.

When visiting Powys, my small daughters were always amused by the way he would stalk about his cramped cottage like a long, lean bird, his noble head with its abundance of white hair hunched into his shoulders, to prevent it from brushing against the ceiling. This posture he would exaggerate in order to provoke them into laughter, a sound he enjoyed. His style of conversation was as startling and original as his prose, and he loved to talk about America, where in his younger days he had traveled from coast to coast living the life of one of W. H. Davies's Super-tramps. He was something of a Beat writer before his time. One of his special cronies was Theodore Dreiser, a man as powerfully built as he was himself, and with whom, when they got drunk together, he would wrestle and roll around on the carpet. For many years James Hanley and I would make an annual spring trip across the mountains from James's home in Montgomery to bring Powys a ceremonial bottle of brandy, which the three of us lost no time in polishing off.

Hanley, unlike Powys, had no Welsh blood but was an Irishman, born in Liverpool, so he qualified as a Celt and almost as a Welshman. He was of middle height, reddish haired, very brawny and tough, and he walked with the rolling gait acquired in his years as a merchant seaman. His novels of the sea have been compared with those of Conrad. His cottage near Llangollen was as small as Powys's, and he lived a similarly simple and industrious life, happy among and endlessly fascinated by the Welsh. His *Welsh Sonata*, his tribute to what he considered his adopted country, is a small masterpiece. He, like Powys, came of a writing family. Timothy Hanley, his wife, was an excellent novelist, and his brother was a biographer. His son Liam, a dozen of whose paintings hang on my walls, is now reaching the fore as a painter. James and I were close friends and constant correspondents for forty years, and I grievously miss him.

As it always does, the Welsh landscape struck me, during my foray to North Wales, as expansive and immense: towering mountains, broad valleys, beetling crags, sweeping estuaries, wide rivers. It takes an exceptionally determined effort of the mind to remind oneself that these incomparable views are actually fashioned on a small scale, as if they were the product of some master craftsman who delighted in producing exquisite miniatures. Wales itself, after all, is a tiny country, only about 130 miles long from north to south. It is only after gazing at some splendid panorama, in awe, for some minutes, that one realizes that it is not really as huge as one assumes but is an effect of trompe l'oeil, a lovely and skillful deception. Wales is like one of those peep shows I dreamed about that night at Crickhowell: you put your eye to the peephole of the shoe box or the school locker, and a fantastic picture leaps out, highly colored, dramatic. That is why Wales can be likened to the work of some master jeweler, to a jewel box crammed with the most various and glittering pieces. Indeed there are times when I think of Wales as being nature's masterpiece, a small canvas on which every aspect of nature's skill is displayed in its most compact and concentrated form. Wales is nature in the mood of Fabergé, her atelier, her private art gallery, her personal sample case.

After returning to Cardiff, and spending time with the

composer Alun Hoddinott and his wife, Rhiannon, I celebrated another old friend in quite a different way: by eating a ceremonial lunch, on my own, at the Angel Hotel, down there across the street from the castle. I would probably have eaten a lunch at the Angel Hotel in any case, since it is Cardiff's grandest hotel, and by doing so I would have reassured myself that I was indeed one of the local boys who made good. But my chief reason for doing it is that I wanted to commemorate another friend, with whom I used to eat there in the 1950s. This was Saunders Lewis, by general consent one of the greatest Welshmen not only of our own century but of all time.

During his lifetime Saunders Lewis knew what it was to be both revered and reviled. Since his death he has been admitted to the pantheon of Welsh heroes. He was born in Liverpool, an English city with a huge and largely Welsh-speaking resident population, the son of a Calvinistic Methodist minister. He was studying at Liverpool University when World War I broke out in 1914, and he joined the South Wales Borderers and went out at once to Flanders. (The Borderers will be known to Americans because of the movie *Zulu*, which dramatizes their defense of Rorke's Drift.) Lewis was promoted to lieutenant and was wounded during the Battle of Cambrai, which witnessed the first use of the tank. His brother was killed at Nieuwpoort in 1916. After the war he finished his studies, became the county librarian for Glamorgan, and began his career as Wales's leading literary critic and the leading playwright in the Welsh language (Emlyn Williams was Wales's leading playwright in English).

In 1925, by which time he was a lecturer at the University College of Wales in Swansea, Lewis acted as a principal founder of the Welsh Nationalist party, the Plaid Genedlaethol Cymru, and later he established and edited its newspaper, *Y Ddraig Goch*, "The Red Dragon." His books and articles grew increasingly critical of the Welsh establishment and his fellow Welshmen, and in 1936, by which time he and Caradoc Evans were probably the two most hated men in the principality, he and two fellow Nationalists decided to draw attention to the grievances of Wales and the plight of the Welsh language by committing, quite literally, an incendiary act. In that year he and his friends set fire to some building materials on a beautiful stretch of the North Wales coast which the RAF had designated a bombing range, demolishing in the process a precious cultural monument. Afterward they gave themselves up to the police, whereupon they were sent for trial at the Old Bailey and sentenced to six months in an English jail. Their action was purely symbolic, not in any way an act of terrorism, though afterward Saunders became jocularly known as "Cinders" Lewis. Subsequently, in an action for which the University of Wales has every cause to feel ashamed, he was dismissed from his job and spent the rest of his life fairly close to the poverty line, eking out a living by means of his pen. The proudest and most flinty of men, he never uttered a word of complaint or self-pity, nor ever truckled to his opponents.

The Welsh, by the way, make rotten terrorists. They may demolish the odd tollgate and incinerate the odd cottage or two, but they lack the stomach for killing women and children and elderly aristocrats. Some years ago a Welsh Nationalist, of the so-called militant wing, was deputed to blow up a dam on Lake Vyrnwy, which supplies water to Birmingham. The Nationalists resent the idea of the English washing their dirty feet in our immaculate Welsh water. So he loaded his pockets with sticks of dynamite and wandered around the reservoir looking for a suitable place to operate. Unfortunately, he discovered that it would be impossible to blow up the dam without also blowing up some of the sheep that were grazing there. The Welsh love sheep. He was unable to face it. He burst into tears and staggered into the local police station to surrender himself. Some terrorist.

In many respects, Lewis resembled my father. Both were in some ways difficult men, obstinate and unyielding, and both possessed a natural authority and inspired a remarkable degree of respect. When I would lunch with Lewis at the Angel, the waiters and other diners would peer at him furtively and whisper to one another, though he would take not the slightest bit of notice. My father too had that kind of presence. This was the more notable because, unlike my father, who was very tall and slender, Lewis was a tiny man, who would scarcely have come up to my father's shoulder. But though he was diminutive, he was dapper, something of a dandy, always beautifully turned out, and as we made our way to our table his step was firm and his shoulders squared, as befitted a former officer in the Borderers, and those who looked up and met his eye quailed at the directness of his gaze. He was an absolutely regal little man. I regarded him as the uncrowned king of Wales. He was Owain Glyndŵr, up too soon.

Not only was he a dandy but he was fond of describing himself as a sybarite, and enjoyed whatever pleasures that he could afford and that came his way—enjoyed them frankly, not in the usual sneaky fashion of politicians who have once described themselves as radicals. We always spent a long time culling the wine list for a promising claret. He favored the French wines because he was a great Francophile, considering himself a disciple of Mauriac, Claudel, Rivière, and Gilson and proclaiming that as a dramatist his chief inspiration was Corneille. Not surprisingly, for an admirer of Claudel and Mauriac, he became a Roman Catholic, though such a step was certainly surprising for a Welshman and positively startling for the son of a Calvinistic Methodist minister.

Like the acts of the heroes of Corneille, everything this gentlemanly man had done had been extreme. His career was extreme, his religion was extreme, his politics were extreme—his poetry and prose were extreme, though extreme in a rigorous, classical fashion and not a florid, romantic one. He was undeniably radical, but the Republicans and Marxists who have now taken over his Plaid Cymru can never have read much of his work. He detested Socialism and Communism, as he detested the

Fascism of the day, though the Socialists and Communists hit back at him by accusing him of Fascist sympathies and of being a Welsh Charles Maurras. He was essentially, I think, an anarchist, with a vision for Wales analogous to the ideas put forth in Prince Kropotkin's *Mutual Help*. In his unique and individual way, he also contrived to be at the same time an anarchist and a royalist (like Herbert Read) and something of a capitalist into the bargain. If our fellow diners at the Angel fancied we were earnestly discussing literature and politics, they were likely to be wrong; what we were probably discussing was the state of the stock market, since we were both at that time, as our means allowed, avid speculators. As for royalism, although his ideas for Wales were revolutionary, he was firmly in favor of the monarchy, which in any case he regarded as more Welsh than British or English, and our first toast in our claret or burgundy, in Welsh or English, was invariably "The Queen."

At the period when we frequented the Angel, we were both writing plays for Emyr Humphreys, who had created a corps of playwrights, some writing in English, some in Welsh, and a repertory company of Welsh actors to present their work. They were stirring days, and when Emyr would sometimes find himself producing pieces by Lewis and me back to back, or even simultaneously, while he was busy in the studio I would take Lewis out for a leisurely lunch. His days as a politician were behind him, he had resigned or been relieved of all his offices, and he regarded himself as a total political failure. None of his prescriptions had been accepted or acted upon, and his campaign for the preservation of the Welsh language, the centerpiece of all his efforts for more than three decades, appeared to have foundered. He talked of his failure not with anger or self-pity but with a kind of blitheness. More even than most Welshmen, he had a certain relish for failure. He showed the fatalism and fortitude of a hero of Corneille. The compensation for his abandonment of politics was that he was able to devote his final years exclusively to poetry and the drama. Yet though he talked about failure in such a debonair fashion, after his death he has turned out to have been truly a remarkable prophet. His chief concern was always to see Wales shed the monstrous apparatus of heavy industry that had deformed it during his lifetime, after which it could reassume its proper and ideal proportions as a country in which agriculture should be supplemented by only the lightest of light industry. With the elimination of coal and the scaling down of steel, this has happened. Although he was a capitalist and not a socialist, the capitalism which he preferred, and which was peculiarly appropriate for a small country like Wales, was a small capitalism, akin to the cooperatives of the anarchist writers, and this too has largely come about. The big combines no longer seem to dominate the scene in the way they still do in England, or where they exist they operate on a less oppressive scale.

What Lewis especially loathed about the Wales of his day was its narrowness of outlook and its provincialism, which could be ascribed to the overriding influence of the Methodists, the Baptists, the Calvinists, and the other sects miscalled Nonconformist which exercised an iron and often callous conformity. He was repelled by the spectacle of a country so inbred, so self-absorbed. He had a fancy that Wales could be like the Catholic Wales of the Middle Ages, when a Gerald the Welshman could go to be educated in Paris and make frequent journeys to Rome, and when the kings and princes of Wales sent embassies and exchanged emissaries with the crowned heads of Europe. For this his contemporaries scoffed at him and called him a reactionary and an obscurantist. But lo, in the course of time, and though he himself is not here to see it, in a curious way this too has come about.

Now that Nonconformism, together with Socialism and Trades Unionism, has lost most of its authority, the suffocating and puritanical atmosphere that I remember from the days of my youth has been largely dissipated. A scant twenty years before our festal meetings at the Angel, Lewis and I would have been hard put to it to find a glass of wine anywhere in Wales. Today, as with everywhere else in the world, the spread of television and the speed up in communications has had a tonic effect on Wales, opening up its hitherto sheltered valleys and shuttered communities and giving it a feeling of kinship with the great world outside. It is harder than it was for religious and political authoritarianism to flourish when, despite all efforts to prevent them from doing so, populations receive tidings of the often far superior way of life enjoyed by societies elsewhere. For some time the writers, composers, and artists of Wales, without losing their own national identity, have been following Lewis's example and launching out into the artistic mainstream. The whole movement, of course, has been given a general and increased impetus by the onset of the Common Market and the European Community. Paris and Rome and the other cities of Europe are now as accessible to Wales as they were in the Middle Ages and have become an even greater part of its conduct and consciousness. My impression is that the Common Market and its extension into Eastern Europe is destined to prove a blessing for small countries. They will find themselves on a much firmer footing of equality with their larger and more powerful neighbors. They will be accorded greater respect, and their voices will be listened to. If the Baltic republics could start to make themselves heard within the stultifying confines of the USSR, how much brighter is the opportunity for little Wales within the immeasurably more enlightened and decent corpus of the European Community?

Only in one area does it appear that Lewis's hopes for Wales have received a setback—and this, unfortunately, was the area to which he attached by far the greatest importance. His main concern was the preservation and propagation of the Welsh language, of which he himself, as poet, essayist, and dramatist, was such an outstanding exponent.

It was to try to stop the shrinkage and possible extinction of the language that he had founded the Plaid and edited *Y Ddraig Goch*. He believed that a nation which has lost its language is a nation which has lost its soul. In 1891, when the first language census was taken, more than half the population spoke Welsh. By the outbreak of World War I in 1914, the proportion had dropped to 40 percent, and by the outbreak of the Second World War in 1939 to 30 percent. By the 1980s it had fallen to below 20 percent. A disastrous and precipitous decline.

Will the death of the language be the stiffest part of the price which Wales may have to pay for that increased and generally beneficial exposure to Europe and the outside world of which I have just spoken? Such a price would, indeed, be a grievous one. I have always found it very difficult to explain to most of my English-speaking friends in England and America the extent of the cultural tragedy that would occur were the language of this small nation to dwindle and perish. The English have always felt resentful of those who refuse to speak the imperial tongue, particularly when, like the Welsh, they persist in speaking their uncouth lingo in the heart of the British Isles itself. Why can't such people see the blessing and beauty of being able to express themselves in the tongue that Shakespeare spoke? Why should they want to cling to their outlandish dialect when so many other nations have been eager to abandon their original language and adopt English? Why should they make such a fuss over their potty little patois when it is so obviously impracticable and such a brake on their progress? The English get quite worked up about it. After all, it was not so long ago that, purely with the best interests of the Welsh in mind, they were making determined efforts to stamp the Welsh language out. Almost within living memory it was an offense for children to be caught speaking Welsh in school. Schoolteachers in Wales were encouraged to make use of a device known as the cribban or "the Welsh Not," a wooden tally which was hung around the neck of any child who inadvertently spoke Welsh in class, as a reminder that the

Welsh language was "a *Not.*" The Not was transferred to the neck of each successive pupil who talked in Welsh, and the pupil round whose neck the tally hung at the end of the day was given a beating, in the good old English fashion.

If the English have had plenty of troubles with their other minorities, Scotch and Irish, at least they have never had to worry about the question of language. Scots Gaelic and Irish Gaelic obligingly died out of their own accord. Only Welsh, by some irritating accident, hung on. How much longer it will be able to do so, with the number of its speakers so dramatically reduced, is open to question. One can only say that, if the Welsh language passes away, something very precious will have vanished from the world. Welsh is no primitive argot, but an ancient and sophisticated language with a peculiarly rich recorded literature that reaches back for almost two thousand years. It has been the instrument of incomparable poets and of very significant novelists and dramatists. I believe firmly in the enriching and enlivening quality of nationalism. Nationalism may have its drawbacks, as a source of conflict and dissension, but it is also a guarantor of physical and spiritual liberty. The Russians could not subdue the Balts, the Poles, the Hungarians, the Czechs because they did not want to be homogenized into the Soviet-style New Man; they wanted to remain Balts, Poles, Hungarians, and Czechs. Similarly, why should we want literature, music, and painting to conform to some featureless and uniform international style? Surely one would prefer French music to sound like French music, Spanish music like Spanish music, Italian music like Italian music?

Therefore, if a language like Welsh is lost, the world will lose just a little of its richness and variety, it will become just a little bit blander. And the Welsh themselves will have lost, if not their soul, at least a sizable portion of it. Even Welsh men and women who are non–Welsh speaking are proud of the language and regard it as a unique possession, although they are sometimes annoyed by the intemperance of the Welsh Language Society and similar groups. They wish the language well and want it to flourish. And indeed, to a hopeful and increasing extent it does in fact flourish. There are indications that it may be on the point of making a recovery. Consider what has been achieved since Lewis founded the Plaid in 1925. Publications in the Welsh language have continued to thrive, and the prospects for the language have certainly been increased by the existence of Welsh radio and Welsh television. Official documents are now bilingual; my father's death certificate did not contain any Welsh, but my mother's did. Accused persons have the right to be tried, if they so desire, before a Welsh-speaking magistrate. When I stepped off the train at Cardiff Station at the beginning of my visit, the first words I saw on the platform were CROESAW Y CYMRU, which would have been a decided novelty when I used to travel down on the old Great Western as a schoolboy. The public signs and street names that I can see from my perch up here, high on the walls of the castle, are written in Welsh as well as in English.

All may not be lost. How can a language be said to be moribund if more than half a million people still speak it, still cherish it, still actively promote it with zest and passion?

Before leaving Tennessee, I had drawn up a list of the places in Glamorgan or not far from its borders that I intended to visit. High on the list were the names of Talgarth and Minsterworth. It took me only a few days to realize that I would visit neither of them.

At Crickhowell, I was only 10 miles from Talgarth. It was not much farther than Llanbedr. I could have walked it in a morning. I had meant to. At the last moment I knew I could not face it.

At Talgarth is the sanatorium where my father spent two of the final years of his relatively short life. It is situated high up on a Breconshire plateau, in the expectation that the cold mountain air would help to heal the lungs of the tuberculosis patients. It is a bleak and windy spot, exceptionally harsh in winter. Once a month, when I was a child, my mother and I would be motored up by my Uncle Arthur to visit my father in the chilly little cubicle where he lay in bed, waiting for the next useless operation, watching the sparrows outside his window feeding on the fat he saved for them from his meals and put out for them in coconut shells.

Talgarth was my Magic Mountain. I was an infant Hans Castorp. I remember the slow and pallid sufferers, the brisk and efficient doctors and nurses, and the large bronze bust of a well-fed and healthy-looking King Edward VII that stood in the hallway. I remember the nervous gaiety with which we set out early from Cardiff for the ride up through the Valleys, bearing the special foods and delicacies that my mother had cooked and baked to try to stimulate my father's appetite. I remember my overwhelming impatience to see him and my puzzlement when I was forbidden to go close to him and embrace him. I remember the long, hushed, white afternoons, playing idly at the foot of the bed while my mother and my uncle tried to make cheerful conversation. And then would come the long ride home again, in the dark, pressed up against my mother, both of us tired now and sad, while the carbide lamps of our car (a Swift—a short-lived and long-dead marque) threw long shadows on the crooked walls of the mining villages, themselves enduring an economic tuberculosis during those years of the Great Depression.

In Tennessee, I had speculated about what Talgarth would look like today. Penicillin had been discovered and had eliminated TB in Britain only a year or two before my father's death— just too late to save him. Had the sanatorium been torn down, like those prisons whose walls had become infected with prison fever? Or had it simply been abandoned by all save the sparrows?

Did the bust of King Edward still preside over the deserted hallway?

I was curious. I had meant to make Talgarth part of my personal pilgrimage. But in the event I found I lacked the courage. Talgarth still represented a raw and ulcerated place in my heart.

But Minsterworth? Surely I could manage to get to Minsterworth. Thirty-five miles from Crickhowell. Fifty miles from Cardiff. What memories did I have of Minsterworth except memories that were happy and radiant?

Of course, I can see now (living life forward but understanding it backward) that my years at Minsterworth Court probably constituted the crown and summit of my life, such as it has been. Perhaps I really knew it even then. That may be why, in the end, I found it too painful to risk going back to take a look at it, any more than I could screw up the courage to walk up the Roman track across the bridge and take a look at Boris and Ida de Chroustchoff's cottage. Once more I wanted to keep the image of the place intact and pristine in my mind, untouched by the intervening years.

I last set eyes on the court on the day in August 1967 when I drove out of the yard and through the white front gates on the way to Southampton. There I would board the *France*, which would take me on the first stage of my journey to West Texas. Dawn was breaking, and it was pelting down with rain. As Valerie and my small daughters ran through the downpour to kiss me good-bye, I felt an excruciating mixture of elation and regret—elation because of the adventure that lay ahead, regret because I somehow sensed that I was not destined to see the court again. My wife was staying behind for only as long as it took to sell it, and would then bring the children and join me in America. All around me in the car, piled high on every seat so that I could scarcely turn the wheel, were the personal possessions I would need during my first weeks in Texas. They hemmed me in, and there were a lot of them, since Siegfried was an enormous car.

Siegfried. He lived up to his name. He was heroic. He was Wagnerian. He had known victory, defeat, Götterdämmerung.

He was a Mercedes 540K, custom-made in 1936 for the chief engineer of the Untertürkheim works, which would be bombed out of existence during World War II. To be a chief engineer of Mercedes in 1936 was a distinguished position. This was the era in which Neubauer was in charge of the Mercedes racing *équipe*, whose brilliant white machines, driven by men like Carraciola, von Brautchitsch, Delius, and Richard Seaman, dominated the European circuits. Siegfried was an opulent tourer, built on elegant and imposing lines and with sumptuous appointments. He weighed 2 tons. His fascia board featured a clock, a cigar lighter, and a car radio which could once be tuned in to such exotic stations as Königsberg and Klaipeda. All of them still worked perfectly when, twenty-five years and God knows how many hundreds of thousands of miles later, I bought the car in Madrid. The gearbox was synchromeshed on all except the first and second gears, one of the first cars to have it.

The car had ended up in Madrid because, according to its logbook, which had by some miracle survived, the chief engineer had surrendered it to one of the generals commanding the German Condor Legion which had fought with the Loyalists in the Civil War. It had stayed in Spain after the Civil War ended, and when I bought it it was still in its wartime livery of *Feldgrau*. On the day I saw it parked outside the Castellana Hilton, where I had been living for two years while working on epics for the Bronston company, it looked battered and forlorn. I knew I had to have it. I waited beside it for its owner to return and bargained for it on the spot. It was a machine made for an author (particularly the author of a biography of Moritz von Sachsen) to parade about in, and the fact that I was British and it could be regarded as the spoils of war was an added fillip.

I took it to a shop at Las Ventas and had it sparklingly repainted in black and yellow and its worn gray upholstery renewed. However, when I first drove it back to Britain, its cylinders were in such bad shape that when I reached the Pyrenees I had to climb them backward, in reverse gear. In Gloucestershire our village blacksmith (always the Wagnerian touch with Siegfried) put the engine back into shape, and in the years that followed I drove it all over Europe, through Mexico and Central America and the American Southwest, and several times back and forth between the Atlantic and Pacific coasts.

Even now, many years after parting with Siegfried, I still often fall asleep soothed by the memory of those long drives. I am bowling along across the deserts of New Mexico or Arizona, the canvas top down, the buttes and the mesas wheeling past. I am wearing my white linen cap with the goggles pushed up on top—what my disrespectful Texas friends called my Desert Fox outfit. The broad, empty road stretches out as far as the horizon, bisected by the sun-struck Mercedes star on the glittering expanse of the radiator. The star rocks gently up and down with the soft motion of the springs, more like the motion of a ship than that of an automobile, and in fact driving Siegfried was more akin to steering an ocean liner than driving a car.

I owned Siegfried for fifteen years. I parted with him in a moment of abstraction that I bitterly regret. After five years in the United States, we had sailed back to Europe with the intention of once more settling there; then we changed our minds and decided to return to Texas. To mark what seemed a definitive break, I divested myself of most of my European possessions, including Siegfried. This was a mistake, a bad example of Welsh impetuosity. And in the case of Siegfried it was more than a mistake; it was a betrayal. He deserved better of me. I have suffered for it. Wherever he is, and whether or not he is still wearing my colors of yellow and black, I think of him and I wish him well.

Of course, personifying an object of metal, rubber, and leather as "he" is an example of the pathetic fallacy. Selling an automobile, even an automobile that has been deeply cherished, can only be described as a relatively minor error of judgment. But selling Minsterworth Court—that was a major blunder. Selling the court was arguably the biggest single mistake I ever made. Why do we do such things?

The lives of all of us probably possess some apogee, some high-water mark, though we often fail to recognize it at the time. We assume that the moment we are now living through is the crest of the wave, but in fact the wave may have crested far back and long ago. It may be only many years later that we realize it. My own personal high-water mark might well have been the years I spent at Minsterworth . . . so what could it have been, apart from that fatal native restiveness, that prompted me to leave it?

When the defeated Napoleon was taken aboard the HMS *Bellerophon*, he was simpleminded enough to believe that his captors were transporting him to England, where he would be allowed to settle down to the agreeable existence of an English country gentleman. Another defeated emperor, William II of Prussia, on his way to exile at Doorn in Holland, also pined for the life of an English country squire, which he declared was the most agreeable on earth. I, having attained the goal to which these august personages aspired, cast it all away.

Minsterworth Court was not particularly large in size or extensive in acreage, but in the way that Wales is the Fabergé of countries, Minsterworth was the consummate jewel of an English country estate—and an hour's drive from Wales and Cardiff into the bargain. It was also in Gloucestershire, one of the most agreeable of English counties.

To reach it, you left the city of Gloucester on its western side, the side on which stood the great Norman cathedral with its massive drum pillars and its soaring square tower. You then crossed on to the far bank of the Severn by means of the medieval bridge at Over, where the monks once made some of the best wine in England, and a couple of miles farther on, tucked between the high road to Wales and the Forest of Dean on the one hand and the Severn on the other, you came to the small and straggling hamlet of Minsterworth. The hamlet, with its public house at one end and its parish church at the other, was already a settlement in Saxon times. The names of several of its modern inhabitants figured in William the Conqueror's Domesday Book.

The Court was situated in the middle, between the church and the pub, on a narrow stretch of what was once a Roman road, not too far from the village school. The village school, which was to be attended by my daughters, was Victorian, and the church, though heavily restored, had Saxon associations. In one corner of its little graveyard, abutting the river, was the grave of the local poet and local drunk, Fred Harvey, known as the Gloucester Lad, in allusion to Housman's Shropshire Lad. Like that other and greatly gifted Gloucestershire poet Ivor Gurney, who died in a lunatic asylum, Harvey had been badly shell-shocked during the First World War. No one returned from Flanders completely sane. Every St. George's Day, when the flag of St. George was flying above the church tower, I would read one of the Gloucester Lad's poems over his grave and place on it, and on those of the four other British soldiers whose graves were in the churchyard, one of my choicest roses.

In the Middle Ages the houses named Courts were actually the residences of the local magistrates, who dispensed justice there and consigned the major offenders to lockups on the premises. I often wondered whether one of the ghosts who were inevitably said to haunt Minsterworth Court may have been one or other of these unfortunates, though I never heard any moaning or clanking of chains. The only ghost I may have glimpsed there I saw in broad daylight. Working at my table in the library window one summer morning, I looked up and caught sight of a broad-shouldered, shortish man strolling away from the house across the lawn, in the direction of the river. He was wearing oxblood leggings, buff-colored breeches, and a coat of some bottle green velvety material. He was bareheaded and carried his black cap in his left hand. I saw the brass buttons on the cuff of his other arm wink in the sunshine as he tapped his thigh with his crop. It struck me that he was a member of one of the local hunts, the Beaufort or the Severn Vale, who for some reason was taking a shortcut across my grounds. The only other thing that crossed my mind was a mild surprise that his clothes were muddy, since it had been a long, dry summer. I went back to my writing, and when I looked up again he had disappeared from sight.

It must have been several months later that an elderly neighbor who had a fondness for local history told me about a harum-scarum character called Dick Hawkins who had owned a house on Elmore Back, on the opposite bank of the Severn, in the 1820s and 1830s. He had sundry lady friends in Minsterworth and its neighboring parishes and used to ride his horse across the river to visit them. He would tie his horse to a tree in my orchard. One day, riding back, he and his horse were caught by the tide or the Severn Bore and drowned. So—just possibly—the sunlit stranger sauntering across my lawn may have been Dick Hawkins. Probably not. However, thinking about it, I realized that neither the members of the Beaufort nor those of the Severn Vale wore bottle green hunting coats.

My library was the oldest portion of the Court, a long, low, irregularly proportioned room with gnarled black beams and with an iron fireback on the broad hearth that was dated 1644. This part of the house dated back to the fourteenth century, when it was built by John of Gaunt, lord of the Duchy of

Lancaster, as a gift for his wife Blanche of Lancaster. It was Blanche of Lancaster's death, at the age of twenty-nine, that prompted Chaucer to write his *Book of the Duchess*. This segment of Gloucestershire, six hundred years later, was still in possession of the Duchy. Being part of the Duchy had its advantages even in my time, since Minsterworth traders and fisherfolk were entitled to use the Severnside harbors and markets free of dues. As Brian Waters, the historian of the river, wrote, "No privilege appeals to countrymen more than one which allows them to go free where others have to pay, and being in the Duchy has made Minsterworth a village of haughty, mellow folk." In the tack rooms below the library the original fourteenth-century walls and some of the ancient pargework could still be seen. Later the house passed into the possession of the Tudors and was bestowed by Queen Elizabeth I, as I mentioned earlier, on her personal genealogist, Gwilym the Herald. It pleased me to have a kind of personal contact, through a man who bore the same name as my father, with our redoubtable Welsh queen, the red-haired Gloriana.

This library and the rooms below it, together with the congeries of outbuildings that surrounded them, no doubt constituted the court of those days. Then, at the end of the seventeenth century, a completely new house was added onto the earlier structure, and the long upper room was converted to a library. This new house was a typical William and Mary box, four rooms up and four rooms down. Perhaps because it was not unduly large, it had an air of exceptional elegance, and in the course of time it had acquired such embellishments as eighteenth-century plasterwork and Adam fireplaces. Then, at some stage, the original house had been stuccoed and washed a dazzling white, and the exterior trim painted a subtle and unusual shade of turquoise.

The setting was as handsome as the house itself. To one side, beyond the paved and sunken Italian garden, was a boxwood walk, with a vegetable garden beyond. Beside the Italian garden, fronting the lawn, was an eighteenth-century gazebo. On the other side were the outbuildings, the yard, the carriage house and garages, the vinery, the orchard. The windows and French window on the eastern side opened on the lawn, with the fountain and goldfish pond, the dovecotes, the ha-ha, the fenced-in paddock running down to a wide vista of the Severn. One side of the paddock was dominated by a huge wellingtonia, one of the tallest trees in Gloucestershire, planted in 1815 to celebrate the Iron Duke's victory at Waterloo.

At the far end of the paddock was a strip of land which, every spring, was smothered in a fantastic profusion of daffodils, jonquils, and hyacinths. A former owner of the court, who belonged to a family that rejoiced in the name of Vyner-Viner-Ellis, had been one of the pioneers in the cultivation of the modern daffodil. These were the trial beds of the varieties for which she had gained many medals at the Royal Horticultural Show. They made a brave display against the slate gray setting of the river. Again, it was a grateful Welsh touch, this array of "St. David's lilies" that attained their glory on the saint's name day, March 1, Wales's national day. It is interesting to note that the tall flower we are familiar with today as the modern daffodil did not exist until fierce old Granny Vyner-Viner-Ellis, reputedly the severest of the local magistrates, produced them. The flowers that St. David saw on the hillsides of Cardiganshire and Words-worth's "host of dancing daffodils" were actually the diminutive and delicate jonquil.

The broad reach of the river itself, beyond the bottom of the paddock and the daffodil beds, possessed its own particular interest. It is here that, at the spring and summer equinoxes, the Severn Bore reaches its maximum height and majesty. The Bore (the word derives from the Anglo-Saxon *bara*, a wave) occurs when the waters of the Atlantic contest for mastery in the estuary of the Severn with the down-flowing waters of the river, at high tide. At that time the waters of the ocean resolutely force back the waters of the river between its ever-narrowing banks. Bores actually occur on many rivers throughout the world, but only on the Red River in China does the water rise as high and spectacularly as it does on the Severn. You can hear the water approaching from a great distance, with a sound like the roar of an express from Paddington; then around the bend comes into sight a solid wall of water, 10 feet high, flinging out in front of it a thick, yellow spume as it shatters itself on the hidden reef of Minsterworth Church Rock. Spectators would come from miles around to gather on the levee at the foot of our paddock to wait and watch for it. There they would be joined by our pony, Serenade, and by our pair of donkeys, the three of them standing with their forelegs planted on the bank, sagely nodding their heads and twitching their tails. Sometimes one of our farmer-friends would bring his canoe, paddle out into the middle of the stream, and meet the wave head-on. The bore would lift him and hurl him upstream as far as Worcester, an exploit that has cost several men their lives.

That part of the bank was also a favored spot, on spring nights, for the fishermen who, with lanterns and triangular nets made of muslin, came to trawl for elvers. The Severn yields many varieties of fish, including the salmon, the lamprey, and the occasional sturgeon and shark, but it is the elver which is the most romantic as well as the most regular and dependable. Elvers are the offspring of the eel, carried in the bodies of their mothers across the Atlantic from the river Severn to be given birth in the spawning grounds of the Sargasso Sea. Thence they make a three-year journey, growing an inch a year, back across the Atlantic to their native waters, where the whole mysterious cycle begins again. It struck me as rather pitiful that many of them should make this dark and arduous passage only to be scooped up and dropped into a bucket at the foot of my paddock. However, they are considered a great delicacy by the local people, and are sold for respectable sums in Gloucester Market. When fried in bacon fat, they have the appearance and taste of spaghetti, and I was not averse to eating them occasionally with my bacon and eggs at breakfast. But then, as a boy in Wales I had been fond of such fishy adjuncts as laver bread, which my mother would sometimes buy at Ashton's, the fishmonger in Cardiff Market whose marble slabs were arranged with a surreal artistry that delighted me. Laver bread is not bread at all, but an edible seaweed which is gathered on the Gower Coast near Swansea. It looks and tastes like spinach, and I had a fondness for it.

I did not wish to intrude upon the elverers when they stole around, whispering and with lanterns twinkling, at the bottom of my orchard in the dead of night. It was a traditional trade. I discovered that that particular stretch of the Severn was not much good for fishing, though now and then I would stroll down and throw a casual line into it. My most serious fishing was done some miles away, mainly on the Wye. One of my chief passions was to angle for pike in the freezing days at the back end of the year, when the pike is most active and predatory. "The mighty Luce or Pike," as Izaak Walton remarked three centuries ago, "is taken to be the tyrant of the fresh waters: solitary, melancholy, and bold." The pike is a fighting fish, mean, murderous, quick, crafty, and fearless. It is a pleasure to kill him. With his glaring eyes, his lean, cartilaginous body, and elongated jaw bristling with teeth, he looks like something out of a horror film. He can bite your steel trace clean in two when you hook him, mangling your fingers as you haul him to the bank. He is too full of bones to be worth cooking, though the French, who cook everything, make rather insipid quenelles out of him, and the Michiganders and Minnesotans possess the secret of baking the northern pike and the wall-eye pike into quite an acceptable dish. In the Severn, however, I was content with catching the occasional eel for the cat's supper. The best lure, I found, was the local one of tying a worm to the end of a stout piece of wool. When the eel took the worm, the wool would wrap itself inextricably around his multiple rows of inward-sloping teeth. Some of these eels were elongated, slime-coated tubes of solid muscle that took a deal of dispatching. The cat, who liked his eels stewed in milk, would invite his friends for supper, and while I fished they would sit in a row beside me on the bank, their gaze fastened on the water, their heads cocked attentively.

After an anxious childhood and adolescence in Cardiff and my English school, and the ragged years of the war, my first years of marriage, at Grange Road in Cambridge and Hamilton Terrace in St. John's Wood, had been passed in pleasant places, but Minsterworth proved truly a kind of idyll. I worked in Gwilym the Herald's library. Valerie brought the gardens into a bountiful condition. I learned how to tend the venerable and abundant vines in the vinery, Black Hamburg and Madresfield Court, and coaxed from them a Tokaylike wine that I called Blanc de Blanc de Blanc. After a glass or two of it, the local postman was discovered, one fine summer afternoon, stretched out fast asleep on a tomb in the nearby churchyard with the contents of his postbag scattered on the grass around him. Remembering my father and his orchids, I cultivated carnations that took prizes at the Gloucester shows. On Sundays we played music. Our friends and neighbors turned their Cromwellian barns into an opera house. There was the Cheltenham Festival and the Three Choirs Festival, held by turns in the cathedrals of Gloucester, Worcester, and Hereford, that dated back to Handel's time and was the oldest music festival in the world. We had Serenade the pony, Crichton and Annabel the donkeys, Paul Clarence the marmalade cat, Tess of the d'Urbervilles the yellow labrador. We had ducks, we had geese, we had a dovecote containing forty white doves.

The doves were a happy accident. I began by stocking the empty dovecote with a single pair of Bohemian Brunners. They multiplied. They multiplied and they multiplied. Occasionally, in a halfhearted effort to make them see sense, I would put some of them into a basket in the boot of my car and release them 30 or 40 miles away. I would suffer agonies of guilt as I watched them wing up and speed away. I prayed that they would find themselves a good home. I need not have bothered. By the time I got back to Minsterworth, they would be waiting for me and would flutter round me with grateful coos. Evidently they thought I had been taking them for a nice little outing in the country. I loved to see Valerie, soon after dawn, standing on the dewy grass in her nightgown, her hair loose around her shoulders, scattering corn for them, some of them perched on her arms and her shoulders, or pecking from her open palms, the others flocking in a foam of white feathers around her naked feet. During the winter, when they were sick or dying, they would make their way to her kitchen door. She would take them in and lay them on straw in a cardboard box beside the stove, feeding them with biscuit soaked in milk.

*Et in Arcadia ego.* "I too have lived in Arcady." The *I* in the quotation is actually the serpent, who is saying, "I too am present in the Garden of Eden."

What serpent was it, who after a few years came creeping to lodge itself in our little West Country Paradise?

There was no specific reason, no particular crisis, for my decision to set out on my travels again. My career as a free-lance writer was modestly thriving. I wrote books, radio plays, television plays. I was engaged increasingly with films. I spent long periods in Paris, Madrid, Berlin, Rome, and made extended trips farther afield to Africa and North America.

Valerie and I had traveled together intensively in Europe, but it may have been my journeys to other and larger continents that had somehow begun to enlarge my sense of perspective and make me dissatisfied with the claustrophobic atmosphere of postwar

Britain. Or perhaps it was simply a case, as I mentioned earlier, of peaking too early. Just as, after six years at Cambridge, I had come to feel that it was too placid a place in which a vigorous young man ought to linger, perhaps I had begun to sense that life in a Gloucestershire village might also turn out to be something of a lotusland. Did I really want to spend the rest of my life reclining on beds of amaranth and moly? Like Cambridge, Minsterworth might be an ideal place in which to spend the evening of one's life, but not its high noon.

What had been driving me hitherto, though it would take me several more years to comprehend it, was the desire to emulate and to surpass my father. From the time I was thirteen, when he had died at the age of forty-nine, I had been spurred on by the desire to avenge him, to vindicate him, to get back at life, to restore the family fortunes. No doubt acquiring Minsterworth Court was all very sweet and gratifying, but perhaps I had done something that a writer and a peripatetic Welshman ought to have taken pains to avoid. Perhaps I had burdened myself down with too much property and too many possessions. They travel fastest, after all, who travel light. Perhaps I had put myself in danger of getting stuck in a groove. Or perhaps, as a Welshman, I felt that in luxuriating in the good life at Minsterworth I was not flirting sufficiently with failure.

An agreeable groove, to be sure. I could have settled into an annual routine: a book, a movie or television play, the odd spot of reviewing. I must have concluded that it would eventually prove stultifying, a trap. Moreover, I had fallen further than I had originally intended into the clutches of the film business. I had entered it inadvertently, when my first novel had been made into a movie and I had written the screenplay. But while I continued to work increasingly for the movies, I also became increasingly aware that my talent and inclination were for writing books.

The film business is addictive. It is also careless and esurient.

It gobbles writers up. It squeezes them dry. Except for an old boxer, nobody is more pathetic than an old screenwriter. The fate of middle-aged actors and directors is bad enough, but the fate of film writers, who are not highly regarded in the first place, is worse. As a thirty-year-old story editor, I was always sick at heart when some distinguished director or writer who was twice my age would come to me begging for a job—any job at all—anything to keep him working.

It was a fate that I was determined to avoid. And so, after fifteen years, I decided to quit while I was still able to do so gracefully, while my energies were still relatively undepleted and the lining of my stomach was still intact. I had also begun to nurse a nagging suspicion that one's creative capacities might not be a renewable resource. What if they were only lent to you on sufferance? What if they were unforgiving, and if you kept forcing and abusing them they got tired of it and decided to leave you? What if you could damage them and destroy them? Writing for the movies was in many ways rewarding and amusing, but in other respects, so far as my own particular case was concerned, I felt it might become a question of an "expense of spirit in a waste of shame." The time had come, I thought, to make a major change, to move on.

Time to move on. Perhaps that was the way I was beginning to feel about Britain. The mood certainly became more acute after my return from Southern Africa. Perhaps I had come to resemble Kipling's "English Irregular," brooding on his impending return to England after service in the Boer War:

> *Me that 'ave been what I've been,*
> *Me that 'ave gone where I've gone,*
> *Me that 'ave seen what I've seen—*
> *   'Ow can I ever take on*
> *With awful old England again? . . .*

*I will arise an' get 'ence—*
*I will trek South and make sure*
*If it's only my fancy or not*
*That the sunshine of England is pale,*
*And the breezes of England are stale,*
*An' there's somethin' gone wrong with the lot . . .*

Unmistakably, England was entering upon an ever more diminished era. This was the 1960s, a decade of intellectual confusion and muddled social change. The country's troubles had been compounded by the accession to the premiership of Harold Wilson. I didn't want to live in Harold Wilson's England.

I do not want to dwell too much on the subject of politics. Briefly, while I have never been active politically, I have always been distrustful of socialism, and by extension of communism. Individualism and individual liberty might really be the paramount theme in my writing. The state has its legitimate claims, but they ought to be strictly delimited and never pressed too hard. With the advent of Mr. Wilson, I knew we were in for another bout of what British Socialists called "social engineering." I didn't want to be engineered. Even the British Society of Authors, an old and up till then independent institution, had elected at about that time to become a trades union, officially affiliated to the British Trades Union Congress, a dubious body at best. I felt that, of all people, authors ought to resist being regimented and ordered about. I suppose I had grown tired, like most of my fellow countrymen, of the boring and sterile confrontation between the left and the right that has characterized British politics since long before the First World War. In the 1960s it was at its height.

I failed to anticipate, of course, that after the decline of the 1960s and 1970s the country would enjoy a dramatic resurgence in the 1980s. Might it have been tempting to go back? After all, the collapse of Socialism in Eastern Europe meant that the

Socialist parties in Western Europe would be required, at least for a time, to keep a lower profile and become a little less given than formerly to rhetoric and exhortation. Can it last? Even on this present trip to Britain, after all, the Trades Union Congress has decreed that I must not send a letter or even a postcard to my sick wife in America. I doubt if the negative confrontations of British politics have ceased; the country appears to be locked in the same old shrill and spiteful cycle. True, today the Socialists do not seem to suffer quite as painfully as they once did from what the early psychologists called *Wahlverbesserungswahn*, "the rage for reforming the world," which was once classified as an actual neurosis. However, old habits die hard. Socialism and Marxism may be discredited in Eastern Europe, but no doubt in many a back room in Hampstead and the Welsh valleys the busts of Lenin and Mao Zedong are still being kept brightly polished.

In the 1960s, with a further dose of Socialist medicine about to be forced down the throats of the British people, I felt it might be possible to live a freer and fuller life elsewhere. Why endure the suffocation of living under a Socialist regime if you don't need to? Why not find some country where the people are not hagridden by ideology, and where almost the last question you would want to ask anybody is what his politics are? Why not follow the example of millions of other people and head for wider horizons while the door is still open?

Fortunately, I had already formed a clear idea of where it was I intended to head: America. I had visited the United States several times during my work in the cinema. I found the atmosphere of America exciting and stimulating. Unlike some of my British friends, I had never harbored silly and tiresome feelings of animosity toward America, not even in its customary mildly jeering guise. After all, unlike them, I had actually been there. I liked America and Americans. I even liked New York. American literature and American jazz had been among my earliest enthusiasms in school and college. I liked the confidence of Americans, their capacity for sustained work, their contempt for the restrictions, pretensions, and inanities of the class system, their absence of pomposity, their lack of the malice and suspicion with which Europeans habitually regard each other. I liked their good nature and civility, the quiet affability which Europeans like to mistake for softness (there is nothing soft about a nation which can produce football teams like the Redskins, the Bears, and the Raiders). Above all I was drawn to the size and to the sheer beauty of the North American continent. That was a place where a man could spread himself and take stock.

It was also fortunate in that around that time I had met the critic and biographer Cleanth Brooks. His work had long been familiar to me, and it was with surprise and delight that I discovered that he was living in London as the cultural attaché at the American embassy. It was this kind and learned man who suggested that I might look out for a position at an American university, and who undertook to recommend me. A Tennessean and an Easterner, he was rather taken back, however, when I expressed an inclination, perhaps stimulated by my recent experience of Africa, to head for the Far West. I thought there was very little point in exchanging England for New England, or Gloucester, Gloucestershire, for Gloucester, Massachusetts. I wanted a thorough change of tempo, a complete change of scene.

A preliminary trip brought me offers of posts in California and Arizona. In the end, after a visit, I accepted an invitation to become writer in residence at the University of Texas at El Paso. The music of its name—El Paso del Norte—enchanted me, and I was enchanted too by its situation on the Rio Grande and the fact that it was a twin city with Juárez, one of the largest of Mexican cities, and was half Hispanic and half Spanish speaking in population. It so happened that at this time I had been commissioned to write a biography of Hernán Cortés. Where better to do so than on the border of Mexico? I might also mention that I was additionally attracted to West Texas by a rather odd coincidence. Years before, when I was studying for my degree in archaeology at Cambridge, and was also studying for the diploma in anthropology, I had elected to write my thesis on the Pueblo peoples of the American Southwest. I had never dreamed that I might one day actually visit, let alone inhabit, that remote corner of the world.

And so I "arose an' got 'ence." Even so, when the moment for departure came, I set off in Siegfried, loaded down to the Plimsoll line, with decidedly mixed feelings. My consolation was the thought that, though I had purchased Minsterworth Court when it was in a considerable state of dilapidation, I had steadily improved and refurbished it. I could at least take comfort in the reflection that I had managed to relinquish a little corner of England in better heart than when I had found it.

Then, as I disembarked from the *France* (a piquant contrast to my Atlantic crossings in the Navy twenty years before), my spirits rose. I set out on the five-day drive from New York to Texas. The sun came out. I put down the hood. Siegfried bestirred his great bulk and hit his stride. When I reached the tawny expanses beyond the Pecos, I experienced the same sense of immediately belonging that I had felt on my first arrival in Spain.

This was a place where I was meant to be.


I stand, high up on the castle wall, staring down through my arrow slit at the crowds strolling along sunlit Duke Street, St. Mary's Street, Queen Street.

If I can take legitimate credit for restoring and improving the house and grounds of Minsterworth Court, I can take no credit, alas, for the improvement I have witnessed in the condition of Cardiff, Glamorgan, Wales. But looking at the throng below me, going busily about its affairs, sauntering around the well-stocked shops, I feel a sense of pride and exhilaration. The citizens of Cardiff look so much more healthy and prosperous than they did when I was last among them, and there is no comparison between their appearance now and their appearance in the years of the Depression, the years of the war, the postwar years.

Cardiff, when it became the official capital of Wales, was the capital of a country whose major industries were either moribund or already dead. Yet somehow or other, in the intervening years, Cardiff has steadily acquired the character of a real capital city—not yet, perhaps, with the style and presence of London, Edinburgh, or Dublin, but in many respects more vibrant and hopeful. The passing of the heavy industries has inflicted serious damage on Wales, but less damage than it seems to have done on neighboring England. Entire regions of England, in spite of the general advances of the 1980s, possess the ravaged aspect of Flanders after a bombardment. Wales, on the contrary, has the air of a patient well on the road to recovery. It is as though, in shrugging off the burden of industrialization it has, as I have said, begun to assume its proper shape and personality. It was a country that was never meant to be industrialized. Industrialization came near to ruining it, as it has ruined the North Country and the Midlands of England and despoiled the countries of Eastern Europe. Mercifully, most of the technologies of the latest industrial revolution, now being introduced to Wales, seem a good deal less gross than those of their predecessors. Even when the depredations of coal mining and steel working have been taken into account, Wales has managed to end up in less of a mess than England.

Looking down from my vantage point at the scene below, it is impossible not to contrast modern Cardiff with what I have seen of modern London, New York, Cairo, Mexico City. Many of the world's cities seem to have reached a stage where they are no longer viable or tolerable places in which to live. Shapeless and disheveled, they may have passed the limit of their usefulness. Perhaps the time has come to give serious thought to the advisability of dismantling them. From where I stand, a city like Cardiff still possesses a feeling of serviceability, of congruity. It has not diffused and dissipated itself. Substantial parts of it have taken their lumps, but it still manages to retain the shape and tautness it possessed when I was a boy.

As a child, traveling backward and forward to school in England, I always had the impression that somehow the British Isles were tilted like a pair of scales, with England and London up in the air and Wales and Cardiff correspondingly sunk down. Now the balance seems to have tilted the other way: it is the turn of Wales to rise, of England to descend. It is England, despite its recent efforts to stop the rot, that cannot slough off its sense of stagnation and distrust of the future. Little Wales, on the other hand, seems to be moving toward Europe and the Common Market with a genuine spring in its step. An extraordinary transformation.

There have been moments in the past few days when I have felt as if I were disembodied, a ghost, a wraith, drifting through the scenes and settings to which I once belonged with the weightlessness of an autumn leaf. There were times when I felt like a stranger, an outsider, even an intruder. This afternoon my sense of malaise has vanished. It has come home to me that I have never really ceased to belong. The youngster who worked on the *Western Mail* and went off to war is somewhere down there among the cheerful, milling throng. Like each one of them, he is an indivisible particle of the Welsh present, moving with them out of the Welsh past and into the Welsh future. Every individual is history. A lifetime of journeying cannot separate him from them. He is down there with Caratacus, Arthur, Hywel Dda, Rhodri Mawr, Owain Glyndŵr. He is there with Rawlins White, Joshua White, Henry Morgan, Evan Evans, Isaac White, Captain Trott, and dear old drunken Uncle Jack. My father, Gwilym, and my mother, Eva, are down there too. We are the Welsh, a peculiar extended family, bound together by our myths and our legends and the heroic or not so heroic sum of our deeds, being swept together with the other peoples of the earth out toward the ocean of eternity. And my Valerie is down there too, not the speechless woman lying abed on a far-off continent, but the laughing, dark-haired girl I danced with in the street outside the Claude Hotel. The Valerie who is in bed in Tennessee will never see her native land again. In a more essential sense, she has never left it.

I remember wishing, an hour earlier, as I was walking down the Cathedral Road from the Lincoln Hotel, that I had something substantial to bequeath to Cardiff, something significant in the way of a memorial. The FitzHamons, the Herberts, the Windsors and Butes planted this towering edifice in the heart of the city. What have I got to offer? A row of books on the shelves of the public library. The ships of the Whites have sailed off into the night. Yet all of those people down there, together with the middle-aged man on the castle wall and his stricken wife in Tennessee, possess a common share in the castle, the books, the departed ships. Wales is us, and we are Wales, forever.

I have labored reasonably hard, I suppose, at my chosen métier, or at the métier which seems to have chosen me, when I was a wild Welsh boy at an English school. On the other hand, I was determined from the outset not to allow my professional activities to devour the whole of my life. Part of it I intended to keep for myself. There is, after all, an art of living, just as there is an art of writing. As Thoreau put it, a man ought to stand up to live before he sits down to write. From the beginning I resolved to enjoy my life, and on the whole I think I have contrived to do so. My lines, as the fishermen put it, have fallen in pleasant places. There surely ought to be a good deal more to one's existence than sitting at a table putting words on paper.

In my diary, whenever I want to celebrate a day that has turned out especially well, I write at the top of the page a small sign that represents what the Romans meant when they declared that they "marked this day with a white stone." I have been fortunate in that the borders of my meandering path have been ornamented with a great many of those shining stones. I have enjoyed writing, yes, but I have enjoyed living, too. My motto has been Robert Herrick's: "Live merrily and trust to good letters." What is it to live merrily? To love with a passion and to be loved with a passion in return. To drink a bottle of good wine. To eat a good dinner accompanied by some lively conversation, and concluded with some music, and perhaps—not only in Wales—a little singing. To drop a fly into a mountain stream. To walk the woods and mountains and deserts, or to drive to the beach, or along unfamiliar roads in search of antiquity, or history, or some majestic spectacle.

"The gods themselves cannot recall their gifts." It is for this among other reasons that the gods can be jealous. In recent months, with Valerie doomed and paralyzed, my luck seems largely to have run out. One must summon up one's courage. One must soldier on. Writing is a prime pleasure.

Who knows, one day I may ramble on farther down the road.

*Heureux qui, comme Ulysse, a fait un beau voyage.*


From where I stand, the white peacocks on the grass below me look like the white doves on my lawn at Minsterworth. High up in the sky, the sunlight bright upon their wings, the gulls fly south, beyond the Angel and the Arms Park, across the Taff, the Esplanade, and Tiger Bay, out across the Bristol Channel and onward to the ocean.

> *What past can be yours, O journeying boy*
> *Towards a world unknown,*
> *Who calmly, as if incurious quite*
> *On all at stake, can undertake*
> *This plunge alone?*